UTB **2053**

W0041641

Eine Arbeitsgemeinschaft der Verlage

Böhlau Verlag · Wien · Köln · Weimar
Verlag Barbara Budrich · Opladen · Farmington Hills
facultas.wuv · Wien
Wilhelm Fink · München
A. Francke Verlag · Tübingen und Basel
Haupt Verlag · Bern · Stuttgart · Wien
Julius Klinkhardt Verlagsbuchhandlung · Bad Heilbrunn
Mohr Siebeck · Tübingen
Nomos Verlagsgesellschaft · Baden-Baden
Orell Füssli Verlag · Zürich
Ernst Reinhardt Verlag · München · Basel
Ferdinand Schöningh · Paderborn · München · Wien · Zürich
Eugen Ulmer Verlag · Stuttgart
UVK Verlagsgesellschaft · Konstanz, mit UVK/Lucius · München
Vandenhoeck & Ruprecht · Göttingen
vdf Hochschulverlag AG an der ETH Zürich

Burkhard Dretzke

Modern British and American English Pronunciation

A Basic Textbook

Ferdinand Schöningh

To Margaret and Janine

Bibliografische Information der Deutschen Nationalbibliothek

Die Deutsche Nationalbibliothek verzeichnet diese Publikation in der Deutschen Nationalbibliografie; detaillierte bibliografische Daten sind im Internet über http://dnb.d-nb.de abrufbar.

© 1998 Verlag Ferdinand Schöningh, Paderborn
(Verlag Ferdinand Schöningh GmbH & Co. KG, Jühenplatz 1, D-33098 Paderborn)

Printed in Germany
Herstellung: Ferdinand Schöningh, Paderborn
Einbandgestaltung: Atelier Reichert, Stuttgart

UTB-Bestellnummer: ISBN 978-3-8252-2053-2

CONTENTS

PART I: PHONETICS AND PHONOLOGY

PART II: A COURSE IN TRANSCRIPTION AND PRO-NUNCIATION EXERCISES

PREFACE

This book is a basic, practical textbook for students of English. It is designed to give students a survey of the main issues pertaining to English phonetics and phonology. The contrastive German-English aspect is of equal relevance. The book should serve as a sound basis in phonetics and phonology and encourage students to look for more specialized information about the topics discussed and to find answers to the questions set throughout the book. To this end, the books recommended in the Bibliography (chapter 0.2) can be consulted. In addition, suggestions for further reading and a key to some of these questions are given at the end of various chapters. Furthermore, a note on pronunciation at the end of each chapter helps students to pronounce difficult words in the text correctly. Since the issues involved in phonetics and phonology are vast, this textbook is far from being comprehensive. Thus students would profit from consulting further publications on aspects such as teaching pronunciation, phoneme theory, intonation, American English pronunciation, changes in pronunciation or contrastive phonetics. After studying the book, students should be able to deal confidently with the fundamental issues discussed in the text and hopefully develop some enthusiasm for phonetics and phonology.

ACKNOWLEDGEMENTS

I would like to thank Margaret for her patience in putting up with my communicating more with the computer than with her. I would also like to thank Janine and Detlef Kurth for some clever computer drawings and advice, Herr Thomas Rönnefarth and Frau Dorothee Mrozek for a preliminary transcription of words and Dr. Daryl Tonkinson for her careful reading of the manuscript. Last but not least, I would like to mention the *Fachbereich Neusprachliche Philologien* of the *Freie Universität Berlin*, which provided some funding for the project.

Part I:
PHONETICS AND PHONOLOGY

0.1 LIST OF PHONETIC SYMBOLS AND SIGNS

British English (RP or BBC pronunciation) and American English (General American English)

vowels

iː	as in *feet*
ɪ	as in *fit*
i	as in *happy*
e	as in *bet*
æ	as in *bat*
ɑː	as in *father* and as in *lot* **(GenAmE only)**
ɒ	as in *hot* **(RP only)**
ɔː	as in *born*
ʊ	as in *put*
uː	as in *pool*
u	as in *situation*
ʌ	as in *hut*
ɜː	as in *bird*
ə	as in *ago*
eɪ	as in *tame*
əʊ	as in *tone* **(RP only)**
oʊ	as in *tone* **(GenAmE only)**
aɪ	as in *time*
aʊ	as in *town*
ɔɪ	as in *boy*
ɪə	as in *fear* **(RP only)**
eə	as in *fair* **(RP only)**
ʊə	as in *tour* **(RP only)**

semi-vowels

j	as in *yes*
w	as in *water*

consonants

p	as in *pan*
b	as in *ban*
t	as in *tan*
d	as in *den*
k	as in *can*
g	as in *gun*
tʃ	as in *chin*
dʒ	as in *gin*
f	as in *fin*
v	as in *van*
θ	as in *thin*
ð	as in *than*
s	as in *sin*
z	as in *zone*
ʃ	as in *shin*
ʒ	as in *genre*
h	as in *hen*
m	as in *man*
n	as in *no*
ŋ	as in *sing*
r	as in *rot*
l	as in *lot*

stress

'	primary stress
ˌ	secondary stress
×	unstressed

juncture and intonation

‖	pause
|	tone-unit boundary
'	high pitch
ˌ	low pitch
↘	falling intonation
`	high-falling intonation

`   low-falling intonation
↗   rising intonation
´   high-rising intonation
ˬ   low-rising intonation
˄   (` ´) falling-rising intonation
    (´ `) rising-falling intonation
→   level intonation

diacritical marks and other symbols

[ ]   phonetic notation
/ /   phonemic notation
< >   written realization
ː   full length as in /fiːl/
ˑ   half length as in *fin* [fiˑn]
̥   loss of voice (devoicing) as in *snow* [sn̥əʊ]
ˌ   syllabicity mark as in *battle* [bætl̩]
*   asterisk in front of word denotes incorrect pronunciation as in *very* */weri/
Ø   zero refers to the absence of an item in a language as in German Ø - English /ð/

0.2 BIBLIOGRAPHY

1. Pronouncing Dictionaries

Ehrlich, E./R. Hand (1984) *NBC Handbook of Pronunciation*. New York: Harper and Row

Jones, D. (1917/89) *English Pronouncing Dictionary*. 14th ed. rev. by A. C. Gimson, rev. by S. Ramsaran. London: Everyman's Reference Library

Jones, D. (1917/97) *English Pronouncing Dictionary*. 15th ed., ed. by P. Roach/J. Hartman. Cambridge: Cambridge University Press

Kenyon J. S./Th. A. Knott (1944/53) *A Pronouncing Dictionary of American English*. Mass.: Merriam Springfields

Pointon, G. E. (1983) *BBC Pronouncing Dictionary of British Names*. London: Oxford University Press

Wells, J. C. (1990) *Pronunciation Dictionary*. London: Longman

2. Phonetic Textbooks

British English

Gimson, A. C. (1962/89) *An Introduction to the Pronunciation of English*. Rev. by S. Ramsaran. London: Edward Arnold

Gimson, A.C. (1962/94) *The Pronunciation of English*. Rev. by A. Cruttenden. London: Edward Arnold

Jones, D. (1918/76) *An Outline of English Phonetics*. Cambridge: Heffers

O'Connor, J. D. (1971/80) *Better English Pronunciation*. London: Cambridge University Press

O'Connor, J.D. (1973/91) *Phonetics*. London: Penguin

Roach, P. (1983/95) *English Phonetics and Phonology*. Cambridge: Cambridge University Press

Roach, P. (1992) *Introducing Phonetics*. London: Penguin

American English (and British English)

Bauer, L./J. M. Dienhart/H. H. Hartvigson/L. K. Jakobsen (1980) *American English Pronunciation*. Copenhagen: Gyldendal

Bronstein, A. J. (1960) *The Pronunciation of American English*. New York: Appleton-Century-Crofts

Cassidy, F.G., ed. (1985) *Dictionary of American Regional English*. Harvard: Belknap Press
Catford, J.C. (1988) *A Practical Course in Phonetics*. Oxford: Clarendon Press
Kenyon, J. S. (1924/69) *American Pronunciation*. Ann Arbor: George Wahr
Kreidler, C.W. (1989) *The Pronunciation of English*. Oxford: Blackwell
Kreidler, C.W. (1997) *Describing Spoken English*. London and New York: Routledge
Kurath, H. (1964) *A Phonology and Prosody of Modern English*. Heidelberg: Carl Winter
Kurath, H./R.F. McDavid (1961) *The Pronunciation of English in the Atlantic States*. Ann Arbor: University of Michigan Press
Ladefoged, P. (1982/93) *A Course in Phonetics*. New York: Harcourt Brace Jovanovich
Prator, C. H./B.W. Robinett (1951/85) *Manual of American English Pronunciation*. New York: Holt, Rinehart and Winston
Wells, J. C. (1982) *Accents of English 1. An Introduction*. Cambridge: Cambridge University Press
Wells, J. C. (1982 a) *Accents of English 2. The British Isles*. Cambridge: Cambridge University Press
Wells, J. C. (1982 b) *Accents of English 3. Beyond the British Isles*. Cambridge: Cambridge University Press

Contrastive German-English

Arnold, R./K. Hansen (1965/92) *Englische Phonetik*. Leipzig: Langenscheidt - Verlag Enzyklopädie
Keutsch, M. (1974) *Praxis der englischen Aussprache*. Tübingen: Niemeyer
Kufner, H. L. (1971) *Kontrastive Phonologie Deutsch-Englisch*. Stuttgart: Klett
Scherer, G./ A. Wollmann (1972/86) *Englische Phonetik und Phonologie*. Berlin: Erich Schmidt

3. General Phonetics

Heffner, R.-M. S. (1950/75) *General Phonetics*. Madison: The University of Wisconsin Press
Laver, J. (1994) *Principles of Phonetics*. Cambridge: Cambridge University Press

4. Dictionaries of Linguistic Terminology

Abraham, W. (1988) *Terminologie zur neueren Linguistik*. Tübingen: Niemeyer
Bußmann, H. (1983/90) *Lexikon der Sprachwissenschaft*. Stuttgart: Kröner
Conrad, R., Hg. (1988) *Lexikon sprachwissenschaftlicher Termini*. Leipzig: Bibliographisches Institut

Crystal, D. (1980/96) *A Dictionary of Linguistics and Phonetics*. Oxford/London: Blackwell/Deutsch
Lewandowski, Th. (1973/94) *Linguistisches Wörterbuch 1, 2 und 3*. Heidelberg: Quelle & Meyer
Richards, J./J. Platt/H. Platt (1985/92) *Dictionary of Applied Linguistics*. London: Longman

Note on pronunciation

phonetic /fə'netɪk/, phonetics /fə'netɪks/, phonology /fəʊ'nɒlədʒi/, preface /'prefəs/, bibliography /bɪbli'ɒgrəfi/, segmental /seg'mentəl/, suprasegmental /suːprəseg'mentəl/, vowel /'vaʊəl/, consonant /'kɒnsənənt/, monophthong /'mɒnəfθɒŋ/, diphthong /'dɪfθɒŋ/, semivowel /'semivaʊəl/, juncture /'dʒʌŋktʃə/, syllable /'sɪləbəl/, assimilation /əsɪmə'leɪʃən/, elision /ɪ'lɪʒn/, basic /'beɪsɪk/, contrastive /kən'trɑːstɪv/, methodology /meθə'dɒlədʒi/, cognitive /'kɒgnətɪv/, psychomotoric /saɪkəʊməʊ'tɒrɪk/, diagnostic /daɪəg'nɒstɪk/, transcription /træn'skrɪpʃən/, primary /'praɪməri/, secondary /'sekəndəri/, pause /pɔːz/, level /'levəl/, diacritical /daɪə'krɪtɪkəl/, phonemic /fəʊ'niːmɪk/, syllabicity /sɪlə'bɪsəti/, asterisk /'æstərɪsk/, zero /'zɪərəʊ/, relevance /'reləvəns/, characteristics /kærəktə'rɪstiks/.

1.0 PHONETICS AND PHONOLOGY

1.1 INTRODUCTION

Phonetics is the science which studies the physical aspect of sounds. It examines the characteristics of human sounds, in particular those sounds used in speech (**phones**). Phonetics deals with any human sound in any language. There are three main areas in the study of sounds: **articulatory phonetics, auditory phonetics** and **acoustic phonetics**. Articulatory phonetics describes sounds in terms of their production by the speech organs. Auditory phonetics describes sounds in terms of the physical effects upon the human ear and brain. Acoustic phonetics describes sounds in terms of the physical properties of sound waves.

Phonology is the linguistic science which studies the functional aspect of sounds in a specific language. It examines how sounds form a system in the language and how they function within the pronunciation system of that language. Its aim is the establishment and the full description of the distinctive sound units of a language (**phonemes**), whose function is to distinguish between meanings. The inventory of phonemes in a language is represented in a phonemic transcription system (cf. chapter 0.1).

As far as the importance of the study of phonetics and phonology is concerned, it seems unavoidable that specialists' and non-specialists' opinions vary considerably. People have different ideas about what is important in the study of English. Some think that literature is more important than linguistics or that cultural studies should be stressed more than they have been so far and that within linguistics, grammar and models of grammar are more important than phonetics and phonology. It seems reasonable to argue that literature, cultural studies, linguistics (including phonetics and phonology) and the study of the history of the English language are all equally necessary. It would be wrong to assume that phonetics and phonology are peripheral to the study of English. Their importance should not be underestimated.

In a book on American Pronunciation, Kenyon writes the following with future teachers of English in mind: "A teacher of speech untrained

in phonetics is as useless as a doctor untrained in anatomy." There are a number of practical reasons why phonetics and phonology are important:
- A teacher's pronunciation is the model for his or her students.
- Teachers should have some knowledge of contrastive phonetics/ phonology to be able to explain differences and similarities between the mother tongue and the target language. They should also have a good idea about the hierarchy of difficulties, ie typical difficulties Germans have with English pronunciations.
Without proper training in phonetics, teachers might invite criticism from their students and encounter difficulties. One can easily imagine the students' reactions to a teacher of English who says: */ˈoːpən zə ˈdoɐ ɛnt zə ˈvɪndoːs ˈpliːs/ (*Open the door and the windows, please*).

It seems that a person's pronunciation is definitely linked to his or her personality and the way people perceive personality. From as early as the beginning of the 20th century, phoneticians have emphasized the fact that pronunciation is an integral part of one's personality. In this context, one could also refer to the flower girl in Shaw's *Pygmalion* who changes her stigmatized accent (Cockney) into a prestigious accent known as Received Pronunciation. (The figure of Professor Higgins was based on the famous British phonetician Henry Sweet). Abercrombie, a Scottish phonetician, writes: "Things such as gait, or the wearing of clothes, can, in addition to their main functions, re-veal personality, but probably no aspect of human behaviour does this so constantly, or so subtly as speech."

Since pronunciation still plays a very important social role in Eng-land, one should not forget G.B. Shaw's sarcastic statement: "It is impossible for an Englishman to open his mouth without making some other Englishman despise him." Consequently, people with the 'right' accent are still regarded as more competent, more intelligent, and socially more desirable than people with the 'wrong' accent. Al-though these remarks apply mainly to native speakers of English, various studies show that foreigners are also judged by their un-English accent. It seems to be the case that a strong German accent sounds rather unpleasant to the English. German English often sounds hard, domineering, guttural, and harsh and can lead to pre-judice and reinforce national stereotypes.

Last but not least, one can quote Wilhelm von Humboldt: "Die Laut-form ist das eigentliche konstitutive und leitende Prinzip der Sprache." Consequently, the motto of this book is taken from the French phonetician Paul Passy: «Peut-on vraiment pénétrer le génie d'une langue, quand on la massacre par une prononciation barbare?»

1.2 SURVEY OF SEGMENTAL AND SUPRASEGMENTAL PHONEMES

In English, phonemes can be divided into segmental phonemes, ie **vowels** and **consonants**, and suprasegmental phonemes, ie **stress**, **juncture** and **intonation**.

Phonetically, **vowels** are sounds in which the airstream from the lungs is not blocked in any way in the mouth or throat. Vowels are pronounced with vibration of the vocal cords. This is known as voicing or voice. All English vowels are voiced. If air escapes through the mouth only, these vowels are said to be oral vowels as is the case in English. From a phonological point of view, vowels are those units which function at the centre of a syllable. Vowels can be divided into short and long vowels, eg /ʊ/ and /uː/ in *pull* and *pool*. If the quality of a vowel remains unchanged, the term pure vowel or monophthong is used, eg *bit, beat, bat, boot*. If there is a change in quality, the term gliding vowel is used. Gliding vowels can be diphthongs with two elements being involved, eg *boy, bait, go, fair,* or triphthongs, where three elements are involved, eg *fire* and *tower*.

Consonants are speech sounds in which the airstream from the lungs is blocked in some way in the mouth or throat. There may be full blockage as for /p/, /g/ or /m/, slight or very slight blockage as for /l/ or /w/ and /j/, or partial blockage where the opening is so narrow that the airstream escapes with audible friction as for /s/ or /v/. Consonants are either voiced or voiceless. From a phonological point of view, consonants are those units which function at the margins of a syllable.

Stress refers to the degree of force used in producing a syllable. More air from the lungs and a greater muscular effort are needed to produce stress. Syllables may or may not be stressed and are known as stressed and unstressed syllables. From a phonological point of view, the main function of stress is to provide a distinguishing clue in words or sentences, eg *'export - ex'port, 'French teacher - French 'teacher.*

Juncture or **pause** refers to the phonetic boundary within a word, between words and between clauses as in *my | train - might | rain, that's | tough - that | stuff, she washed | and combed her hair - she washed and combed her hair.* The pause is marked by a vertical line | .

Intonation refers to the melody of a language. In speech, an utterance is rarely spoken on the same note all the time, rather the pitch of a speaker's voice is raised or lowered continuously to create a melody. Vowels, consonants, stress, juncture and intonation are used to distinguish between utterances. This distinctive function can be seen in the following examples.

1. Segmentals: vowels and consonants

- **vowels***: bit - bat; rob - rub; boy - buy*
- **consonants**: *bat - cat; wing - ring; thin - sin*
- **sequence of vowels and consonants**: *pit - tip; but - tub; nip - pin*

2. Suprasegmentals or prosodic features: stress, juncture (pause), intonation

- stress
'conjure - con'jure; 'import - im'port; 'blackbird - black 'bird; 'White House - white 'house; 'English teacher - English 'teacher

Q(uestion) 1 Explain the difference in meaning of the above words and word groups.

- juncture
*night rate - nitrate; an aim - a name; I scream - ice cream
It's the doctor, Mr. Nester. - It's the doctor, Mr. Nester.
There were few passengers on the train who escaped unhurt. - There were few passengers on the train, who escaped unhurt.*

Q2 Explain the difference in meaning of the above words and sentences.

- intonation
Who did it, Peter? - Who did it? Peter. - Who did it? Peter?

3. Summary of segmentals, suprasegmentals and paralinguistic features in English

As far as vocal means in communication are concerned, voice can distinguish between meaning by producing different vowels, conso-nants, stress patterns, junctures and intonational patterns. In addition, voice can also be used to add meaning to utterances: words or senten-ces spoken with a yawning, breathy, laughing or creaky voice can sig-nal a certain attitude or social role for example. These are called par-alinguistic features. The vocal means are summarized in the following diagram. The term phonation is used to refer to any vocal activity.

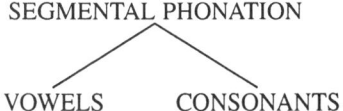

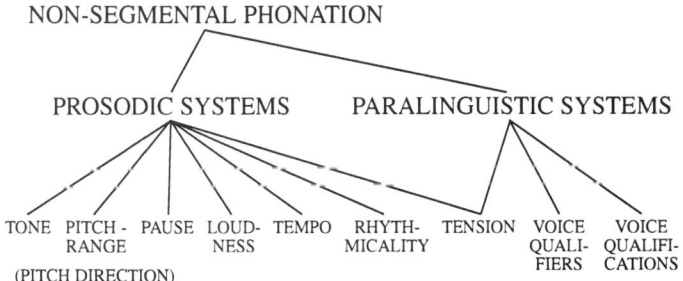

INTONATION PAUSE STRESS
(cf. Crystal 1969: 177)

Q3 In communication, one uses vocal and verbal means, vocal and non-verbal means and non-vocal and non-verbal means. What is meant by these terms? What are paralinguistic and **extralinguistic** features in communication?

1.3 ORGANS OF SPEECH AND CLASSIFICATION OF SEGMENTALS

1. Introduction: Speech Organs

Articulatory phonetics is based on the study of the mechanism for the production of speech sounds by the human speech organs. The vocal organs or organs of speech are the **lungs**, the **larynx** containing the **vocal cords** (or **vocal folds**), the **pharynx** containing the **epiglottis**, the **nasal cavity** and the **oral cavity** containing the **soft palate** (or **velum**) and the **hard palate**, the **tongue**, the **teeth** and the **lips** (cf. diagrams below). The function of these organs in speech is as follows.

Lungs: sounds are generally produced with the help of outgoing breath from the lungs. This direction of air is called egressive. In some languages, the direction can be ingressive, where air is breathed in. With egressive breath, the air travels from the lungs up the **windpipe** or **trachea**, past the larynx with its vocal cords and pharynx and then reaches the nasal and the oral cavity. The air can either be expelled through the mouth only as is the case with oral sounds, or through the nose only as is the case with nasal sounds, or through both the mouth and nose as is the case with nasalized vowels.

Larynx: when air is pushed up from the lungs, it first passes through the larynx. Inside the larynx are the **vocal cords** which interfere with the airstream. The vocal cords are two bands of muscles, whose functions vary depending on the different opening space between them. This space between the vocal cords is called **glottis**. There are at least four major positions of the vocal cords based on differences in the opening.

1st position: The vocal cords are tightly closed, ie the air stream is completely blocked by the vocal cords, air pressure builds up from the lungs and is then released explosively when the vocal cords are suddenly opened. The sudden release of the compressed air produces a kind of coughing noise, which is called a glottal stop. The symbol for the glottal stop is /ʔ/.

2nd position: The vocal cords are wide apart and the flow of air passes through them without any interference as, for example, with [s]. This results in glottal friction which is responsible for all voiceless consonants. The interference is in the mouth, but not between the vocal cords. The vocal cords do not vibrate, consequently a voiceless sound is produced.

3rd position: The vocal cords are loosely together and vibrate with the outgoing airstream. They act as a vibrator like the string of a guitar. The continuous vibration is called **voice** or **voicing**. Vibration is the normal feature of all vowels and voiced consonants.

There are two other functions controlled by voice. The first refers to the control of **pitch**, which is the auditory sensation in terms of a scale of high and low notes. The difference in the rate of vibration corresponds to differences in pitch - the slower the rate the lower the pitch and the quicker the rate the higher the pitch. A rate of seventy vibrations per second corresponds to a very low note and one thousand vibrations per second corresponds to a very high note. The second function relates to **loudness**. The amplitude, ie the amount of horizontal opening of the vocal cords, is responsible for the loudness of an utterance. The further the vocal cords move apart in the open phase the louder is the resultant sound. The smaller the gap the softer the sound. In addition, loud sounds need extra air pressure from the lungs.

4th position: If the vocal cords are close together with the exception of a small part which remains open, ie if they have a position somewhere between voiced and voiceless, then devoiced sounds are produced. Devoicing can mean less voice (slight vibration of the vocal cords) or no voice (no vibration of the vocal cords). This is also the position of a whisper and /h/.

Pharynx: Above the larynx there is a tube-like cavity, which is called the pharynx. Two more cavities, the oral cavity and the nasal cavity branch off the pharynx. One important organ can be found in the pharynx, ie the **epiglottis**. The epiglottis has no direct function in speech. Its function is to close the trachea while swallowing food. In other words, the epiglottis folds over the top of the larynx to prevent food from getting into the trachea or windpipe.

Oral cavity: The oral cavity is the most important of the three cavities, because it is the most variable in dimension and in shape. This is due to the mobility of the lower jaw, of the lips and especially of the tongue. The tongue is the speech organ par excellence and in many languages, it is synonymous with the word for language (cf. *lingua, lengua, langue*). The top part of the oral cavity is called the **palate**.

Palate: The front part of the palate is bony and fixed (**hard palate**), whereas the back part is moveable and soft (**soft palate**). The palate can be divided into four parts, the **uvula**, the **soft palate** or **velum**, the **hard palate** and the **alveolar ridge**. The general function of the palate in speech is to serve as an articulatory background to the tongue. The soft palate is a moveable organ and it has the additional function to close and open the nasal cavity. Its position determines three different types of sounds - oral sounds, nasal sounds and nasalized sounds. If the soft palate is raised, it blocks off the nasal cavity and all the air from the lungs escapes through the oral cavity only. All English sounds except the nasals /m, n, ŋ/ are produced in this way. If the soft palate is lowered and if the mouth is completely blocked at the same time, the air passes through the pharynx and nasal cavity and escapes through the nose only. All English nasals are produced in this way. If the soft palate is lowered to a certain degree and if air escapes through the mouth and nose at the same time, then nasalized vowels as in French *bon, blanc, fin* are produced.

The uvula, which is in some way independent of the palate, can be used to produce uvular sounds such as the French and German /r/.

Tongue: The tongue consists of a complex bunch of muscles, which are highly moveable. The tongue is usually divided into five major parts, the tip (or **apex**), the blade (or **corona**), the front, the back (or **dorsum**) and the root of the tongue. The edges of the tongue are called the rims. The tongue not only articulates with the palate, but also with the teeth. In addition, the part of the tongue and the degree of raising determine the differences in sounds. If the rims of the tongue make contact with the sides of the palate along the line of the teeth, the result is a lateral sound like English /l/.

Teeth: the teeth are bony and fixed and serve as an articulator for the tongue.

Lips: the lips are soft and moveable and can close the oral cavity as in /p/ or can be held apart in various ways. If held apart, four major positions are possible.

1st position: the lips are spread as in /iː/.
2nd position: the lips are neutrally open as for /e/.
3rd position: the lips are open-rounded as for /ɒ/.
4th position: the lips are close-rounded as for /ʊ/.

Nasal cavity: this cavity is used as a resonator in the production of nasal sounds, where the oral cavity is completely closed, and for nasalized sounds, where both the oral cavity and the nasal cavity are open.

Q4 Describe the production of any sound.

2. ARTICULATORY ORGANS (DIAGRAM)

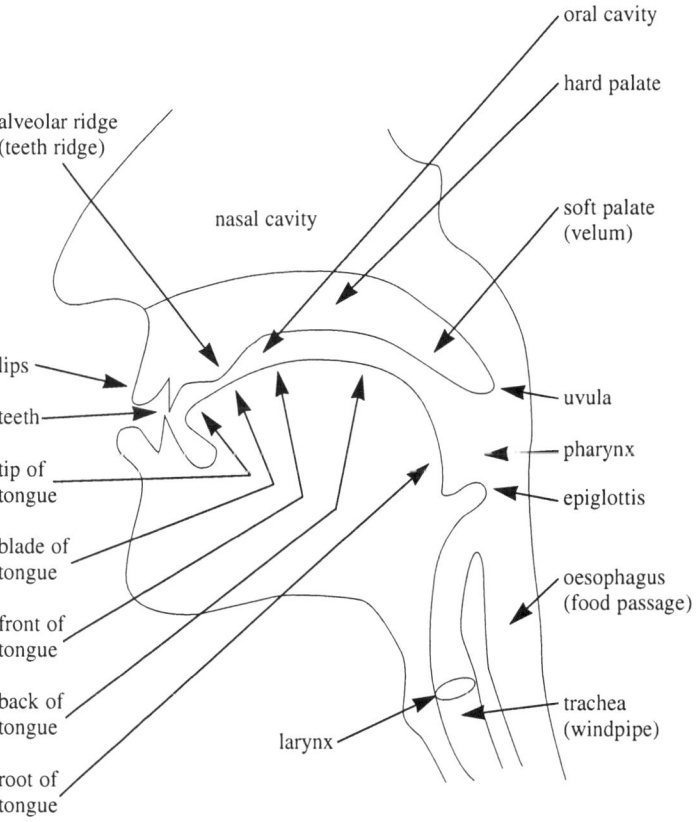

3. LARYNX

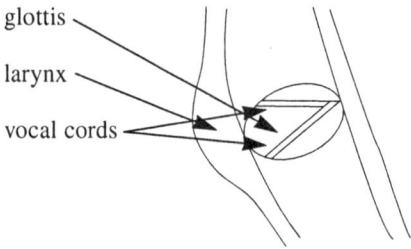

glottis

larynx

vocal cords

Q5 Find the German equivalents for the English terms.

4. THE VOCAL CORDS (DIAGRAM)

The four main positions of the vocal cords are as follows.

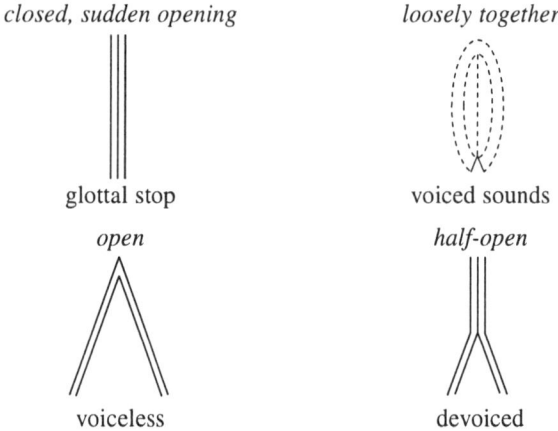

closed, sudden opening   *loosely together*

glottal stop   voiced sounds

open   *half-open*

voiceless   devoiced

5. TESTING FOR VOICED SOUNDS

The vibration of the vocal cords can be tested for in several ways. If one has difficulty in hearing the difference between a voiced and a voiceless sound, one should make a long hissing sound [ssss] and alternate this sound with a long buzzing sound [zzzz]. By putting one's fingers in one's ears, one should be able to hear the difference. The vibration can also be felt by putting a finger on the Adam's apple, by placing the backs of the fingers on the neck to the right and left of the chin or by placing a hand flat on the top of the head.

6. LENIS AND FORTIS CONSONANTS AND THE PROBLEM OF DEVOICING

German speakers do not normally have any great difficulty in pronouncing familiar voiced and voiceless consonants. The only problem lies in the pronunciation of final voiced obstruents (cf. chapter 2.2) in English, because in German all final obstruents are voiceless (*Auslautverhärtung*). The final consonants in the words *Hand, Tag* or *brav* are pronounced with /t/, /k/ and /f/. In English, final voiced consonants are, from a phonetic point of view, devoiced or even voiceless. If one whispers the words *his* and *hiss*, no final voiced sound will be heard in either case, one will nevertheless perceive two different final sounds. The difference is no longer between voiced and voiceless, but in their different **force of articulation**. The final sound in the word *his* is pronounced with relatively weak friction, whereas the final /s/ in the word *hiss* has quite a strong friction. In other words, force of articulation refers to the intensity of the tenseness of the muscles and to the strength of the airstream. From an articulatory point of view, one can distinguish between consonants which are pronounced with relatively strong energy (**fortis** consonants) and those which are pronounced with relatively weak energy (**lenis** consonants). All fortis consonants are voiceless, all lenis consonants are either fully voiced (ie between vowels), devoiced or even voiceless.

Apart from the differences in the force of articulation, there is another feature that separates *his* and *hiss*. The quantity (length) of the vowels is different. The vowel in *his* is longer than the vowel in *hiss*. There is a general rule in English pronunciation stating that all final lenis consonants lengthen the preceding vowel and all final fortis consonants shorten the preceding vowel. Examples are *cap-cab, tripe-tribe, rope-robe, bet-bed, heart-hard, brought-broad, pick-pig, back-bag, dock-dog, leaf-leave, life-live, safe-save, rice-rise, fuss-fuzz* and *race-raise*. German only has final fortis obstruents, therefore care must be taken to articulate final lenis obstruents as weakly as possible. Furthermore, the preceding vowel has to be pronounced with relatively great length.

Q6 Are the following two statements correct?
a) All *fortis* consonants are voiceless.
b) All *lenis* consonants are voiced, devoiced or even voiceless.

7. CLASSIFICATION OF VOWELS: MONOPHTHONGS AND DIPHTHONGS

7.1 General approach

The vowel type can be described as follows (in auditory and articulatory terms).
- The type of vowel: monophthong, diphthong, (triphthong)
- The position of the lips: spread, neutral, rounded
- The position of the tongue: the part of the tongue which is used, ie
                                front, middle, back
                                the degree of raising, ie close (high),
                                open (low)
- The force of articulation: tenseness or laxness of muscles
- The length of vowels: short, long
- The position of the velum: raised, lowered

7.2 English and German vowels (diagrams)

- English monophthongs

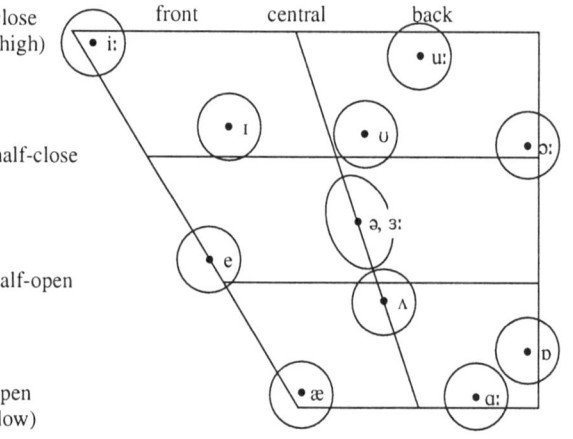

(cf. Wells 1990 and Hartman/Roach 1997)

- English diphthongs

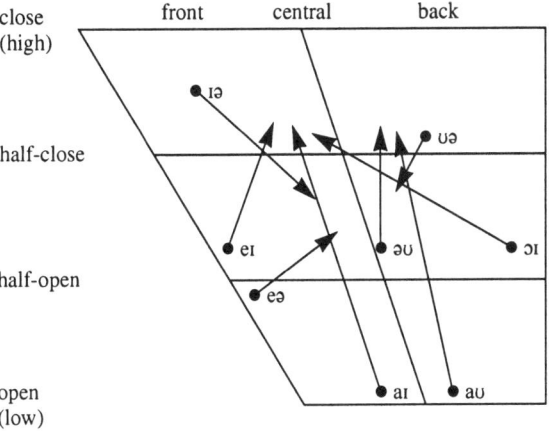

(cf. Wells 1990 and Hartman/Roach 1997)

- German monophthongs

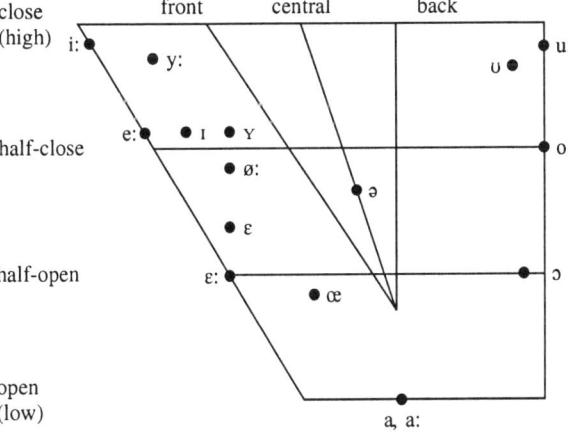

(Kohler 1977/97: 174)

- German diphthongs

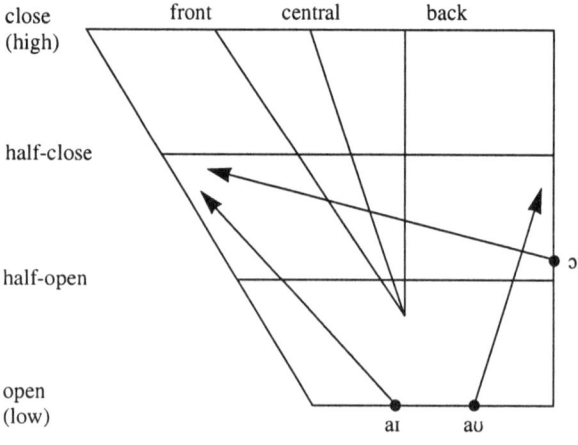

(Kohler 1977/97: 174)

8. CLASSIFICATION OF CONSONANTS

8.1 General approach

The consonantal type can be described as follows (mainly in articulatory terms):
- Place of articulation
- Manner of articulation
- Presence and absence of voice
- Force of articulation
- Position of the soft palate

8.2 Detailed approach

With the help of a detailed description of the articulatory organs, consonants are classified according to the **places of articulation** and the **manner of articulation**. The major places of articulation at which the airstream can be interfered with are as follows:

- places of articulation
bilabial as in /p, b, m, w/

labio-dental as in /f, v/
dental as in /θ, ð/
alveolar as in /t, d, n, l, s, z/
post-alveolar as in /r/
palato-alveolar as in /ʃ, ʒ, tʃ, dʒ/
palatal as in /ç/
velar as in /k, g, ŋ, x/
uvular as in /ʀ, ʁ/
glottal as in /h, ʔ/

- **manner of articulation**
Sounds are normally also classified according to the manner of articulation or manner of interference. Basically there are three possibilities: **complete closure** of the air passage, **narrowing** of the passage
so that the air forced through the narrowing causes audible friction
and more **open positions** which do not result in friction.

complete closure: some sounds are produced with complete closure
at some point in the mouth. The articulating organs move together to
form a complete obstruction followed by a release stage. The sounds
formed in such a manner are **stops** (or **plosives**) and **affricates**.
Examples of stops are bilabial /p, b/, alveolar /t, d/, velar /k, g/, the
glottal stop and the affricates /tʃ, dʒ/. There is also complete closure
as far as nasals are concerned, where the oral cavity is closed. Nasals
are nevertheless not included in the category of stops. They are
classified independently under nasals.

narrowing: if the articulating organs are brought very close together
and the air is forced through this narrowing, the air becomes turbulent
resulting in a friction noise. Sounds with such friction are called **fricatives**. Examples of fricatives are labiodental /f, v/, dental /θ, ð/,
alveolar /s, z/ and palato-alveolar /ʃ, ʒ/.

open positions: if the articulating organs are not too close together
and do not cause friction, the various shapes of the articulating organs
produce the following types of sounds - vowels, glides (semi-vowels)
and liquids (/l, r/). The sounds with very open positions are vowels
and the sounds with quite open positions are the semi-vowels /j/ and
/w/. English /r/, which is classified as a frictionless continuant, is produced with quite a narrow opening. Because English /l/ is frictionless,
it is usually listed in this category, although the passage of air is blocked

in the middle of the mouth, where the air passes out over the rims of the tongue and around the alveolar closure. Consequently, the category of 'partial closure' is sometimes used by some phoneticians.

8.3 English consonants (chart)

Manner ----- Place	Plosives	Rolls and Taps	Affri-cates	Fricatives	Nasals	Laterals	Frictionless Continuant	Semi-Vowels
Bilabial	p, b				m			w
Labio-dental				f, v				
Dental				θ, ð				
Alveo-lar	t, d	[r, ɾ]		s, z	n	l		
Post-alveolar							r [ɹ]	
Palato-alveolar			tʃ, dʒ	ʃ, ʒ				
Palatal				[ç]				j
Velar	k, g			[x]	ŋ			
Glottal				h				

9. DIFFERENCE BETWEEN VOWELS AND CONSONANTS

A vowel is a speech sound in which the airstream from the lungs is not blocked in the pharynx or oral cavity. The different positions of the tongue do not cause any audible friction. English vowels are pronounced with vibration of the vocal cords.

A consonant is a speech sound where the airstream from the lungs is either completely blocked and then released (plosive), partially blocked (lateral) or where the opening is so narrow that the air escapes with audible friction (fricative). In the case of nasals, the air stream is blocked at different places in the mouth and released through the nose.

Key to some questions

Q1 '*English teacher* means that the teacher teaches English, whereas *English* '*teacher* means that the teacher is English.

Q2 *It's the doctor, Mr. Nester.* Read without a pause, this sentence means that one introduces the doctor to Mr. Nester.
It's the doctor, Mr. Nester. Read with a pause after *doctor,* this sentence means that Mr. Nester is the doctor.
There were few passengers on the train who escaped unhurt. Read without a pause, this sentence means that only a minority of the many passengers escaped unhurt.
There were few passengers on the train, who escaped unhurt. Read with a pause after *train,* this sentence means that there were only few passengers on the train and that they all escaped unhurt.

Q3 By vocal and verbal means one understands the use of the voice and words. Non-verbal and vocal communication consists of the use of the voice without words, ie permanent traits (voice qualifiers) in one's voice like nasalization, hoarseness, creakiness or temporary traits (voice qualifications) like sighing, laughing, breathiness or nasalization because of a cold. Non-verbal and vocal features are also called paralinguistic features. Non-vocal and non-verbal means are extralinguistic features like kinesics (gestures, posture, nodding), oculesics (eye contact), haptics (tactile contact) and proxemics (spatial distance in communication), which play a very important role in correct communicative behaviour.

Q4 All sounds are produced with the help of air. The airstream comes out of the lungs, goes into the trachea (ie wind pipe) and then passes through the larynx which contains the vocal cords or vocal folds. Its forward position is prominent and is called the Adam's apple. The trachea can be closed by the epiglottis, which prevents food from getting into the trachea. The larynx with its vocal cords is important, because it is mainly responsible for the production of voiced and voiceless sounds. The air goes past the larynx into the pharynx and is then pushed out through the mouth via the oral cavity (oral sounds) with the soft palate being raised, or through the nose via the nasal cavity (nasal sounds) with the soft palate being lowered. When air escapes through the nose and the mouth, nasalized vowels are produced as in French *bon, vin, banque* for example.

Q6 Both statements are correct.

Further Readings

Crystal, D. (1969) *Prosodic Systems and Intonation in English*. Cambridge: Cambridge University Press
Crystal, D. (1975) *The English Tone of Voice*. London: Edward Arnold
International Phonetic Association (1949) *The Principles of the International Phonetic Association*. London: Department of Phonetics, University College
Kohler, K. (1977/97) *Einführung in die Phonetik des Deutschen*. Berlin: Erich Schmidt
Oksaar, E. (1988) *Kulturemtheorie*. Göttingen: Vandenhoeck & Ruprecht
Scollon, R./S. Wong (1994) *Intercultural Communication*. Oxford: Blackwell
Valdes, J.M. (1986) *Culture Bound*. Cambridge: Cambridge University Press

Note on pronunciation

phone /fəʊn/, phoneme /ˈfəʊniːm/, distinguish /dɪˈstɪŋgwɪʃ/, articulatory /ɑːˈtɪkjʊlətəri/, auditory /ˈɔːdɪtəri/, acoustic /əˈkuːstɪk/, linguistics /lɪŋˈgwɪstɪks/, peripheral /pəˈrɪfərəl/, anatomy /əˈnætəmi/, hierarchy /ˈhaɪərɑːki/, stigmatized /ˈstɪgmətaɪzd/, Cockney /ˈkɒkni/, personality /pɜːsəˈnæləti/, phonetician /fəʊnɪˈtɪʃən/, clothes /kləʊðz/ (/kləʊz/), subtly /ˈsʌtli/, sarcastic /sɑːˈkæstɪk/, guttural /ˈgʌtərəl/, prejudice /ˈpredʒədɪs/, stereotype /ˈsteriətaɪp/, vocal /ˈvəʊkəl/, audible /ˈɔːdəbəl/, prosodic /prəˈsɒdɪk/, 'conjure /ˈkʌndʒə/, con'jure /kənˈdʒʊə/, paralinguistic /pærəlɪŋˈgwɪstɪk/, phonation /fəʊˈneɪʃən/, rhythmicality /rɪðmɪˈkæliti/, cavity /ˈkævɪti/, velum /ˈviːləm/, uvula /ˈjuːvjʊlə/, pharynx /ˈfærɪŋks/, epiglottis /epɪˈglɒtɪs/, oesophagus /iːˈsɒfəgəs/, trachea /trəˈkiːə/, fortis /ˈfɔːtɪs/, lenis /ˈliːnɪs/, triphthong /ˈtrɪfθɒŋ/, spread /spred/, close (adj.) /kləʊs/, diagram /ˈdaɪəgræm/, affricate /ˈæfrɪkət/, lateral /ˈlætərəl/, continuant /kənˈtɪnjuənt/, bilabial /baɪˈleɪbiəl/, labiodental /leɪbiəʊˈdentəl/, postalveolar /pəʊstælviˈəʊlə/, palato-alveolar /ˈpælətəʊævlviˈəʊlə/, palatal /ˈpælətəl/, velar /ˈviːlə/, glottal /ˈglɒtəl/, trait /treɪ/ (/treɪt/), nasalization /neɪzəlaɪˈzeɪʃən/, hoarseness /ˈhɔːsnəs/, kinesics /kaɪˈniːsɪks/ (/kɪˈniːsɪks/, /kaɪˈniːzɪks/), gesture /ˈdʒestʃə/, posture /ˈpɒstʃə/, oculesics /ɒkjʊˈliːsɪks/ (/ɒkjʊˈliːzɪks/), haptics /ˈhæptɪks/, tactile /ˈtæktaɪl/, proxemics /prɒkˈsiːmɪks/, spatial /ˈspeɪʃəl/, communicative /kəˈmjuːnɪkətɪv/.

2.0 DESCRIPTION OF VOWELS AND CONSO-NANTS

2.1 VOWELS: MONOPHTHONGS AND DIPHTHONGS

There are twenty vocalic phonemes in British English (RP). They can be categorized in terms of their type (monophthongs, diphthongs), their production (position of the lips, the tongue, the part of the tongue used and the degree of raising), their position in the mouth (front, central, back, close/high and open/low), the force of articulation (tense, lax), the length of the vowel (short, long) and the position of the velum (raised, lowered). Monophthongs are the front vowels /iː, ɪ, e, æ/, the central vowels /ʌ, ə, ɜː/ and the back vowels /ɑː, ɒ, ɔː, ʊ, uː/. Diphthongs ('twice sounding') are sequences of vocalic elements which form a glide within one syllable. As the stress and the length associated with the glide is usually concentrated on the first element, the diphthongs are said to be falling. The diphthongs can be categorized as closing diphthongs (gliding from a more open to a closer position, as the second element is a close vowel, ie /ɪ/ and /ʊ/ as in /eɪ, əʊ, aɪ, aʊ, ɔɪ/) and central diphthongs (the second element is an /ə/ as in /ɪə, eə, ʊə/). Triphthongs, which have no phonemic status, are closing diphthongs followed by /ə/ within a word, either as an inseparable part of the word (*mayor, boa, fire, sour, soya*) or as a suffix added to the root (*player, slower, higher, defiant, greyer, employer, joyous*) or as a separable element in a composite form (*nowadays, throwaway*). All vowels are voiced.

VOWELS: monophthongs

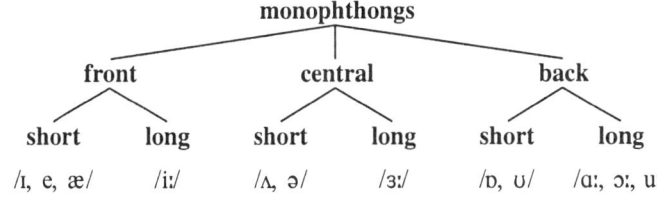

Inventory of English vowels (monophthongs)

VOWELS: diphthongs and triphthongs

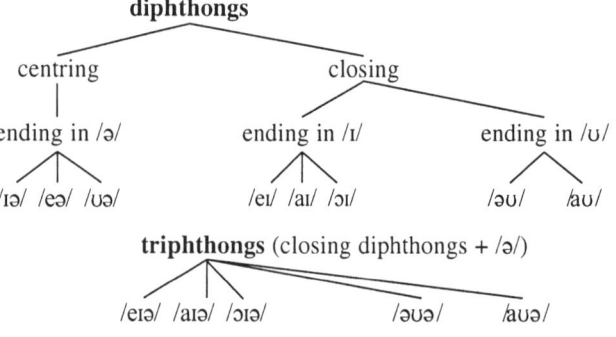

Inventory of English vowels (diphthongs and triphthongs)

1. The vowel /iː/

Description and position in the mouth: The front of the tongue is raised to a high position slightly behind and below the close front position. The lips are spread, the tongue is tense, with the side rims making firm contact with the upper back teeth.

Classification of /iː/: vowel, monophthong, front, close, tense, spread, long.

Variants: The vowel is often diphthongized in final position resulting in [ɪiː].

General cognitive difficulties:

- *quay, people, Beauchamp, cedar, ether, Edith, niece, demon, species, heathen, receipt, veto, unique, technique, epoch, lever, penalize.*
- Latin and Greek words having <ae> and <oe>: *Caesar, aesthetics, encyclopaedia, Croesus, phoenix, amoeba.*

Cognitive difficulties relating to differences between BrE (RP) and GenAmE: *epoch* and *lever* have /e/, *penalize* has /e/ or /iː/ in GenAmE.

Psychomotoric difficulties: no major difficulties for German speakers. Diphthongization should be taken into account.

2. The vowel /ɪ/

Description and position in the mouth: The part of the tongue between front and centre is raised just above the half-close position. The lips are loosely spread, the tongue is lax, with the side rims making light contact with the upper back teeth.

Classification of /ɪ/: vowel, monophthong, front to middle, half-close, lax, loosely spread (nearly neutral), short.

Variants: no major variants exist in RP. The use of unstressed [i] in certain positions is nowadays common in words such as *happy, happier, react, appreciate, Sunday, twentieth.*

General cognitive difficulties:

- *build, business, women, minute, England, guinea, kindle, kindred, pigeon, Hereford, lettuce, forehead, preface, biscuit, breeches* (also /ˈbriːtʃəz/), *Greenwich, sieve, mischief, surfeit.*
- Latin and Greek words ending in <e> preferably have [i]: *apostrophe, recipe, simile, Dante, Athene, Irene.*

Cognitive difficulties relating to differences between BrE (RP) and GenAmE: *been* has /bɪn/ or /ben/, *anti-* and *semi-* have /aɪ/ or /ɪ/ ([i]) in GenAmE.

Psychomotoric difficulties: no major difficulties for German speakers. Southern German speakers and speakers from the Rhineland sometimes use a tense /i/ instead of a lax /ɪ/.

3. The vowel /e/

Description and position in the mouth: The front of the tongue is raised between the half-open and half-close positions. The lips are loosely spread, and are slightly wider apart than for /ɪ/. The tongue is between lax and tense, with the side rims making light contact with the upper back teeth.

Classification of /e/: vowel, monophthong, front, half-open, half-close, half-tense, slightly spread, short.

Variants: The vowel is often more open before dark /l/ resulting in [ɛ].

General cognitive difficulties:

says, said, bury, burial, Canterbury, Geoffrey, Leicester, friend, sweat, zealous, Leonard, leopard, jeopardy, threepence, lieutenant, leisure, any, many, Thames, Pall Mall (formerly /e/, nowadays /æ/), *heifer, Reading, cleanse, deaf, tread, cleanly* (adj.), *ate* (also /eɪ/), *again* (also /eɪ/).

Cognitive difficulties relating to differences between BrE (RP) and GenAmE: GenAmE has *lieutenant* /luː-/, *ate* /eɪ/ (non-standard AmE /et/), *leisure* /iː/. Some American speakers use the same pronunciation for the words *Mary, marry* and *merry,* ie /e/ ([ɛ]).

Psychomotoric difficulties: no major difficulties for German speakers. Sometimes hypercorrection can be observed resulting in a very open realization of the vowel as in /æ/.

4. The vowel /æ/

Description and position in the mouth: The front of the tongue is raised to a position between half-open and open and the jaw is slightly dropped. The lips are neutrally open, the tongue is slightly tense, with the side rims making very light contact with the back teeth.

Classification of /æ/: vowel, monophthong, front, half-open to open, half-tense to tense, neutral, short (between short and long).

Variants: no major variants exist in RP.

General cognitive difficulties:

- *ass, bass (= fish), bade* (also /beɪd/), *balcony, finance, romance, expand, gas, scalp, Pall Mall* (also formerly /pel mel/), *The Mall, salmon, glacier, gravel, mass (= mass of people), mass (= eucharist)* (also /mɑːs/), *agile, raven* (v.), *plait, garage, Japan, patronize, chamois/chammy/shammy* (*leather*).
- Variation: either /æ/ or /ɑː/ in RP: *lather, trans-, elastic, plastic.* (Formerly also very conservative RP variants: *Atlantic, gymnastics*).
- Variation: either /æ/ or /eɪ/: *apical, azure.*

Cognitive difficulties relating to differences between BrE (RP) and GenAmE: GenAmE *plait* /pleɪt/ or /plæt/; free variation in GenAmE between /æ/ and /eɪ/ in *apical, apricot, azure, matrix, patronize.*

Psychomotoric difficulties: a major problem for German speakers, who replace /æ/ by /ɛ/ or /e/ in words like *action, back, sack* etc (cf. chapter 9). The mispronunciation of *man* */men/ consequently results in the incorrect pronunciation of *men* */mɪn/: thus one hears singular */men/ (for *man*) and plural */mɪn/ (for *men*).

5. The vowel /ɑː/

Description and position in the mouth: The part of the tongue between the centre and back is in the fully open position and no contact is made between the rims of the tongue and the upper back teeth. The lips are neutrally open, the jaws are quite apart, and the tongue is tense.

Classification of /ɑː/: vowel, monophthong, back to middle, open, tense, neutral, long.

Variants: no major variants exist in RP.

General cognitive difficulties:

- *cigar, Derby, Berkeley, clerk, sergeant, alms, ah, aha, ma, pa, amen* (also /eɪmen/).
- French words <a>, <-oir> and <-ois>: *garage* (also /ɪ/), *moustache, vase, promenade, reservoir, abattoir, boudoir, memoir, bourgeois, chamois*.
- loanwords from other languages (eg from Latin, Italian): *bravo, cantata, drama, lava, sonata, soprano, sultana, pyjamas, banana, lager, saga, tomato*.

Cognitive difficulties relating to differences between BrE (RP) and GenAmE: *staff, bath, glass, rather, aunt, command, dance, plant, laugh, ask, bath, path, rather, example* have /æ/; *vase* /veɪs/ or /veɪz/, *tomato* has /eɪ/; *Derby, Berkeley, clerk* have /ɜː/; in certain environments GenAmE retains /ɑː/ (cf. 8.2 American English).

Psychomotoric difficulties: no major difficulties for German speakers.

6. The vowel /ɒ/

Description and position in the mouth: The back of the tongue is in the fully open position. The lips are open and slightly rounded, the tongue is lax with the side rims making no contact with the upper back teeth. The jaw is wide open.

Classification of /ɒ/: vowel, monophthong, back, open, lax, rounded, short.

Variants: no major variants exist in RP. Occasionally, a very old-fashioned pronunciation /ɔː/ can still be heard.

General cognitive difficulties:

cough, Gloucester, trough, swan, sovereign, product, barometer, speedometer, biology, geology, philosophy, Maurice, yacht, hover, wan, wrath (also /rɔːθ/).

Cognitive difficulties relating to differences between BrE (RP) and GenAmE: The vowel /ɒ/ is not used in GenAmE, it is usually replaced by /ɑː/ or /ɔː/ (cf. 8.2 American English). The word *wrath* is usually /ræθ/ in GenAmE.

Psychomotoric difficulties: no major difficulties for German speakers, but Germans should produce a very open vowel, since the German /ɒ/ is half-open. In other words, Germans have to drop their jaw to produce the correct English vowel.

7. The vowel /ɔː/

Description and position in the mouth: The back of the tongue is raised between the half-open and half-close positions. The lips are medium-rounded, the tongue is half-tense, with the side rims making no contact with the upper back teeth.

Classification of /ɔː/: vowel, monophthong, back, half-open, half-close, tense, rounded, long.

Variants: no major variants exist in RP.

General cognitive difficulties:

Magdalen (College), appal, Sean, mall (also /mæl/).

Cognitive difficulties relating to differences between BrE (RP) and GenAmE: The vowel /ɔː/ is used in GenAmE, but can be replaced by /ɑː/. There is often free variation between /ɔː/ and /ɑː/. (cf. 8.2 American English).

Psychomotoric difficulties: no major difficulties for German speakers.

8. The vowel /ʊ/

Description and position in the mouth: The part of the tongue between the centre and back is raised just above the half-close position. The lips are closely but loosely rounded, the tongue is lax, with the side rims making no contact with the upper back teeth.

Classification of /ʊ/: vowel, monophthong, back to middle, half-close, lax, rounded, short.

Variants: no major variants exist in RP. The use of unstressed [u] in certain positions is nowadays common in words such as *situation* and *annual*.

General cognitive difficulties:

cushion, wool, woollen, wolf, worsted, Worcester, Wolsey, cuckoo, courier, bosom, woman, soot, brook, Boleyn, Pembroke, Woolwich, hook, hood, foot.

Cognitive difficulties relating to differences between BrE (RP) and GenAmE: no major differences exist.

Psychomotoric difficulties: no major difficulties for German speakers.

9. The vowel /uː/

Description and position in the mouth: The back of the tongue is raised to a high position. The lips are closely rounded, the tongue is quite tense with the side rims making no contact with the upper back teeth.

Classification of /uː/: vowel, monophthong, back, close, tense, rounded, long.

Variants: The vowel is often diphthongized in final position resulting in [ʊuː].

General cognitive difficulties:

canoe, tomb, womb, Ouse, coup, rouge, route, menu, cue, bugle, nucleus, eucalyptus, eunuch, Teutonic, adieu, deuce, pseudo, nephew, ague, Sioux, ouzel, impugn, fuchsia, manoeuvre, wound (n.), *bamboo, Sue, Susan, newt, nude, Jew, juice, loot, loose.*

Cognitive difficulties relating to differences between BrE (RP) and GenAmE: the word *route* is /raut/ or /ruːt/ in GenAmE.

Psychomotoric difficulties: no major difficulties for German speakers. Diphthongization should be taken into account.

10. The vowel /ʌ/

Description and position in the mouth: The centre of the tongue is raised just above the fully open position. The lips are neutrally open, the tongue is lax, with the side rims making no contact with the upper back teeth. The jaw is fairly open.

Classification of /ʌ/: vowel, monophthong, centre, half-open to open, lax, neutral, short.

Variants: no major variants exist in RP.

General cognitive difficulties:

onion, London, oven, blood, flood, stomach, twopence, wonder, hiccough, Douglas, Doug, hurry, curry, courage, worry.

Cognitive difficulties relating to differences between BrE (RP) and GenAmE: *hurry, curry, courage* and *worry* have /ɜː/ in GenAmE. *Note*: Words which have intervocalic /r/, but which are derived from base forms with /ɜː/, keep /ɜː/ as in *purring, furry.*

Psychomotoric difficulties: no major difficulties for German speakers.

11. The vowel /ɜː/

Description and position in the mouth: The centre of the tongue is raised between half-close and half-open. The lips are neutrally spread, the tongue is tense, with the side rims making no contact with the upper back teeth.

Classification of /ɜː/: vowel, monophthong, centre, half-close to half-open, tense, spread to neutral, long.

Variants: no major variants exist in RP.
General cognitive difficulties:
myrtle, myrrh, err, er, purr, purse, worse, journey, courtesy, scourge, colonel, sterling, Stirling, worm, attorney, were, connoisseur, Persia, surgeon.
Cognitive difficulties relating to differences between BrE (RP) and GenAmE: no major differences exist, but GenAmE always has /ɜːr/, where BrE (RP) has /ɜː/ (cf. also RP /ɑː/ and /ʌ/).
Psychomotoric difficulties: no major difficulties for German speakers.

12. The vowel /ə/

Description and position in the mouth: The centre of the tongue is raised between half-open and half-close position. The lips are neutrally spread, the tongue is lax, with the side rims making no contact with the upper back teeth.
Classification of /ə/: vowel, monophthong, centre, half-close to half-open, lax, neutral, short.
Variants: no major variants exist in RP.
General cognitive difficulties:
The schwa sound, which is the usual name for the neutral vowel [ə], is the most frequent sound in English. It is used for any unstressed vowel, eg <a> (*woman*), <e> (*gentlemen*), <i> (*possible*), <o> (*oblige*) and <u> (*suppose*). It is also normal in unaccented function words such as *a, an, at, but, for, from* etc (cf. weak forms, chapter 4.1). The former contrast between unstressed /ɪ/ and /ə/ in words like *affect - effect, accept - except, officers - offices, razors - raises, grocers - grosses, battered - batted, chattered - chatted* is nowadays lost in RP. It might be retained in *allusion - illusion.* In contrast to English, only a weakened <e> can be reduced to schwa in German. The distribution is thus different and may cause cognitive problems. Examples are *Lincoln, London, monarch, purchase, breakfast, trespass, comfort, effort, borough, succeed, bonus, thorough, gentleman.*
Cognitive difficulties relating to differences between BrE (RP) and GenAmE: in unstressed <ar>, <er>, <ir>, <or> and <ur> American English has /ər/, where BrE has /ə/. Examples are *sugar, better, Virginia, information, survive.*
Psychomotoric difficulties: no major difficulties for German speakers. Speakers from the North of Germany and Berlin sometimes use an /ɐ/, especially in final position.

13. The vowel /eɪ/

Description and position in the mouth: The glide starts from slightly below the close-mid front position and then moves in the direction of RP /ɪ/, which is accompanied by a slight closing movement of the lower jaw. The lips are loosely spread.

Classification of /eɪ/: vowel, closing diphthong, front, tense, spread, long.

Variants: no major variants exist in RP, although the first element can have a latitude of variation.

General cognitive difficulties:

halfpenny, sleigh, steak, gauge, gaol (jail), Cambridge, chamber, pastry, ballet, café, née, début, résumé, communiqué, fiancée, précis, Gaelic, chaos, fragrance, manger, patent, vacant, radar, yea, Abraham, mania, raven (n., adj.), *steak, Yeats, bass (= in music), base, champagne, dahlia, eh.*

Cognitive difficulties relating to differences between BrE (RP) and GenAmE: no major differences exist. The word *patent* is /pætənt/ in GenAmE, but also /peɪtənt/ meaning *obvious* (cf. also individual cases dealt with under RP /e/, /æ/ and /ɑː/).

Psychomotoric difficulties: no major difficulties for German speakers.

14. The vowel /aɪ/

Description and position in the mouth: The glide starts at a point slightly behind the front open position and then moves in the direction of RP /ɪ/, which is accompanied by a closing movement of the lower jaw. The lips move from a neutral position to a loosely spread position.

Classification of /aɪ/: vowel, closing diphthong, from between centre and front to front, tense, from neutral to spread, long.

Variants: no major variants exist in RP, although the first element can have a latitude of variation.

General cognitive difficulties:

aye, live (adj.), *pint, bias, diverse, choir, lilac, viscount, horizon, indict, height, alibi, aisle, minute (= tiny), franchise, psychology, geyser, bacilli, nuclei, stimuli, missile, finite, wild, climb, wind* (v.), *malign, sleight, dye, thyme, paradigm, fertile, hostile, docile.*

Cognitive difficulties relating to differences between BrE (RP) and GenAmE: *fertile, hostile, docile* have /ɪl/ or /əl/ in GenAmE.

Psychomotoric difficulties: no major difficulties for German speakers.

15. The vowel /ɔɪ/

Description and position in the mouth: The glide starts at a point between the back half-open and open positions and then moves in the direction of RP /ɪ/, which is accompanied by a closing movement of the lower jaw. The lips move from an open rounded position to a loosely spread position.

Classification of /ɔɪ/: vowel, closing diphthong, from back to front, tense, from rounded to neutrally spread, long.

Variants: no major variants exist in RP, although the first element can have some variation.

General cognitive difficulties:

buoy, buoyant.

Cognitive difficulties relating to differences between BrE (RP) and GenAmE: no major differences exist.

Psychomotoric difficulties: no major difficulties for German speakers.

16. The vowel /əʊ/

Description and position in the mouth: The glide starts at a central position between half-close and half-open and then moves in the direction of RP /ʊ/, which is accompanied by a slight closing movement of the lower jaw. The lips move from a neutral position to a loosely rounded position.

Classification of /əʊ/: vowel, closing diphthong, from centre to back, tense, from neutral to loosely rounded, long.

Variants: no major variants exist in RP, although the first element can have a more rounded and backer variant with conservative speakers.

General cognitive difficulties:

doe, sloe, foe, hoe, mauve, beau, bureau, causerie, brooch, Holborn, Moscow, sew, shew, cocoa, tobacco, folk, yolk, comb, gross, Job, fore-castle /fəʊksl/, row (= use oars, line, trip in rowing boat), bow (= knot, also for arrows, for violin), yeoman.

Cognitive difficulties relating to differences between BrE (RP) and GenAmE: The usual realization in AmE is /oʊ/; *brooch* has /oʊ/ or /uː/ in GenAmE.

Psychomotoric difficulties: some difficulties for German speakers, who should make a conscious effort to start with an /ə/ and then glide to /ʊ/.

17. The vowel /aʊ/

Description and position in the mouth: The glide starts at a point between the back and front open positions and then moves in the direction of RP /ʊ/, which is accompanied by a slight closing movement of the lower jaw. The lips move from a neutrally open position to a weakly rounded position.

Classification of /aʊ/: vowel, closing diphthong, from between centre and back to back, tense, from neutral to rounded, long.

Variants: no major variants exist in RP, although the first element can be extra long.

General cognitive difficulties:

Macleod, cowl, bough, plough, bow (= *act of bending, bend the body or head forward; front of a boat*), *owl, vow, drought, slough* (= *swamp*), *row* (= *quarrel*), *sow* (= *female pig*), *wound* (= past and pp of *wind*), *Cowley.*

Cognitive difficulties relating to differences between BrE (RP) and GenAmE: no major differences exist.

Psychomotoric difficulties: no major difficulties for German speakers.

18. The vowel /ɪə/

Description and position in the mouth: The glide starts at a front half-close position and then moves in the direction of RP /ə/. The lips are neutral, with a slight movement from loosely spread to open.

Classification of /ɪə/: vowel, centring diphthong, from front to centre, tense, from between neutral and spread to open, long.

Variants: no major variants exist in RP, although /ə/ can be more open in final position.

General cognitive difficulties:

hero, Ian, Iain, dreary, weary, Deirdre, weird, fakir, tear (= *drop of liquid*), *imperialism.*

Cognitive difficulties relating to differences between BrE (RP) and GenAmE: This diphthong does not exist in GenAmE, where one has the combination of /ɪ/ and /r/ (/ɪr/).

Psychomotoric difficulties: no major difficulties for German speakers. Sometimes the second element is incorrectly replaced by an /ɐ/.

Note: /ɪə/ is usually a falling diphthong, but it is a rising diphthong in unstressed syllables where /ɪ/ is often realized as /j/ (examples are *windier, serious, idiom*).

19. The vowel /eə/

Description and position in the mouth: The glide starts at a half-open front position and then moves in the direction of RP /ə/. The lips are neutrally open throughout.

Classification of /eə/: vowel, centring diphthong, from front to centre, tense, neutral, long.

Variants: no major variants exist in RP, although the first element is sometimes extra long and the second element is sometimes dropped.

General cognitive difficulties:

mare, pear, heir, there, their, Mary, Sarah, scarce, mayor, prayer (= act of praying).

Cognitive difficulties relating to differences between BrE (RP) and GenAmE: This diphthong does not exist in GenAmE, where one has the combination of /e/ and /r/ (/er/ or /ɛr/).

Psychomotoric difficulties: no major difficulties for German speakers. Sometimes the first element is incorrectly replaced by an /eː/ and the second element by an /ɐ/.

20. The vowel /ʊə/

Description and position in the mouth: The glide starts at a back half-close position and then moves in the direction of RP /ə/. The lips move from a weakly rounded position to a neutrally spread position.

Classification of /ʊə/: vowel, centring diphthong, from back to centre, tense, from rounded to neutral, long.

Variants: one major variant exists in RP. In frequently used monosyllabic words like *poor, your, you're* and *sure,* the diphthong changes into /ɔː/.

General cognitive difficulties:

bourse, jewel, Europe, fluent, truant, urine, dour, gourd, pleurisy.

Cognitive difficulties relating to differences between BrE (RP) and GenAmE: This diphthong does not exist in GenAmE, where one has the combination of /ʊ/ and /r/ (/ʊr/).

Psychomotoric difficulties: no major difficulties for German speakers. Sometimes the second element is incorrectly replaced by an /ɐ/.

Note: /ʊə/ is usually a falling diphthong, but it is a rising diphthong in unstressed syllables where /ʊ/ is often realized as a weakened /w/ (examples are *influence, valuable, vacuum, jaguar*).

2.2 CONSONANTS AND SEMI-VOWELS

There are twenty-four consonantal phonemes in British English (RP). They can be divided into **obstruents** and **sonorants**. In the articulation of obstruents, one can find either total closure (**plosives** or **stops** and **affricates**) or a stricture causing friction (**fricatives**). Obstruents include the bilabial plosives /p, b/, alveolar plosives /t, d/, velar plosives /k, g/ and the palato-alveolar affricates /tʃ, dʒ/. The fricatives are the labiodental /f, v/, dental /θ, ð/, alveolar /s, z/, palato-alveolar /ʃ, ʒ/ and glottal /h/. In the articulation of sonorants, one can find only partial closure combined with an unimpeded oral escape of air (**approximants**) or nasal escape of air (**nasals**). There are three English nasals: bilabial /m/, alveolar /n/ and velar /ŋ/. Approximants can be divided into the lateral approximant /l/ (**liquid**), the postalveolar approximant /r/ (**liquid**), the palatal approximant or **semi-vowel** or **glide** /j/ and the (labio-)velar approximant or semi-vowel or glide /w/.

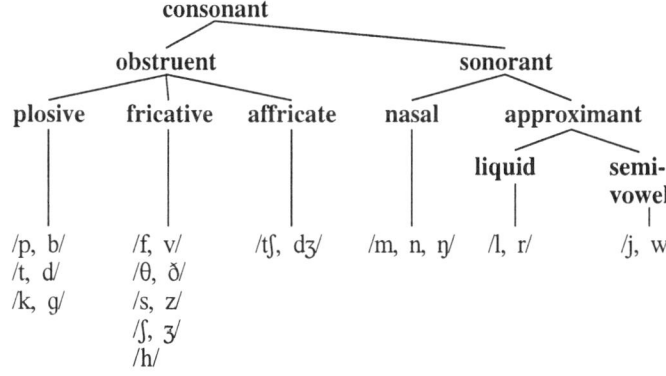

Inventory of English consonants

Plosives

Plosives or stops are sounds which are produced by stopping the air-stream from the lungs completely and then suddenly releasing it with an explosion. The articulation of plosives consists of three stages:

1st stage: **closing stage**, during which the articulating organs move together in order to form the obstruction.

2nd stage: **hold (compression) stage**, during which the air is compressed behind the closure. In this stage, the vocal cords or vocal folds may or may not vibrate.

3rd stage: **release (explosion) stage**, during which the organs involved are opened abruptly thus allowing the air to escape with an explosion.

1. The consonants /p/ and /b/

Description and position in the mouth: The consonants /p/ and /b/ are formed by closure of the lips.

1.1 Classification of /p/: consonant, plosive, bilabial, fortis, voiceless.
Realization: /p/ is strongly aspirated initially in accented syllables (*pin, appear, pray*), relatively unaspirated in unaccented syllables (*upper, capable, simply*) and always unaspirated after /s/ (*spin, sprain*).
Variants: no major variants exist in RP.
General cognitive difficulties:
- *hiccough.*
- silent /p/: *receipt, corps, pneumonia, pneumatic, Ptolemy, coup, cupboard, raspberry.*
- most words with <ps-> have either /s/ or /ps/ : *psalm, pseudo-, psychology.*

Cognitive difficulties relating to differences between BrE (RP) and GenAmE: no major differences exist.
Psychomotoric difficulties: no difficulties for German speakers.

1.2 Classification of /b/: consonant, plosive, bilabial, lenis, voiced.
Realization: /b/ is fully voiced between vowels (*rubber, labour*), partially devoiced in initial position (*beauty, brand*) and fully devoiced in final position *(robe, ebb).*
Variants: no major variants exist in RP.
General cognitive difficulties:
silent /b/: *limb, thumb, comb, debt, subtle, subtlety, tomb, dumb, bomb, bomber, bombing, climb, plumber, lamb, succumb.*
Cognitive difficulties relating to differences between BrE (RP) and GenAmE: no major differences exist.
Psychomotoric difficulties: German speakers have difficulty in pronouncing final /b/ (cf. devoicing).

2. The consonants /t/ and /d/

Description and position in the mouth: The consonants /t/ and /d/ are formed by a closure made between the tip and the rims of the tongue and the upper alveolar ridge and side teeth.

2.1 Classification of /t/: consonant, plosive, alveolar, fortis, voiceless.
Realization: /t/ is strongly aspirated initially in accented syllables *(tin, attain, tray)*, relatively unaspirated in unaccented syllables *(utter, outward, entry)* and always unaspirated after /s/ *(stone, strain)*.
Variants: no major variants exist in RP.
General cognitive difficulties:
- /t/ pronunciation in words with <th>: *Esther, Thames, thyme, Theresa, Thomas, Thompson.*
- past marker <ed> is pronounced /t/ after voiceless consonants (except /t/): *stopped, laughed, hissed.*
- silent /t/: *castle, Christmas, glisten, listen, mortgage, chestnut, wrestle, moisten, mistletoe, depot, bouquet, ballet.*
- either with /t/ or with /θ/: *Anthony, Bentham.*
Cognitive difficulties relating to differences between BrE (RP) and GenAmE: The flap [D] occurs in GenAmE intervocalically and between vowel+certain consonants+vowel in words like *matter, writer, winter, wanted, porter* (cf. chapter 8.2).
Psychomotoric difficulties: no difficulties for German speakers.

2.2 Classification of /d/: consonant, plosive, alveolar, lenis, voiced.
Realization: /d/ is fully voiced between vowels *(rudder, rider)*, partially devoiced in initial position *(duty, drink)* and fully devoiced in final position *(rode, bad)*.
Variants: no major variants exist in RP.
General cognitive difficulties:
- silent /d/: *handsome, handkerchief.*
- past marker <ed> is pronounced /d/ after vowels and voiced consonants (except /d/): *booed, barred, begged.*
- past marker <ed> pronounced /əd/ or /ɪd/ after /d / or /t/: *waited, waded.*
- generally silent /d/, but also with /d/: *landlady, Windsor, sandwich.*
Cognitive difficulties relating to differences between BrE (RP) and GenAmE: The flap [D] occurs in GenAmE intervocalically and between vowel+certain consonants+vowel in words like *rider, rudder, harder* (cf. chapter 8.2).

Psychomotoric difficulties: German speakers have difficulty in pronouncing final /d/ (cf. devoicing).

3. The consonants /k/ and /g/

Description and position in the mouth: The consonants /k/ and /g/
are formed by the closure made between the back of the tongue and
the soft palate.

3.1 Classification of /k/: consonant, plosive, velar, fortis, voiceless.
Realization: /k/ is strongly aspirated initially in accented syllables
(kin, account, came), relatively unaspirated in unaccented syllables
(baker, anchor, biscuit) and always unaspirated after /s/ *(skin, screen).*
Variants: no major variants exist in RP.
General cognitive difficulties:
- with /k/: *scholar, schooner, ache, anchor, archives, choir, Czech,
  machination, mechanic, Michael, stomach, technique, archangel,
  chaos, echo, scheme, quay, banquet.*
- silent /k/: *knave, knife, knock, Knorr (soup), Knirps (umbrella),
  Connecticut, indictment, muscle, victuals.*
Note: In foreign words beginning with <kn->, /k/ is usually dropped
as in *knackwurst, Knirps, Knorr.* Sometimes variant pronunciations
can be heard with /k/, with /k/ followed by an epenthetic /ə/ or without /k/ as in *Knesset, Knossos, Knauss, Knopf.*
**Cognitive difficulties relating to differences between BrE (RP)
and GenAmE:** /sk/: *schedule* in GenAmE, BrE (RP) has /ʃ/ or /sk/.
Psychomotoric difficulties: no difficulties for German speakers.

3.2 Classification of /g/: consonant, plosive, velar, lenis, voiced.
Realization: /g/ is fully voiced between vowels *(rugger, eager),* partially devoiced in initial position *(go, great)* and fully devoiced in
final position *(rogue, egg).*
Variants: no major variants exist in RP.
General cognitive difficulties:
- silent /g/: *sing, singer, singing, tongue, gnaw, gnu, gnome, gnosis,
  gnat, diaphragm, malign, phlegm, paradigm.*
- /g/ in Germanic words: *geese, Gilbert, Gertrude.*
**Cognitive difficulties relating to differences between BrE (RP)
and GenAmE:** no major differences exist.

Psychomotoric difficulties: German speakers have difficulty in pronouncing final /g/ (cf. devoicing).

Note: **The glottal plosive** or **glottal stop** /ʔ/, which can sometimes be heard in the speech of RP and GenAmE speakers, is not part of the phonemic system of RP or GenAmE. Some speakers use the glottal plosive as a means of emphasis before a stressed vowel. It is also used in interjections. Examples are *ge* /ʔ/ *ography, co* /ʔ/ *operate, re* /ʔ/ *action* and *it was* /ʔ/ *awful, the bottle is* /ʔ/ *empty, I haven't seen* /ʔ/ *anybody,* /ʔ/ *ow,* /ʔ/ *oops,* /ʔ/ *oh.*
The glottal stop is more common in RP than in GenAmE .
Description and position in the mouth: The glottal plosive /ʔ/ is formed by the closure of the vocal cords, where the air-stream is obstructed. The air pressure below the glottis is released by the sudden separation of the vocal cords and the air escapes through the mouth.
Classification of /ʔ/: consonant, plosive, glottal, fortis, voiceless.
Psychomotoric difficulties: no difficulties for German speakers in producing a glottal plosive, but the use (and over-use) is not to be recommended.

Affricates

The term **affricate** refers to a combination of a plosive and a fricative sound. It refers to a sound made when the air-pressure behind a complete closure in the oral cavity is gradually released and considerable friction occurs approximately at the point where the plosive is made. The friction present in an affricate is of shorter duration than that which characterizes an independent fricative.

4. The consonants /tʃ/ and /dʒ/
Description and position in the mouth: The consonants /tʃ/ and /dʒ/ are formed by a closure made between the tip and the rims of the tongue and the upper alveolar ridge and side teeth. The closure is released slowly with a fricative release stage.

4.1 Classification of /tʃ/: consonant, affricative, palato-alveolar, fortis, voiceless.
Realization: no allophone exists in RP.
Variants: no major variants exist in RP (cf. semi-vowels).

General cognitive difficulties:
- /tʃ/: *mischief, feature, orchard, cello, concerto, Czech.*
- /tʃ/ or /dʒ/: *Harwich, Norwich, Greenwich, Woolwich, spinach.*
- /tʃ/ or /k/: *conch.*
- /tʃ/ or /ʃ/: *niche.*
- /tʃ/ or /ʃ/ in clusters starting with <n> in final or sometimes medial positions: *pinch, pinching, branch, French, luncheon.*

Cognitive difficulties relating to differences between BrE (RP) and GenAmE: no major differences exist. GenAmE usually prefers /tʃ/, where there is variation between /tʃ/ and /dʒ/ in BrE.

Psychomotoric difficulties: some German speakers omit the plosive element. They should make a conscious effort to pronounce the first element of the affricate (cf. German *Tschechin, Tschako, Tscherkessen, tschüs*).

4.2 Classification of /dʒ/: consonant, affricative, palato-alveolar, lenis, voiced.

Realization: /dʒ/ is fully voiced between vowels (*pidgin, reject*), partially devoiced in initial position (*joke, jam*) and fully devoiced in final position (*village, rage*).

Variants: no major variants exist in RP (cf. semi-vowels).

General cognitive difficulties:
- /dʒ/: *ginger, longevity, manger, digest, singe, gauge.*
- /dʒ/ or /tʃ/: *Harwich, Norwich, Greenwich, Woolwich, spinach.*
- /dʒ/ or /ʒ/ in clusters starting with <n> in final and sometimes medial positions: *strange, revenge, tinge, stranger, danger.*

Cognitive difficulties relating to differences between BrE (RP) and GenAmE: no major differences exist. GenAmE usually prefers /tʃ/, where there is variation between /tʃ/ and /dʒ/ in BrE.

Psychomotoric difficulties: some German speakers omit the plosive element. They should make a conscious effort to pronounce the first element of the affricate (cf. German loan words such as *Jungle, Jazz*). German speakers also have difficulty in pronouncing final /dʒ/ (cf. devoicing).

Note: **Special kinds of explosion**
As far as the release stage of plosives is concerned, there are three kinds of explosion with plosives depending on the following consonant.
- **incomplete explosion** for the combination plosive+plosive:
When one plosive is immediately followed by another, the closure of

the speech organs for the second plosive is made, while the closure and the hold stage of the first plosive is still in position. Thus there are two compression stages. Only then are the lips opened and the air is released in one explosion for the two plosives.

Examples are *kept, act, hot temper, stop talking, what chance.*

- **nasal explosion** for the combination plosive+nasal:

When /t/ or /d/ in particular are followed by an alveolar nasal, the explosion of the stop takes place through the nose. Thus the air explodes out of the nose rather than out of the mouth.

Examples are *written, Britain, ridden.*

- **lateral explosion** for the combination plosive+lateral:

When /t/ or /d/ in particular are followed by a lateral, the explosion takes place laterally, ie the air escapes from the sides of the tongue.

Examples are *middle, title, little, good luck.*

Fricatives

Fricatives are sounds which are produced by allowing the airstream from the lungs to escape with friction. Thus, two organs are brought and held sufficiently together for the escaping air-stream to produce friction.

1. The consonants /f/ and /v/

Description and position in the mouth: The consonants /f/ and /v/ are formed by the inner surface of the lower lip making light contact with the edge of the upper teeth, so that the escaping air produces friction.

1.1 Classification of /f/: consonant, fricative, labiodental, fortis, voiceless.

Realization: no major allophone exists in RP.

Variants: no major variants exist in RP.

General cognitive difficulties:

- *draught, trough, slough (= cast off skin), lieutenant, Stephanie, alpha, phonetics.*

- /f/ or /p/: *diphthong, triphthong, diphtheria.*

Cognitive difficulties relating to differences between BrE (RP) and GenAmE: no major differences exist.

Psychomotoric difficulties: no difficulties for German speakers.

1.2 Classification of /v/: consonant, fricative, labiodental, lenis, voiced.

Realization: /v/ is fully voiced between vowels (*even, oven*), partially devoiced in initial position (*veal, vermin*) and fully devoiced in final position (*love, move*).

Variants: no major variants exist in RP. In the West Country, voiceless /f/ is pronounced as voiced /v/. See also influence on Standard English in words such as *vane* (German *Fahne*), *vat* (German *Faß*) and *vixen* (German *Füchsin*).

General cognitive difficulties:

- *of, Stephen, Stephenson, eisteddfod.*
- /v/ or /f/: *nephew.*

Cognitive difficulties relating to differences between BrE (RP) and GenAmE: no major differences exist.

Psychomotoric difficulties: some German speakers either use too weak a contact for /v/ thus pronouncing [ʊ] or use bilabial friction [β]. There is also **hypercorrection**, which results in /w/, eg *very well* */weri wel/ or *voice* */wɔɪs/. Germans also have difficulty in pronouncing final /v/ (cf. devoicing).

2. The consonants /θ/ and /ð/

Description and position in the mouth: The consonants /θ/ and /ð/ are formed by putting the tip and the rims of the tongue either between the teeth (interdental position) or behind the upper teeth (postdental position).

2.1 Classification of /θ/: consonant, fricative, dental, fortis, voiceless.

Realization: /θ/ is normally produced in post-dental position.

Variants: no major variants exist in RP. In Cockney, /θ/ is replaced by /f/.

General cognitive difficulties:

- usually silent /θ/: *asthma, isthmus.*
- either with /t/ or with /θ/: *Anthony, Bentham.*
- /θ/ or silent /θ/: *months.*

- /t/ pronunciation in words with <th>: *Thames, thyme, Theresa, Thomas, Thompson*
(cf. also **Note on distribution**).
Cognitive difficulties relating to differences between BrE (RP) and GenAmE: no major differences exist.
Psychomotoric difficulties: German speakers have great difficulty in pronouncing /θ/, especially in combination with other fricatives (cf. **Note on psychomotoric difficulties**).

2.2 Classification of /ð/: consonant, fricative, dental, lenis, voiced.
Realization: /ð/ is fully voiced between vowels (*either, father*), partially devoiced in initial position (*then, there*) and fully devoiced in final position (*smooth, breathe*).
Variants: no major variants exist in RP. In Cockney, /ð/ is replaced by /v/.
General cognitive difficulties:
- /ð/ or silent /ð/: *clothes.*
- /ð/ or /θ/: *booth, bequeath, betroth, earthen, with, baths, laths, sheaths, wreaths, oaths, truths, youths.*
(cf. also **Note on distribution**).
Cognitive difficulties relating to differences between BrE (RP) and GenAmE: no major differences exist. GenAmE prefers /θ/ in final position with words written <-th> or <-ths>, eg *booth, betroth, with, paths, truths.*
Psychomotoric difficulties: German speakers have great difficulty in pronouncing /ð/, especially in combination with other fricatives (cf. **Note on psychomotoric difficulties**). They also have difficulty in pronouncing final /ð/ (cf. devoicing).

Note on distribution of /θ/ and /ð/
Initial position
- /θ/ is the normal case: *thin, thistle, through, three, thing, thumb* (German /d/: *dünn, Diestel, durch, drei, Ding, Daumen*).
- /ð/ is the exception, but occurs very often, as words (function words) of very high relative frequency are pronounced in this way: *the, that, those, this, these, they, them, their, there, than, then, though, thus*. Also *thither* (RP /ðɪðə/, GenAmE /θɪðə/ and /ðɪðə/), *thence, thou, thee, thy, thine.*

Medial position

- /θ/ in words of Greek and Latin origin: *method, author, cathedral, pathos, sympathy, panther*.
- /ð/ in words of Germanic origin: *brother, either, father, mother, other, northern, weather, worthy*.

Final position

- /θ/ is the normal case: *bath, birth, breath, faith, health, fifth, north, mouth, path, youth*.
- /ð/ (spelling <-th>): *smooth, mouth* (v.).
- /ð/ (spelling <-the>): *bathe, breathe, clothe, loathe, seethe, soothe, scythe*.

Note on psychomotoric difficulties

If students cannot pronounce /θ, ð/ at all, ie not even in isolation, they should put their tongue between their teeth and push air through the oral cavity. Students can control this position easily, as they can see the interdental position clearly by looking in the mirror. Once students have mastered the interdental position, they should try the post-dental position for the simple reason that, in combinations such as /θ, ð/ with /s, z/, the distance the tongue has to move is shorter and thus easier to manage. The combination of dental and alveolar sounds can best be achieved by letting the tongue glide continuously from one place of articulation to another. The movement of the tongue from one position to the next should be uninterrupted. In other words students should not stop the articulation after one sound and then start anew, as such an interruption in the articulation could result in typical mispronunciations.

"The difficulty of /θ, ð/ lies not so much in their articulation, which most learners can perform correctly in isolation, as in their combination with other fricatives, especially /s/ and /z/. Learners should, therefore, practise with drills containing such combinations involving rapid tongue glides, e.g. /s+θ/ *this thing, sixth,* /z+θ/ *his thumb,* /s+ð/ *pass the salt,* /z+ð/ *is this it?,* /θ+s/ *fifths,* /θ+s+ð/ *Smith's there,* /ð+z+ð/ *soothes them;* (Gimson 1962/94:168-169)."

3. The consonants /s/ and /z/

Description and position in the mouth: The consonants /s/ and /z/ are formed by the tip and blade of the tongue making light contact with the upper alveolar ridge.

3.1 Classification of /s/: consonant, fricative, alveolar, fortis, voiceless.

Realization: no special realizations of /s/.

Variants: no major variants exist in RP. In the West Country, voiceless /s/ is pronounced as voiced /z/.

General cognitive difficulties:

- *cease, increase, decrease, crease, dose, promise, precise, basis, crisis, oasis, analysis, excited, paradise, loose, sausage, cedar, close* (adj., adv.).
- plural marker, genitive and third person <s> is /s/ after voiceless consonants (except sibilants): *pants, months, puffs, stops.*
- silent /s/: *isle, island, aisle, viscount, corps, debris.*

Cognitive difficulties relating to differences between BrE (RP) and GenAmE: no major differences exist.

Psychomotoric difficulties: German speakers have no difficulty in pronouncing /s/. Daniel Jones mentions the fact that Germans often use a slightly different articulation, which results in 'a particularly penetrating **s**'.

3.2 Classification of /z/: consonant, fricative, alveolar, lenis, voiced.

Realization: /z/ is fully voiced between vowels (*fuzzy, hazy*), partially devoiced in initial position (*zone, zeal*) and fully devoiced in final position (*his, buzz*).

Variants: no major variants exist in RP.

General cognitive difficulties:

- *desert* (n.)*, desert* (v.)*, dessert, hussar, muslin, Missouri, Ms, Mrs, venison, schism, scissors, possess, disease, house* (v.)*, houses, use* (v.)*, exam, example, exhibit, Wednesday, Tuesday, Thursday, species, series, bases, crises, oases, analyses, lose, close* (v.)*, dissolve, cleanse, blouse, erase.*
- plural marker, genitive and third person <s> is /z/ after vowels and voiced consonants: *bees, beds, John's, Sarah's, rides, sees.*
- plural marker, genitive and third person <s> is /əz/ or /ɪz/ after sibilants, ie /s, z, ʃ, ʒ, tʃ, dʒ/: *wishes, horses, hisses, budges, Jones's, George's, camouflages, itches.*

Cognitive difficulties relating to differences between BrE (RP) and GenAmE: *blouse* and *erase* always have /s/, *houses* has /z/ or /s/ in GenAmE.

Psychomotoric difficulties: (Northern) German speakers have no difficulty in pronouncing /z/. They do have difficulty in pronouncing final /z/ (cf. devoicing).

Note: Traditionally <x> has been pronounced /ɪgz/ if the primary stress follows <x>, eg *exam, example, exhaust, exhibit, exact*, and /eks/ if the primary stress precedes <x>, eg *exhibition, exit, excavator, exile*. There is now quite a lot of variation resulting in the pronunciations *exit* /eksɪt/ or /egzɪt/, *exert* /ɪgzɜ:t/ or /ekzɜ:t/ and *exam* /ɪgzæm/ or /ekzæm/.

The prefix <ex-> (= *formerly*) is always pronounced /eks/ as in *ex-husband, ex-girlfriend*.

4. The consonants /ʃ/ and /ʒ/

Description and position in the mouth: The consonants /ʃ/ and /ʒ/ are formed by the tip, the blade and the front of the tongue making light contact with the alveolar ridge as well as with the hard palate and the upper side teeth.

4.1 Classification of /ʃ/: consonant, fricative, palato-alveolar, fortis, voiceless.
Realization: no special realizations of /ʃ/ (cf. semi-vowels for cases of assimilation).
Variants: no major variants exist in RP.
General cognitive difficulties:
- *Russia, pension, censure, herbaceous, Sean, schmaltz, schmuck, schwa, schlep.*
- (Modern) French borrowings: *Michigan, Chicago, Charlotte, Charlemagne, champagne, chauffeur, chivalry, parachute.*
- assimilations: *issue, this year, miss you.*
- with /ʃ/ or /sk/: *schedule.*
- with /ʃp/ or /sp/: *spiel.*
Cognitive difficulties relating to differences between BrE (RP) and GenAmE: the word *schedule* is pronounced with /sk-/ in GenAmE. Sometimes BrE (RP) and GenAmE have different preferences: *Asia, Persia, version* are pronounced /ʒ/ or /ʃ/ in BrE (RP) and /ʃ/ or /ʒ/ in GenAmE.
Psychomotoric difficulties: German speakers have no difficulty in pronouncing /ʃ/.

4.2 Classification of /ʒ/: consonant, fricative, palato-alveolar, lenis, voiced.
Realization: /ʒ/ is fully voiced between vowels (*illusion, allusion*), partially devoiced in initial position (*gigolo, genre*) and fully devoiced

in final position (*rouge, beige*).
Variants: no major variants exist in RP.
General cognitive difficulties:
- *gigolo, gendarme, genre, garage* (also /-dʒ/), *allusion, illusion, rouge, beige.*
Cognitive difficulties relating to differences between BrE (RP) and GenAmE: no major differences exist.
Psychomotoric difficulties: (Northern) German speakers have no difficulty in pronouncing /ʒ/; a starting point can be German words like *Genie, Loge* or *Genre*. They do have difficulty in pronouncing final /ʒ/ (cf. devoicing).

5. The consonant /h/

Description and position in the mouth: The consonant /h/ is glottal, ie the friction is caused by the narrowing of the space between the vocal cords. The upper part of the vocal tract is shaped in readiness for the articulation of the following vowel.
Classification of /h/: consonant, fricative, glottal, fortis, voiceless.
Realization: no special realizations of /h/, but it must be noted that there is a voiced allophone medially between vowels in words like *anyhow, perhaps, ahead*.
Variants: one variant exists in RP. In stressed initial position, the sequence /hj/ can be replaced by /ç/ as in *human, huge, hue*.
General cognitive difficulties:
- /h/ or silent /h/: *hysterical, historical, horizon, hotel, habitual* (the indefinite article *an* can be used before a word beginning with <h> when the initial syllable is unstressed, eg *an hotel, an hysterical outburst, an historian, an hereditary title, an habitual offender*).
- initial silent /h/: *honour, hour, hourly, heir, heiress* and in weak forms like *tell her, tell him*.
- medial silent /h/: *shepherd, Durham, Birmingham, Clapham, Buckingham, exhaust, exhilarate, exhibit, vehicle, vehement, annihilate, forehead* (also with /h/).
- always final silent /h/: *oh, ah, hurrah*.
Cognitive difficulties relating to differences between BrE (RP) and GenAmE: the word *herb(s)* (but not the name *Herb*) is always pronounced without /h/ in GenAmE.
Psychomotoric difficulties: German speakers have no difficulty in pronouncing /h/.

Nasals

The three nasal consonants /m, n, ŋ/ are produced by a complete clo-sure within the mouth, the soft palate is in its lowered position and the air escapes entirely through the nasal cavity and the nose. They are usually voiced and resemble vowel-type sounds in that they can perform the syllabic function of vowels (syllabic nasals).

1. The consonant /m/

Description and position in the mouth: The consonant /m/ is formed by a closure of the lips as for /p, b/, the soft palate is lowered adding the resonance of the nasal cavity to those of the pharynx and the oral cavity. The tongue usually retains or anticipates the adjacent sound.

Classification of /m/: consonant, nasal, bilabial, lenis, voiced.

Realization: no special realizations of /m/. If /m/ is preceded by a voiceless consonant there is devoicing (*smoke, topmost, bottom*).

Variants: no major variants exist in RP, but there are some inciden-ces of assimilation (cf. chapter 4.2) in words like *comfort, come first, warm vest* (labiodental /ɱ/) and *one mile, ten pairs, tenpence, hap-pen, ribbon* (/n/ changes into /m/).

General cognitive difficulties:

- consonant after /m/ is silent: *comb, autumn, damn, solemn, lamb, tomb, bomb, bomber, bombing, thumb, climb, limb, succumb, suc-cumbed.*

- silent /m/: *mnemonic.*

Cognitive difficulties relating to differences between BrE (RP) and GenAmE: no differences exist.

Psychomotoric difficulties: German speakers have no difficulty in pronouncing /m/.

2. The consonant /n/

Description and position in the mouth: The consonant /n/ is formed by a closure of the tongue with the teeth ridge and the upper side teeth as for /t, d/. The soft palate is lowered adding the resonance of the nasal cavity to those of the pharynx and the oral cavity behind the alveolar closure. The lip position depends on that of the adjacent vowels, eg rounded lips in *noon*, neutrally open lips in *nark* and spread lips in *neat*. The tongue usually retains or anticipates the adjacent sound.

Classification of /n/: consonant, nasal, alveolar, lenis, voiced.

Realization: no special realizations of /n/. If /n/ is preceded by a voiceless consonant there is devoicing (*snake, chutney, cotton*).

Variants: no major variants exist in RP, but there are some incidences of assimilation (cf. chapter 4.2) in words like *infant, invoice, on fire* (labiodental /ɱ/), *tenth, when they* (dental /n̪/), *ten miles, ten people* (/m/) and *ten cups, ten girls* (/ŋ/).

General cognitive difficulties:
- silent /n/: *autumn, damn, solemn, hymn, column*.
- /n/ or silent /n/: *kiln*.

Cognitive difficulties relating to differences between BrE (RP) and GenAmE: no differences exist.

Psychomotoric difficulties: German speakers have no difficulty in pronouncing /n/. A dental realization instead of the alveolar realization should be avoided.

3. The consonant /ŋ/

Description and position in the mouth: The consonant /ŋ/ is formed by a closure in the mouth between the back of the tongue and the velum as for /k, g/, the soft palate is lowered adding the resonance of the nasal cavity to those of the pharynx and the small part of the oral cavity behind the velar closure. The lip position depends on that of the adjacent vowels and the tongue usually retains or anticipates the adjacent sound.

Classification of /ŋ/: consonant, nasal, velar, lenis, voiced.

Realization: no special realizations of /ŋ/.

Variants: no major variants exist in RP, but there are some incidences of assimilation, eg *ten kilos* (cf. chapter 4.2).

General cognitive difficulties: Cognitive difficulties arise from some different distributions of velar /ŋ/ in German and English.

In English, words with final <ng> and words in which final <ng> becomes medial by adding suffixes are always pronounced with /ŋ/. Exceptional cases are the comparative and superlative of adjectives, where one regularly has /ŋg/, and words ending in <-ish>, which can either have /ŋ/ or /ŋg/.

Words where final or medial <nk> is preceded by a stressed syllable have /ŋk/ only. Words where medial <nk> is preceded by an unstressed syllable have /nk/ or /ŋk/.
The prefix <un-> followed by a velar consonant is always pronounced /ʌnk/ or /ʌng/

- /ŋ/ only: *sing, sings, singing, singer, wronged, belonged, slangy.*
- /ŋ/ or /ŋg/: *longish, youngish, England, English.*
- /ŋg/ only: *longer, longest, younger, youngest, linger, finger.*
- /ŋk/ only: *sink, blinker, handkerchief.*
- /nk/ or /ŋk/: *conclusion, concussion.*
- /nk/ or /ng/ only: *unkind, ungrateful.*

Cognitive difficulties relating to differences between BrE (RP) and GenAmE: no major differences exist.
Psychomotoric difficulties: German speakers have no difficulty in pronouncing /ŋ/ (or /ŋg/ or /ŋk/).

Note on syllabic nature of nasals

Nasals are often **syllabic**, ie they have vocalic character in words ending in /n/ (*written*) and less commonly in words ending in /m/ (*rhythm*) or /ŋ/ (*bacon*).

- /t/ or /d/+unstressed syllable ending in /n/ usually has syllabic [n̩], eg *written, mutton, Britain, ridden, harden.*
- /s/, /z/, /ʃ/, /ʒ/, /tʃ/, /dʒ/, /f/, /v/+unstressed syllable ending in /n/ have syllabic [n̩] or /ən/, eg *person, raisin, occasion, fashion, illusion, kitchen, region, hyphen, even.*

Nasals are **not syllabic** in final position
- if preceded by nasal+unstressed vowel: *common, canon, German.*
- if preceded by nasal+stop+unstressed vowel: *London, Washington, badminton.*

Approximants (oral frictionless continuants)

Approximants are a group of voiced sounds where the airstream escapes through a relatively narrow opening in the mouth without friction. In being frictionless and continuant, approximants are vowel-like. However, they function phonologically as consonants, ie they appear at the edges of syllables. Approximants can be divided into the **lateral approximant** /l/ (from Latin *latus* = side), where the air escapes on both sides of the tongue, the **postalveolar approximant** or **postal-**

veolar frictionless continuant /r/, the **palatal approximant** or **semi-vowel** or **glide** /j/ and the **(labio-)velar approximant** or **semi-vowel** or **glide** /w/.

1. The consonant /l/

Description and position in the mouth: The consonant /l/ is formed by the tip of the tongue being in contact with the alveolar ridge thus creating a partial closure of the mouth. The soft palate is raised and the air escapes on both sides of the tongue through the mouth. For clear [l] the front of the tongue is raised in the direction of the hard palate at the same time as the tip contact is made. For dark [ɫ] the tip contact is also made on the teeth ridge, but the front of the tongue is slightly depressed and the back is raised in the direction of the soft palate. The lip position depends on that of the adjacent vowels, eg rounded lips in *loop* and *pool*, neutrally open lips in *lark* and *Carl* and spread lips in *least* and *peel*. The tongue usually retains or anticipates the adjacent sound.

Classification of /l/: consonant, lateral, alveolar, lenis, voiced.

Realization: /l/ is normally voiced, but it is voiceless when a voiceless consonant precedes /l/ as in *play, clay, flow, slow* or *hopeless*. Apart from differences in voicing, the major difference is in the realization of a clear allophone [l] and a dark allophone [ɫ]. The latter can also be syllabic. Thus one can find four major allophones, ie a voiced clear [l], a voiceless clear [l̥], a voiced dark [ɫ] and a syllabic voiced dark [ɫ̩].

Variants: no major variants exist in RP.

General cognitive difficulties:

- distribution of clear [l] and dark [ɫ]: a clear [l] is used when a vowel or /j/ follows as in *light, loot, failure, million, fill it, filling*. A dark [ɫ] is used in final position after a vowel and before a consonant as in *feel, fool, help, elbow, cruel.*
- silent /l/: *alms, almond, folk, should, could, half, salmon, Holborn, talk, yolk, Lincoln, colonel.*

Cognitive difficulties relating to differences between BrE (RP) and GenAmE: dark [ɫ] can be found in all positions in GenAmE.

Psychomotoric difficulties: German speakers with the exception of people coming from the Ruhr area usually have difficulty in pronouncing dark [ɫ]. One can practice dark [ɫ] by inserting /uː/ in words like *table, cable, people* and then slowly reducing the /uː/.

Note on syllabic nature of /l/

Dark [ɫ] is often **syllabic**, ie it has vocalic qualities in words ending in <-l>.

- after the stop consonants and affricates /p, b, t, d, k, g, tʃ, dʒ/, a syllabic [ɫ] is preferred, eg *apple, trouble, kettle, medal, tackle, giggle, Rachel, cudgel.*
- after fricatives, there is a choice between a syllabic dark [ɫ] or /ə/ + dark [ɫ], eg *parcel, measles, level, offal, Ethel, betrothal, bushel.*

2. The consonant /r/

Description and position in the mouth: The consonant /r/ is formed by the tip of the tongue being near to, but not touching the rear part of the upper teeth. The back rims of the tongue touch the upper teeth and the central part of the tongue is lowered, with a general contraction of the tongue. This leads to a hollowing of the tongue. There is also a slight retroflexion of the tip of the tongue. The soft palate is raised and the air escapes freely over the centre part of the tongue without friction. The lip position is usually rounded, but is also determined by that of the following vowel, eg rounded lips in *root* and *poor*, neutrally open lips in *raspberry* and *barrage* or spread lips in *reach* and *peering.*

Classification of /r/: consonant, postalveolar, frictionless continuant, lenis, voiced.

Realization: /r/ has several realizations.

It is a voiced postalveolar frictionless continuant if followed by a vowel (*red, round*), if placed between vowels (*mirror, parade, far away, our aunt*) and if preceded by a lenis consonant except /d/ (*brief, agree*).

It is a voiced postalveolar fricative if preceded by /d/ (*dry, bedroom*). It is a voiceless postalveolar fricative after stressed /p, t, k/ (*proud, trout, cream*).

It is a devoiced postalveolar fricative after unstressed /p, t, k/ (*apron, nitrate, acronym*), after /sp, st, sk/ (*spring, string, scream*) or after stressed or unstressed voiceless fricatives (*thrive, shrink, frame, three, belfry, saffron, mushroom*).

Variants: there are two major variants in RP, ie the **alveolar tap [ɾ]** and the **linguo-alveolar roll** or **trill [r]**. (The phonetic symbol for the 'normal' English /r/ is [ɹ].)

The alveolar tap is produced by a single tap of the tip of the tongue against the alveolar ridge, with the side rims of the tongue making light contact with the upper teeth. (The articulation of the tap differs from that of /d/ in that the contact required for the tap is of shorter duration and less complete than that for /d/).

The trill or roll is produced by a rapid succession of taps of the tip of the tongue on the alveolar ridge.

The tap is sometimes used in intervocalic position (*very, sorry, for ever*), after voiceless /θ/ (*three, forthright, with respect*) and after /b, d/ (*bright, dry*).

The trill is used in all positions in very highly stylized speech in RP (and usually in Scottish English).

Note: In different areas of the UK, one can also find a **uvular roll [ʀ]** or a **uvular fricative [ʁ]** (North East England, some Scottish areas), a **retroflex [ɻ]** (South-West England and Northern Ireland) and a **rolled [r]** in Scotland.

General cognitive difficulties:
- *wring, wretched, Wright.*
- silent /r/: *acre, centre, iron.*

Cognitive difficulties relating to differences between BrE (RP) and GenAmE: As GenAmE is a rhotic accent, /r/ is pronounced in any environment, even in words such as *car* or *park*, where /r/ is not pronounced in BrE (RP).

Psychomotoric difficulties: German speakers have difficulty in pronouncing /r/.

Several methods to achieve the correct pronunciation have been suggested.
- One can first pronounce /ʒ/, then retract the tongue, hollow and lower it slightly, have the jaws apart and the lips rounded. One can also push the tongue further back by a mechanical device such as a pencil or a bent thumb.
- One can start off by pronouncing /ɜː/. This sound should then be pronounced with exaggerated length, a weak breath effort, with rounded lips and the retraction and hollowing of the tongue.
- For students who have mastered dark [ɫ], another method is recommended. One should start off with dark [ɫ], then retract the tip of the tongue a bit further, hollow the tongue, open the jaws and round the lips.

Note on linking /r/ and intrusive /r/:
- **linking /r/:** RP retains word final postvocalic /r/ as a linking form when the following word begins with a vowel, eg *far off, her aunts, answer it, poor Albert.*

- intrusive /r/: By analogy, this linking usage has extended to other cases, even when there is no spelling justification. Extra sounds ie epenthetic sounds are used in many languages and English avoids the hiatus as far as possible by using extra sounds to link syllables together. The intrusive /r/ is such an epenthetic sound. Thus one hears an intrusive /r/ in word groups like *Russia* /r/ *and China, drama* /r/ *and music, idea* /r/ *of it* and *I saw* /r/ *it.* It is obvious that the RP system of linking words strongly favours this tendency. Spelling might still constitute an inhibiting factor, but there is a very strong tendency to use an intrusive /r/ among the majority of RP speakers. The tendency only varies according to different environments. The tendency is strongest in the environment /ə/+/ə/ or /ɪ/ (*idea* /r/ *of it, idea* /r/ *is*), still quite strong in /ɑː/ or /ɔː/+/ə/ or /ɪ/ (*Shah* /r/ *of Persia, the spa* /r/ *is well-known*, *law* /r/ *and order*) and least strong within one word (*draw*/r/*ing*).

3. The semi-vowels /j/ and /w/

Semi-vowels are, in phonetic terms, vocalic, but they are normally treated within the consonantal class, because they function as consonants. In other words, they have a marginal rather than a central position in the syllable. They are also referred to as **glides**, because they glide from a slightly closer position than /iː/ or /uː/ to the position of the following vowel.

3.1 The semi-vowel /j/
Description and position in the mouth: The semi-vowel **/j/** is formed by the tongue assuming a position higher than for a front close vowel and then moving away to the position of the following vowel. The lips are neutral, spread or rounded depending on the lip position of the following vowel.

Classification of /j/: semi-vowel, palatal, close, lenis, voiced.

Realization: /j/ is normally voiced, but it is voiceless when stressed voiceless /p, t, k, h/ precede /j/ as in *pew, tune, queue, cure, accuse, huge.*

/j/ is devoiced after /sp, st, sk/, after voiceless fricatives and after unstressed /p, t, k/ as in *stew, spurious, askew, enthusiasm, pursue, refuse, opulent, spatula, help you.*

Variants: major variants exist in RP in the following cases:
- /j/ is pronounced after /t, d, n/ +/uː/ as in *tune, duke, new.*

- /j/ is dropped after /tʃ, dʒ, ʃ, r/ + /uː/ as in *chew, June, chute, rumour* and consonant + /l/ + /uː/ as in *blue, clue, plume.*
- either /j/ or /Ø/ after /s, z, θ/ + /uː/ as in *assume, resume, enthusiasm.*
- either /j/ or /Ø/ after a syllable with primary or secondary stress as in *absolute, revolution, lunatic,* whereas /j/ is always pronounced in words such as in *value, failure.*
- Assimilation of /j/ in the following cases:
  /tj/ → /tʃ/ as in *virtue, actual, Christian, don't you.*
  /dj/ → /dʒ/ as in *educate, soldier, duration, did you.*
  /sj/ → /ʃ/ as in *issue, this year, miss you.*
  /zj/ → /ʒ/ as in *casual, visual, usual.*
  /hj/ → /ç/ as in *human, humane, huge, humour.*

General cognitive difficulties:
The distribution of variants with /j/ or without /j/ may cause problems. Sometimes there are incidences of hypercorrection, where words like *yesterday* or *young* are pronounced with */dʒ/ instead of /j/.

Cognitive difficulties relating to differences between BrE (RP) and GenAmE: no major differences exist. In GenAmE, assimilated /tʃ, dʒ, ʃ/ are more common than in BrE (RP). The word *figure* is pronounced /fɪgjər/ in GenAmE.

Psychomotoric difficulties: German speakers have no difficulty in pronouncing /j/.

Note on linking /j/
When two vowels come together across a boundary, a rapid and weak linking /j/, normally represented in phonetic transcription by a raised [ʲ], is used after a front vowel followed by another vowel in order to avoid the hiatus. Examples are *free again* /friː ʲ əgen/, *the ears* /ði ʲ ɪəz/, *lovely evening* /lʌvli ʲ iːvnɪŋ/.

Compare short and weak [ʲ] to long and strong /j/:
the ears /ði ʲ ɪəz/ - *the years* /ði jɪəz/,
three oaks /θriː ʲ əʊks/ - *three yolks* /θriː jəʊks/.

3.2 The semi-vowel /w/
Description and position in the mouth: The semi-vowel **/w/** is formed by the tongue assuming a position higher than for a back close vowel (depending on the openness of the following sound) and then

moving away immediately to the position of the following vowel. The lips are generally rounded.

Classification of /w/: semi-vowel, labio-velar, close, lenis, voiced.

Realization: /w/ is normally voiced, but it is voiceless when stressed voiceless /t, k/ precede /w/ as in *twin, quarter, request, quiet.*

/w/ is devoiced after /sk/ or a voiceless fricative as in *square, sweat, thwart* and after unstressed /t, k/ as in *outward, quotation, sequel.*

Variants: one major variant exists in RP. Lexical words with the spelling <wh> are sometimes pronounced /hw/ or, more usually, with the fortis labio-velar voiceless fricative /ʍ/. In such speech, which contains a number of oppositions like *wine - whine* and *Wales - whales,* /ʍ/ has phonemic status. Function words with the spelling <wh> are usually pronounced /w/, but may have /hw/ or /ʍ/ in emphatic speech.

General cognitive difficulties:
- /w/ is pronounced in *one, once, language, linguistics, anguish, choir, suite.*
- silent /w/: *write, wriggle, whore, sword, wrap, wrath, wreath, wretched, wrist, Greenwich, War<u>w</u>ick, Norwich, Harwich.*

Cognitive difficulties relating to differences between BrE (RP) and GenAmE: In GenAmE /hw/ or /ʍ/ are heard more frequently than in BrE (RP).

Psychomotoric difficulties: German speakers have difficulty in pronouncing /w/, as this sound does not exist in modern German.

One can practice /w/ by producing a strong rounded full /uː/ as one syllable followed by the next vowel and then reduce the first syllable until the /uː/ loses its syllabic function. Thus the word *wine* can first be pronounced as /uː+aɪn/ and then as /waɪn/.

Note on linking /w/:

When two vowels come together across a boundary, a rapid and weak linking /w/, normally represented in phonetic transcription by a raised [ʷ], is used after a back vowel followed by another vowel in order to avoid the hiatus. Examples are *how old* /haʊ ʷ əʊld/, *two eights* /tuː ʷ eɪts/, *do ask* /duː ʷ ɑːsk/.

Compare short and weak [ʷ] to long and strong /w/:
two eights /tuː ʷ eɪts/ - *two weights* /tuː weɪts/,
new age /njuː ʷ eɪdʒ/ - *new wage* /njuː weɪdʒ/.

Suggested readings (cf. **Bibliography**, chapter 0.2)

Note on pronunciation

inseparable /ɪn'sepərəbəl/, composite (adj.) /'kɒmpəzɪt/, loosely /'luːsli/, preferably /'prefərəbli/, Rhineland /'raɪnlænd/, hypercorrection /haɪpəkə'rekʃən/, medium /'miːdiəm/, diphthongized /'dɪfθɒŋgaɪzd/, schwa /ʃwɑː /, latitude /'lætɪtjuːd/, monosyllabic /mɒnəʊsɪ'læbɪk/, obstruent /'ɒbstruənt/, sonorant /'sɒnərənt/, unimpeded /ʌnɪm'piːdɪd/, approximant /ə'prɒksɪmənt/, obstruction /əb'strʌkʃən/, pressure /'preʃə/, surface /'sɜːfɪs/, origin /'ɒrɪdʒɪn/, genitive /'dʒenətɪv/, preference /'prefərəns/, resemble /rɪ'zembəl/, anticipate /æn'tɪsɪpeɪt/, adjacent /ə'dʒeɪsənt/, suffixes /'sʌfɪksɪz/, syllabic /sɪ'læbɪk/, recommend /rekə'mend/, analogy /ə'nælədʒi/, epenthetic /epen'θetɪk/, hiatus /haɪ'eɪtəs/, marginal /'mɑːdʒɪnəl/.

3.0 DESCRIPTION OF STRESS, RHYTHM AND INTONATION

3.1 SYLLABLE, WORD, STRESS AND WORD STRESS

1. What is understood by syllable and word?

Words are linguistic units which carry meaning and which, phonetically and phonemically speaking, are composed of one or more phones/phonemes. Words can be monosyllabic or polysyllabic. For example, the word *no* consists of one syllable, the word *a-go* consists of two syllables, and the word *ne-ver-the-less* consists of four syllables. A syllable is a unit of pronunciation which can consist of one or more sounds, but which is smaller than a word. It seems that native speakers have an intuitive feeling for what a syllable is, even though there can also be disagreement as far as syllabic divisions are concerned: the word *extra* may be interpreted as having the syllables /e+kstrə/, /ek+strə/ or /eks+trə/. The linguistic definition of a syllable is highly complicated and several theories have been put forward.

In phonetics, syllables can be defined in terms of the articulatory effort or chest pulses. In other words, the contractions of certain chest muscles, which are accompanied by increased air pressure, make up the syllables. When the articulatory effort is most noticeable, one speaks of the **peak** of a syllable. In auditory terms, sonorous sounds, especially vowels, are most prominent in a syllable and thus produce the peak of a syllable.

In phonology, the syllable is defined by the way in which vowels and consonants combine in individual languages to produce typical sequences. Vowels and, to a certain extent, syllabic consonants such as nasals and laterals can form syllables, but only vowels can occur on their own. Consonants occur at the edges of a sequence of sounds, ie at the beginning or at the end of a syllable. Syllables are classified according to whether they end in a vowel (**open syllable**) or in a consonant (**closed syllable**), where the consonant 'closes' the syllable. The words *show*, *too* and *law* have open syllables exhibiting a consonant-vowel (CV) sequence, whereas the words *bed*, *tap* and *cup* have closed syllables with a CVC sequence.

The syllable can also be divided into parts:
- the opening segment of the syllable, called the **onset**
- the closing segment of the syllable, called the **coda**
- and the central segment of the syllable, called the **nucleus** (or **peak** or **centre**).

Speech segments which form the nucleus of a syllable are **syllabic** (vowels and syllabic consonants), speech segments which cannot form the nucleus of a syllable are **non-syllabic**.

The sequential arrangement of the phonological units (phonemes) in a language is called **phonotactics**. For example, in English, not more than three consonants can occur initially resulting in CCCV. Basically, the following consonantal groups (clusters) are possible: /s/+/p/+/l/ or /r/ or /j/ (*splash, sprout, spew*), /s/+/t/+/r/ or /j/ (*strain, stew*) and /s/+/k/+/l/ or /r/ or /j/ or /w/ (*sclerosis, scratch, skew, squash*). Up to four consonants can occur finally, although final VCCCC is quite rare (*prompts, glimpsed, thousandths*). In contrast to English, one can find the combination /strtʃ/ and other consonantal combinations in Czech (cf. Czech *'Strč prst skrz krk'* = *'Put your finger through your neck'*). There are also restrictions concerning the combination of consonant +vowel: long vowels and diphthongs do not precede /ŋ/, and /e, æ, ʌ, ɒ/ do not occur finally. In other words, English does not exploit all the possible combinations of its phonemes (cf. Gimson 1962/94: 216ff; chapter 4: Connected Speech).

Postal (1968: 138) mentions four types of consonantal clusters:
- possible and actual, *eg <u>br</u>ick*
- possible but not actual, eg **<u>pl</u>ig*
- impossible but actual, eg *<u>sph</u>ere*
  impossible and not actual, eg **<u>fn</u>es*

Q1 How would one classify the following initial clusters /ps+vowel/, /sg+vowel/, /fk+vowel/, /fn+vowel/, /ts+vowel/, /tsg+vowel/ and /zg+vowel/? Which English words or word groups begin with these clusters?

2. What is understood by stress?

Stress can be defined as emphasis on or prominence of a word or syllable so that it stands out from other words or syllables. It refers to the degree of force of articulation used in producing a syllable, ie the degree of muscular tension involved and the amount of air expelled from the lungs. Stress is normally perceived as greater loudness and/or longer duration and/or better quality and/or higher pitch than the surrounding words or syllables by the listeners. A syllable is stressed because the accent is on that syllable, eg *con'fusion*, *'nature*, *maga'zine* or speakers wish to emphasize a syllable or a word, eg *I said 'consult, not 'insult*; *I think 'she did it*.

Within words, some syllables seem to be 'strong syllables', ie they receive a stress, and others seem to be 'weak syllables', ie they receive a weak stress or no stress at all. Words such as *'father*, *'mother* or *'sister* are stressed on the first syllable, *to'mato*, *po'tato* or *su'ppose* are stressed on the second syllable and *prepa'ration*, *hesi'tation* or *suppo'sition* are stressed on the third syllable, whereas the rest of the syllables are not so prominent. The strongest stress in a syllable is called **primary stress** or **main stress**.

The identification of stress can be studied from two angles: it can be studied from the point of view of the speaker, ie **production**, and from the point of view of the hearer, ie **perception**.

The production of stress normally depends on muscular tension and air pressure. In other words, the more muscular tension and air pressure used, the more prominent are the sounds produced. The perception of more prominent sounds depends on several factors, ie **loudness**, **pitch**, **quality** and **quantity** (**length**).

- It can be said that stressed syllables are perceived as louder than unstressed syllables. Voiced sounds are principally louder than voiceless sounds.
- All syllables are pronounced with some sort of pitch. Pitch is related to the frequency of vibration of the vocal cords and is interpreted in musical terms as low pitched notes and high pitched notes. If one syllable is spoken at a different pitch to all other syllables, then this syllable is perceived as more prominent than the others by the hearer. The effect is even stronger, if movement of pitch (falling or rising melody) is involved. Pitch is probably the most important factor in rendering syllables more prominent than others.
- The centre of a stressed syllable is the vowel with its unique quality compared to the neighbouring vowels, which are normally weakened vowels such as /ɪ, i, ə, ʊ, u/ or syllabic consonants. It is the contrast between a full vowel and weakened vowels or syllabic consonants that renders a syllable more prominent.
- Finally, the length of a syllable also plays a part in making it more prominent. Long vowels and diphthongs are longest, followed by

short vowels and then weakened vowels. Length is probably the
least decisive factor as far as prominence is concerned.

To summarize, one can state that prominence can be achieved by any
one factor alone, but more probably by more than one of the four factors stress, pitch, quality and quantity. Generally, all four factors combine to render a syllable more prominent than others.

3. Degrees of stress

Apart from syllables with **primary stress** and **no stress**, one can also
identify intermediate degrees of stress. One-syllable words like *hat*,
coat or *bag* obviously have one centre and are said to have one primary or main stress. In two-syllable words such as *begin*, *about* or
ago, the main stress falls on the second syllable and the first syllable
is unstressed or weak. The prominence of the second syllable can be
explained by the pitch movement from a low level to a high falling
level. In words with more than two syllables such as *supposition* or
definition, the stress on the first syllable is weaker than on the third
syllable, but stronger than on the second or fourth syllable. This intermediate stress is called **secondary stress**. It has less prominence than
the main stress, but more prominence than no stress at all. It serves to
keep the rhythm natural - the alternation of a stressed and an unstressed
syllable can be considered in terms of the natural rhythm of the heart-
beat - and it also allows vowels to keep their full quality as does the
primary stress. Vowels which receive a secondary stress always keep
their full vowel quality and are thus never weakened.
In three syllable-words, the position of the secondary stress is determined by the position of the main stress. If the words have their main
stress on the third syllable, then the secondary stress is placed on the
first syllable, eg ˌcontriˈbution or ˌsuppoˈsition. The place of the
secondary stress in words which have their main stress on the fourth
syllable, fifth syllable or sixth syllable, has, to a large extent, to be
learned separately and individually. If the main stress is on the fourth
or fifth syllable, the secondary stress is usually placed on that syllable which receives the primary stress in the base word. The different
stress patterns can be illustrated in the following words: ˌcharacteˈri-
stic and faˌmiliˈarity (main stress on the fourth syllable), ˌnationa-
liˈzation (main stress on the fifth syllable) and inˌdustrialiˈzation
(main stress on the sixth syllable).

In syllables with **no stress** at all (weak stress or non-stressed), any vowel is usually reduced to /ə/, eg *apply*, *polite*, *figure*. Unstressed written <i> is often reduced to /ɪ/, so that in certain cases the phonemic difference between /ə/ and /ɪ/ is preserved, eg *allusion - illusion*.

In a highly complex analysis of degrees of stress, a fourth stress, ie **tertiary stress**, could be introduced, in addition to primary, secondary and weak stress. In hard words, ie in words of Latin and Greek origin, an unstressed vowel is often not reduced. The word *poetic* /pəʊˈetɪk/ has a tertiary stress on the first syllable, a primary stress on the second syllable and a weak stress on the third syllable. Unstressed syllables containing /ɪ, i, ə, ʊ, u/ or a syllabic consonant are always less prominent than unstressed syllables under tertiary stress.

Q2 Where does the **main stress** fall in the following words? *father, terrible, answer, develop, prefer, nature, courage, define, prepare, suppose, confirm, reform, interpret, character, recommend, English teacher (teacher from England), English teacher (somebody teaching English).*

Q3 Use the marks ' (for main stress), ˘ (for unstressed syllables and tertiary stress) and ˌ (for secondary stress) to indicate the varying prominence of the syllables in the following words: *definition, preparation, supposition, confirmation, reformation, interpretation, characterization, recommendation, peculiarity.*

4. Placement of stress in words

The stress pattern of English words is fixed, in the sense that the main stress always falls on a particular syllable of any given word, but free in the sense that the main stress is not tied to any particular position in the chain of syllables constituting a word. As the position of the accentual pattern of a word is highly unpredictable and as there is no simple way of knowing which syllable or syllables in an English word must be stressed, it follows that every time one learns a new word with more than one syllable, one must learn that particular stress pattern. In contrast, Czech words are always stressed on the first syllable, French words have their stress on the last syllable and in Polish, the syllable before the last, ie the **penultimate** syllable, is stressed.

The complex nature of stress placement in English and the existence of a large number of exceptions is a constant challenge to linguists, who have tried to come up with a set of stress rules, but their solutions are often too complex and theoretical to be of any practical use to students (cf. Chomsky/Halle 1968: 70ff.). The following approach tries to tackle the problem from a more practical point of view and summarizes a few rules in the simplest possible form. As nearly all the rules have quite a number of exceptions, students might be better advised to learn the stress pattern of each word individually.

Before students can decide on the stress pattern of words, the following questions must be considered:

a) Is the word **morphologically simple** or is it **complex**?

Morphologically **simple words** consist of a **root** or **stem** only. A root is the base form of a word which cannot be further divided or analyzed without total loss of identity.

Morphologically **complex words** contain one or more **affixes**, ie **prefixes** or **suffixes**, or are **compounds**, which consist of two (or more) free morphemes. Affixes are (bound) morphemes which are added to the root. Prefixes come before the root and suffixes follow the root.

b) What **grammatical category** does the word belong to? Is it a noun, an adjective, a verb etc?

c) **How many syllables** does the word have?

d) What is the **phonological structure of the syllables**?

4.1 Stress rules for simple words

Simple words are words that are composed of not more than one morphological unit. The position of the main stress is influenced by the word class, ie different stress patterns are often found in verbal and adjectival roots on the one hand and nominal roots on the other.

The following rules apply to **two-syllable words**:

- **verbs:** The basic rule is that if the second syllable of the verb contains a long vowel or diphthong, or if it ends with more than one consonant, then the second syllable is stressed. Examples are *apply* /əˈplaɪ/, *arrive* /əˈraɪv/, *attract* /əˈtrækt/ and *assist* /əˈsɪst/.

If the final syllable contains a short vowel and one (or no) final consonant, the first syllable is stressed. Examples are *enter* /ˈentə/, *envy* /ˈenvi/, *open* /ˈəʊpən/ and *equal* /ˈiːkwəl/.

A final syllable is also unstressed if it contains /əʊ/, eg *follow* /ˈfɒləʊ/ and *borrow* /ˈbɒrəʊ/.

Note: Words such as *per'mit* or *ad'mit* which do not fit the above descriptions can either be interpreted as being morphologically complex (*per+mit* or *ad+mit*) or can simply be put into the category of exceptions.

- **adjectives:** Adjectives are stressed according to the same rules that apply to verbs. Examples are *lovely* /'lʌvli/, *even* /'iːvən/, *hollow* /'hɒləʊ/, *divine* /dɪ'vaɪn/, *correct* /kə'rekt/ and *alive* /ə'laɪv/.
  There are also exceptions like *honest* /'ɒnəst/ or *perfect* /'pɜːfəkt/.

- **nouns:** If the second syllable contains a short vowel the stress will usually come on the first syllable. Otherwise it will be on the second syllable. Examples are *money* /'mʌni/, *moment* /'məʊmənt/, *product* /'prɒdʌkt/ versus *estate* /ɪ'steɪt/, *idea* /aɪ'dɪə/ and *balloon* /bə'luːn/.

The following rules apply to **words with three syllables**:
- **verbs:** If the last syllable contains a short vowel and ends with one consonant, then the stress is placed on the penultimate syllable. Examples are *as'tonish, en'counter, e'xamine.*
  If the last syllable contains a long vowel or diphthong, or ends with more than one consonant, then the final syllable is stressed. Examples are *ascer'tain, resu'rrect.*
- **adjectives:** If the last syllable contains a short vowel and ends with one consonant, then the stress is placed on the penultimate syllable. Examples are *e'ffective, im'plicit, dy'namic.*
  If the last syllable contains a long vowel or diphthong, or a vowel followed by two consonants, the first syllable is stressed. Examples are *'paranoid, 'opportune, 'prominent, 'moribund.*
- **nouns:** If the last syllable contains a short vowel or /əʊ/, and if the penultimate syllable contains a long vowel or diphthong or if it contains more than one consonant, the stress is placed on the penultimate syllable. Examples are *um'brella, to'mato, di'saster, mu'seum, sy'nopsis.*
  If the last syllable contains a short vowel and the middle syllable also contains a short vowel with no more than one consonant, the first syllable is stressed. Examples are *'quality, 'cinema, 'emperor, 'capital.*

Note: With words of more than two syllables, the question of root and affix is not always treated consistently.

4.2 Stress rules for complex words

Complex words are composed of more than one morphological unit. There are basically two different types of complex words, ie words that consist of a **root** and an **affix**, and **compounds** or **compound words** which in general are made up of two (sometimes more) **free morphemes**.

Affixes can be either **prefixes** or **suffixes**. Prefixes come before the root and are morphemes such as *de-, mis-, in-* or *un-* as in *defrost, mislead, insecure* and *unclear*. Other prefixes are *dis-, non-, mal-, co-, hyper-, mini-, out-, over-, sub-, under-, anti-, counter-, inter-, trans-, ex-, fore-, pre-, post-, semi-, neo-, tele-* for example. Suffixes follow the root and are morphemes such as *-less, -ness, -ish or -ful* as in *careless, happiness, youngish* and *fearful*. Other suffixes are *-able, -age, -ant, -ing, -ism, -eer, -ette, -let, -ity, -like, -ly, -esque, -ist, -ite, -ive, -ify, -ize* for example (cf. Quirk/Greenbaum/Leech/Svartvik 1985: 1540ff).

Compounds consist of two words that can usually occur independently of one another such as *bank* and *account* (*bank account*), *dark* and *room* (*darkroom*) or *duty* and *free* (*duty-free*).

5. Complex words: stem and affix

5.1 Stem and prefix

As far as the first category of complex words is concerned, **prefixes** normally do not affect the accentual pattern of a word, eg *'necessary - un'necessary, co'rrect - inco'rrect, 'honest - dis'honest*. Exceptions can occur with the prefixes *'fore-* (*'forearm, 'forename*), *'mini-* (*'mini-skirt, 'minibus*), *'sub-* (*'subway*), *'super-* (*'superman, 'supermarket*), *'sur-* (*'surcharge, 'surtax*), *'bi-* (*'biplane, 'bicycle*), *'poly-* (*'polyglot*), *'tele-* (*'telegram, 'telephone*), *'auto-* (*'autocrat*) and others.

5.2 Stem and suffix

Suffixes, on the other hand, can affect the accentual pattern in three possible ways: there are stress-attracting suffixes where the affix itself is stressed (*mountai'neer* vs. *'mountain*), stress-neutral suffixes where the affix does not affect the word stress at all (*'punishment - 'punish*) and stress-changing suffixes where the affix will change the stress pattern of the stem (*re'ality* vs. *'real*). It should be noted that the following rules are guidelines only and that because of countless exceptions, different rules may apply.

Stress-attracting suffixes are as follows

-'*ade: charade, escapade, lemonade*
-'*ain (v.): entertain, ascertain, attain*
-'*aire: questionnaire, millionaire, doctrinaire*
-'*ation: nationalization, privatization, provincialization*
-'*ee: interviewee, employee, nominee*
-'*eer: auctioneer, engineer, racketeer*
-'*ese: Chinese, journalese, officialese*
-'*esque: burlesque, Daliesque, picturesque*
-'*ette: kitchenette, suffragette, usherette*
-'*ier: brigadier, cavalier, gondolier*
-'*ific: honorific, terrific, scientific*
-'*ique: antique, oblique, unique*
-'*itis: appendicitis, laryngitis, pharyngitis*
-'*osis: hypnosis, tuberculosis, thrombosis*
-'*oon: lampoon, balloon, spittoon*

Stress-neutral suffixes are as follows

-*able: acceptable, distinguishable, answerable*
-*age: baggage, mileage, breakage*
-*al: revival, refusal, personal*
-*ary: honorary, momentary, imaginary*
-*en: deepen, ripen, widen*
-*er: Londoner, villager, boiler*
-*ery: machinery, nursery, slavery*
-*ful: handful, glassful, spoonful*
-*fy: glorify, testify, justify*
-*ing: farming, amazing, building*
-*ish (adj.): childish, snobbish, youngish*
-*ism: despotism, collectivism, imperialism*
-*ist: extremist, idealist, terrorist*
-*ize: atomize, finalize, familiarize*
-*like: childlike, statesmanlike, x-like*
-*less: careless, colourless, harmless*
-*ly: friendly, cowardly, manly*
-*ment: arrangement, amazement, equipment*

-ness: happiness, meanness, kindness
-or: executor, persecutor, vivisector
-ous: famous, nervous, poisonous
-ry: rivalry, charlatanry, heraldry
-ship: authorship, friendship, bachelorship
-ster: gangster, trickster, gamester
-ure: exposure, departure, legislature
-wise: moneywise, clothes-wise, weatherwise
*-y (*adj.*): funny, hairy, creamy*
*-y (*n.*): delicacy, intimacy, presidency*

Note: There is vacillation as far as this stress pattern is concerned. The rules, to a large extent, depend on the word class and the meaning of the suffix. Some exceptions to the above mentioned rules are:
-al: 'sentiment - senti'mental, 'medicine - me'dicinal, 'origin - o'riginal.
-ous: 'moment - mo'mentous, 'miracle - mi'raculous, 'courage - cou'rageous
-fy: 'person - per'sonify, 'solid - so'lidify
Another example is the suffix *-ish*, which is stress-neutral in adjectives. Verbs with stems of more than one syllable always have the stress on the syllable immediately preceding *-ish*, eg *re'plenish, as'tonish* and *de'molish.*

Stress-changing suffixes that affect stress in the stem
-eous: ad'vantage - advan'tageous, 'courage - cou'rageous, 'error - e'rroneous
-ian: 'civil - ci'vilian, 'history -his'torian, 'Canada - Ca'nadian
-ic: 'atom - a'tomic, 'poet - po'etic, 'chaos - cha'otic
-ical: 'history - his'torical, 'allegory - alle'gorical, e'conomy - eco-'nomical
-ity: 'curious - curi 'osity, 'rapid - ra'pidity, 'person - perso'nality
-ious: 'victory - vic'torious, 'melody - me'lodious, 'mystery - mys'terious
-ual: 'habit - ha'bitual, 'intellect - inte'llectual, 'concept - con'ceptual

Q4 Explain the word stress in the following words: *Arabic, momentous, outrageous, denial, proverbial, demolish, replenish, devotion, perfection, furious, injurious.*

Q5 Define the following terms: **affix, suffix, prefix, simple words, complex words, compounds, stem, root** and **free morpheme.**

5.3 Word-class pairs with changing stress

There are a number of words with identical spelling which have a different stress pattern depending on the word class (noun, adjective or verb). They are composed of a prefix and stem and have initial stress in the case of nouns or adjectives and final stress as verbs. The following examples can be given:

	noun or **adjective**	**verb**
absent		
abstract		
accent		
cement		
combine		
comment		
compress		
concert		
conduct		
confine		
conflict		
consort		
contact		
contest		
contract		
contrast		
convert		
convict		
desert		
digest		
discount		
dispute		
escort		
exploit		
export		
extract		
frequent		
impact		
implant		
import		

noun or **adjective**	**verb**

incline
increase
insult
intercept
intimate
object
perfect
permit
pervert
present
proceeds
produce
progress
project
protest
rebel
record
refill
refuse
segment
separate
subject
survey
suspect
torment
transfer
transport

Q6 Transcribe the above words and translate them into German.

5.4 Variable stress

In a number of English words, the stress pattern varies with RP speakers. Words like *'controversy - con'troversy, 'hospitable - hos'pitable* or *'comparable - com'parable* are often stressed differently. These **divided usages**, ie usages which constitute competing forms and which are equally correct, reflect a more liberal attitude towards pronunciation in general. It must be pointed out that the different stress patterns are equally acceptable to educated native speakers, although some prescriptivists may still oppose the more modern forms of pronunciation (cf. chapter 8.1.1 for a list of divided usages).

6. Stress in compounds

Compounds are composed of more than one word, which function grammatically and/or semantically as a single word. They normally consist of free morphemes, where each individual word can be used independently as an English word. They are written in three different ways: some of the compounds are written as one word as in *keyboard* and *guidebook*, sometimes they are written as two words as in *ghetto blaster* and *theme park*, and they can also be separated by a hyphen as in *job-sharing* and *clear-cut*. There is also vacillation in so far as words with primary stress on the first syllable are either written with a hyphen or as one word ('*weather-wise* or '*weatherwise*) and words with primary stress on the second syllable are normally written as two words as in *acid* '*rain* and *rice* '*pudding*.

As far as the stress pattern is concerned, only certain guidelines can be given, as there are quite a number of exceptions. Basically, compounds are most commonly stressed on the first element as in '*daybreak,* '*bank account* and '*racehorse.* In these cases, a secondary stress is normally retained in the second element. However, the main stress can also occur on the second syllable. Then the first element normally receives a secondary stress. The following cases can be distinguished.

6.1 Compounds functioning as nouns

- **'noun+noun:** '*bar code,* '*birthplace,* '*bodyscanner,* '*crow's nest,* '*job centre,* po'*lice force,* '*shopping centre,* '*phonecard,* '*toilet roll,* '*screen saver,* '*textbook,* '*wheelie bin.*

Note: There are some exceptions, where one finds the stress pattern noun+'noun. These cases can be categorized as follows:
- man-made items: *apple* '*pie, brick* '*wall, cotton* '*wool, fruit* '*salad.*
- the first noun is a name: *Christmas* '*pudding* (but '*Christmas cake,* '*chocolate cake,* '*cheesecake), Highland* '*fling, London* '*Road* (but '*Oxford Street), Norfolk* '*terrier.*
- the first noun is a number or value: *100 percent* '*achievement, fifty pound* '*fine, second-*'*class, twopence* '*piece.*

- **'noun+adjective, 'noun+verb, 'adverb+noun, 'adjective+noun, 'adjective+verb, 'verb+noun:**
  '*home-sick,* '*joy-riding,* '*landfill,* '*background,* '*faintheart,* '*white-wash,* '*small-talk,* '*eating apple,* '*building society.*

Note: There are also exceptions, especially in the case of adjective+'noun and verb-ing+'noun, eg *alternating 'current, black 'economy, flying 'saucer.*

- **phrasal and prepositional verbs used as nouns stressed on the first syllable:** *'burn-out, 'cock-up, 'lay-offs, 'showdown.*

6.2 Compounds functioning as adjectives and verbs
- Adjectives can have either initial or final stress and have thus to be learned individually, eg *'headstrong, 'sell-by (date), 'waterproof* vs. *deep-'seated, rent-'free, user-'friendly.*
- Verbs normally have initial stress, eg *'babysit, 'backbite, 'headhunt,* but take final stress, if the first element is an adverb, eg *back-'pedal.*

6.3 Compounds functioning as adverbs
Compounds functioning as adverbs usually have final stress, eg *head-'first, down'stream, South-'West, through'out.*

7. The so-called level stress in individual words or groups of words

The concept of level stress has often been used to refer to the double primary stress in individual words, compounds and groups of words. Examples are *'thir'teen, 'New 'York, 'London 'Road, 'home 'rule, 'prime 'minister* and *'public 'school.*
The following combinations of level stress can be listed:
- noun+noun as in *'Victoria 'Station, 'mountain 'railway, 'garden 'wall, 'Hyde 'Park*
- adv.+noun as in *'down'hill, 'down'stairs, 'over'seas*
- v.-en (past participle)+noun as in *'mounted po'lice, 'Promised 'Land*
- noun+adj. as in *'court 'martial, 'Prince 'Consort*
- adj./adv.+adv. as in *'half-'yearly, 'hard-'up*
- phrasal verbs (v.+adv.) as in *'bring 'up, 'get 'out, 'call 'off*
- adj./adv.+v.-ing as in *'ever'lasting, 'over'whelming, 'under'lying*
- adj./adv./noun+v.-en (past participle) as in *'far-'fetched, 'out' spoken, 'well-'made*
- adj./adv./noun+noun-ed as in *'cold-'blooded, 'ill-'mannered, 'silver 'haired*

As the first stress is accompanied by a **static tone** and the second by a **kinetic tone** (see below 3.3), the second primary stress is perceived as a fully stressed syllable, whereas the first stress is perceived as a secondary stress. Thus one hears ˌthir'teen, ˌNew 'York, ˌLondon 'Road, ˌhome 'rule, ˌprime 'minister and ˌpublic 'school. This concept is usually favoured by linguists.

Nevertheless, from a contrastive point of view, Germans have to be careful not to miss the primary stress in English words such as ˌfar 'reaching (German 'weitreichend), ˌfour'teen (German 'vierzehn) and ˌduty-'free (German 'zollfrei).

When the stress pattern is the same in German and English ('car owner, 'birdcage, 'shoemaker), there are usually no problems for German speakers. Occasionally, mistakes are made because of hypercorrection.

8. Summary

The description of stress in English words has made it clear that the pattern is rather complex, often unpredictable and full of exceptions. An additional difficulty lies in the fact that the dividing line between the different types of complex words is often impossible to draw. Last but not least, more difficulties may arise from so-called pseudo-compounds, which are normally of Greek and also Latin origin, eg 'telephone, 'photograph, 'circumflex, 'monochrome, 'prototype.

3.2 SENTENCE STRESS AND RHYTHM

When words are used in a sentence, the stress pattern of the sentence is determined by a number of factors. These are usually grammar, the general rhythm pattern of the sentence, the context, the individual speakers and the listeners. Thus it is quite difficult to formulate definite rules and one can only offer sign-posts. Broadly speaking, it may be said that a strong stress is placed on those words in the sentence which are most important from the viewpoint of sense or implication. In other words, **content words** are normally stressed, whereas **function words (grammatical words)** are not stressed. The following 'rules' can only serve as guidelines.

1. Stressed and unstressed words in a sentence

1.1 stressed words (words with primary stress)
- nouns
- demonstrative and interrogative pronouns
- verbs
- adverbs
- adjectives
- interjections

1.2 unstressed words (normally not stressed)
- conjunctions
- all pronouns except demonstratives and interrogatives
- auxiliaries
- prepositions

As a rule of thumb, one can say that in any given text about fifty per cent of the total number of words is stressed.

2. Shift of emphasis in a sentence (tonicity)

The term tonicity refers to the position of the stressed word or syllable within a tone unit. The tonic syllable carries maximal prominence which is usually due to a pitch change. The change in tonicity gives the sentence different implications. This is an important aspect of communication in conversation, where the change draws attention especially to a new aspect in a sentence.

Compare the following sentences:
'Jane was walking home. (*It was Jane, not Christine.*)
Jane was 'walking home. (*She was walking, not driving.*)
Jane was walking 'home. (*She was on her way home, not on her way to work.*)

Note: Because of the different factors involved in the determination of sentence stress, one should be aware of the fact that normal stress patterns will probably *not* be used when the speakers are
- expressing emphasis: *It was 'my idea.*
- making a contrast or comparison: *It's not 'him, it's Jim.*
- expressing some feeling such as anger, fear or surprise: *I 'am cross!*

Q7 Read the following passage aloud and indicate the primary stress.
George: The air's quite fresh, isn't it? We're in for a fine day, I should think. I wish I'd put a coat on though.
Mary: You'll warm up when we've been walking for a bit. Not so fast, though, George. You're not running for the train this morning.
George: Sorry. I get so used to hurrying down this road in the mornings. How's that? Is this a more reasonable speed?
Mary: Yes, that's better. I don't expect you'll be quite so energetic on the way home, when it's up-hill all the way. Oh, have I brought my purse? Thank goodness!
(Arnold/Gimson 1965/70:78)

3. Rhythm

3.1 Introduction
The rhythm of a language refers to the perceived regularity of peaks of prominence in speech and is determined by a regular and noticeable beat. It is assumed that in English each stress group within a word is given about the same amount of time regardless of the number of intervening unstressed syllables between the stressed syllables. In other words, the rhythmic beats of an utterance occur at fairly equal intervals of time (**isochronism** or **isochrony**). As a result of this, the speed at which the unstressed syllables are uttered - and the length of each - will depend upon the number of unstressed syllables occurring between the strong beats. Thus several unstressed syllables have to be articulated rapidly in order to fit them into the allocated time span. English is said to have a **stressed-timed rhythm**. Other languages such as French and Spanish have a different rhythmical structure. Stressed and unstressed syllables occur at fairly equal intervals of time (**isosyllabism**). The term **syllable-timed rhythm** is used for such languages.

3.1.1 Compare the following utterances
I'm   'going to   'Perth for the   'day.
I'm   'going to   'Perth   to'day.
I'm   'going to   'Perth   'now.

Q8 Analyze the speed and the length of the sounds in these sentences.

3.1.2 Pronounce the following sentence
He went into a shop to purchase a halfpennyworth of cheese.
/hiː ˈwent ɪntu ə ˈʃɒp tə ˈpɜːtʃəs ə ˈheɪpəniwəθ əv ˈtʃiːz/

Q9 Count the number of unstressed syllables between the stressed syllables.

3.2 Rhythmical variation in the stress pattern
3.2.1 Change of primary stress
Variation of stress in a sentence is natural. The stress placed on words can vary in a sentence depending on their environment. If for example one has three consecutive main stresses in a word group, one will tend not to stress all the syllables with the same force. One will follow a kind of natural rhythm pattern of fully stressed and weaker stressed syllables identical to the natural beat of the heart. Thus one can expect eg *'hot roast 'beef, 'late fourth 'century, 'John went 'out* (but: *She 'went 'out*).

Note: Loss of stress for rhythmical reasons is not always essential for correct pronunciation. It would be unlikely, but nevertheless not incorrect for a speaker to say *'hot 'roast 'beef.*

Verb and adverb
- Verb and adverb stressed, eg *She 'got 'up, to 'sit 'down.*
- If the adverb is in the middle of two stressed words, there is no primary stress on the adverb, eg *He 'took off his 'hat* (rhythmical variation).
- If a stressed noun is between a verb and an adverb, there is no primary stress on the adverb, eg *He 'took his 'hat off. 'Put the 'coat on.* (But: *He 'took it 'off, 'Put it 'on*).

Auxiliaries
- Auxiliary verb is stressed, if linked with a weakened *not*, eg *You 'shouldn't have 'done it.*
- Auxiliary verb is stressed, if it introduces a question and if no stressed word follows, eg *'Have you 'seen him*?
- Auxiliary verb is stressed in final position, eg *'Yes, I 'have.*
- Auxiliary verb in question tags is stressed, eg *They'll 'come, 'won't they*? *He 'can't 'swim, 'can he*?

3.2.2 Change of secondary and primary stress

When a simple or complex word pattern in isolation has a primary stress preceded by a secondary stress, the primary stress will move back to the place of the secondary stress, if the following word starts with another primary stress, eg

ˌfif'teen vs. 'fifˌteen 'people
ˌWest'minster vs. 'Westˌminster 'Abbey
ˌafter'noon vs. 'afterˌnoon 'session
'leather + 'armˌchair vs. 'leather ˌarm'chair
ˌfull'grown vs. 'fullˌgrown 'man
ˌChi'nese vs. 'Chiˌnese 'tea

Q10 Explain the terms **content word, function word, level stress, tonicity, isochronism** and **isosyllabism**.

3.3 INTONATION

1. Introduction

Intonation means tune or melody. Every language incorporates a melody - no language is spoken on the same musical note all the time. The voice goes up and down and the different pitches of the voice, which are made up of voiced segments, combine to make tunes. The pitch depends on how fast the vocal cords vibrate: if they vibrate rapidly, the result is a high pitch, and if they vibrate slowly, the result is a low pitch. The pitch of voiced segments can either be level or variable. In some languages the tune mainly belongs to the word (Chinese for example). There are four tones in Modern Standard Chinese, high, rising, low, and falling, which can be indicated by the symbols ˉ(macron), ↗(upward diagonal arrow), _(under-bar) and ↘ (downward diagonal arrow) in front of the respective word; thus ˉba, ↗ba, _ba and ↘ ba have four different meanings: ˉba means *eight*, ↗ba means *to pull out*, _ba means *to take* and ↘ ba means *to quit*. In many other languages of which English is one, the tune belongs not to the word but to the word group or tone group. If you say the English word *yes* with different tunes, it has the status of a one-word-sentence. *Yes* spoken with different tunes will keep its meaning - it is still the same word. The individual words do not change their meaning, but the tune may add the speaker's feelings at that moment.

2. Division of utterances into tone units

When people speak, they normally express their thoughts in closely-knit groups of words or units of information, which are called **tone units** or **tone groups**. Tone units refer to a distinctive sequence of pitches or tones in an utterance and can consist of a single word or a number of words. The whole tone unit stands between a double vertical line (double bars) ‖. Longer tone units are normally separated from each other by pauses, which are marked by a single vertical line |. Tone units most commonly correspond with clauses, but also with smaller syntactic constituents than the clause. The following examples illustrate the different tone units: ‖ *They usually start at eight* ‖. ‖ *The workers normally start work very early in the morning* ‖ or ‖ *The workers | normally start work | very early in the morning* ‖. ‖ *She worked hard | and earned a lot of money* ‖. ‖ *The new sensational film | which was released yesterday | and shown all over London | attracted thousands of people* ‖. The pauses depend to a great extent on the situation, speech style and idiosyncratic factors in general. Studies have suggested that in conversation and in lectures about half the tone units are three to four words in length, and that less than 10 per cent of tone units will be more than eight words long (cf. Gimson 1962/94: 241).

A longer tone group can be analyzed as follows: all the unstressed syllables or syllables with secondary stress before the first stressed syllable make up the **prehead**, the first stressed syllable makes up the **head**, all the other stressed and unstressed syllables following the head before the last stressed syllable make up the **body**, the last stressed syllable makes up the **nucleus**, and all the following unstressed syllables make up the **tail** (cf. Kingdon 1958. Crystal 1969 divides the tone group into prehead, head, nucleus and tail. Halliday 1970 uses the terms pretonic and tonic and Brazil/Coulthard/Johns 1980 speak of proclitic segments, tonic segments and enclitic segments).

The prehead is spoken either on a low note or notes rising to the note of the head, which is usually spoken on the highest note and which is higher than its equivalent in German. The stressed syllables of the

body are spoken on **static notes** which gradually and smoothly de-
scend to the last stressed syllable. The static notes, ie the stressed syllables before the nucleus, are indicated here by a superior vertical
stroke ('). The unstressed syllables follow the same pattern as the
stressed syllables of the body and are spoken approximately on the
same notes as the stressed syllables. The last stressed syllable is the
nucleus, which constitutes the most important part as far as the grammatical, attitudinal and informational role is concerned. It is here
where the decisive and audible pitch change (**kinetic tone**) occurs
and where a statement can be changed into a question, or a polite
request into a rude order. This pitch change can either be a glide on
the nuclear syllable itself or a jump from the nuclear syllable to the
following syllable or syllables. The nucleus with its obligatory primary stress is therefore the most prominent syllable in a tone-unit.
The nucleus can have a falling tone indicated here by a downward
diagonal arrow (↘), it can have a rising tone indicated by an upward
diagonal arrow (↗), it can have a falling-rising tone indicated by a
wedge (ˇ) and it can have a rising-falling tone indicated by a circumflex (ˆ). Exceptionally, the nucleus can also have a level tone
indicated here by a horizontal level arrow (→). All the unstressed syllables following the nucleus are normally spoken on the same notes
as the last note of the nucleus or on slightly falling notes with a falling intonational pattern and rising notes with a rising intonational
pattern. If a tail follows a level nucleus, the unstressed syllables
remain on the same level. A sentence can consist of a prehead, head,
body, nucleus and tail, but also of a nucleus only in a one-word-sentence, which underlines the outstanding significance of the nucleus.
In other words, the nucleus is the only obligatory constituent, whereas the prehead, head and the tail are optional elements. A tone unit
can thus be represented as follows: (prehead) (head) (body) nucleus
(tail)

Tone unit

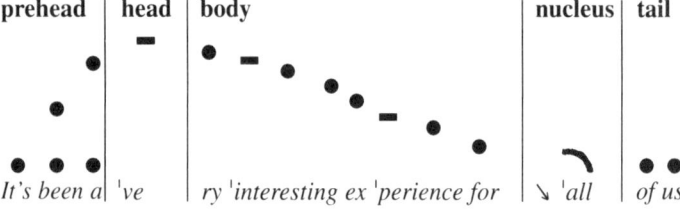

prehead	head	body	nucleus	tail
It's been a	've	ry 'interesting ex 'perience for	↘ 'all	of us.

The German equivalents of the above terms are *Vorlauf, erste Haupt-tonsilbe, Binnenlauf, letzte Haupttonsilbe* or *Schwerezentrum* and *Nachlauf* (cf. v. Essen 1953/79: 196).

Q11 Compare the two utterances: *It's been a* 'very 'interesting ex-'perience for ↘'all of us. - It's been a* 'very 'interesting ex 'perience for ↗'all of us.

3. Main types of intonation and examples

3.1 Falling intonation (↘)
A falling intonation is characterized by a movement from relatively high to relatively low. The fall can be divided into high falling and low falling. The difference in fall is indicated by ˎ (low fall) and by ˋ (high fall). ↘ stands before the nucleus and ' stands before the stressed syllables.
Examples:
	↘*No!*		,		↘*Excellent.*		,		↘*Fivepence.*	
	'*What's* ↘*that?*		,		*I was* 'very 'pleased and ↘*flattered.*	
	'*How can I* 'possibly 'pay him	'three 'thousand ↘*pounds?*	

3.2 Rising intonation (↗)
A rising intonation is characterized by a movement from relatively low to relatively high. The rise can be divided into high rising and low rising. The difference in rise is indicated by ˏ (low rise) and by ´ (high rise). ↗ stands before the nucleus and ' stands before the stressed syllables.
Examples:
	↗*Ten?*		,		↗*Why?*		,		↗*Fivepence?*	
	'*Fifty* ↗*pounds?*		,		*Was she* 'very ↗ *pleased?*	
	'*Have you* 'heard the 'latest 'news?*	

3.3 Falling-rising intonation (ˇ)
A falling-rising intonation is characterized by a movement from relatively high to relatively low and then back to (mid-) high. The fall-rise is indicated by ˇ. The fall and rise can be confined within one syllable. When this pattern has two nuclei, it is labelled fall-plus-rise and is indicated by ˋ+´. The symbol ˇ stands before the nucleus or ˋ and ´ stand before the two nuclei. ' stands before the stressed syllables.

Examples:
‖ ˇ *Why?*‖, ‖ ˇ *Five?*‖, ‖ ˇ *Fivepence?*‖
‖ *I* `hope | *she is* 'not 'late.‖, ‖*We* 'didn't `know | *it would be so* ´dangerous.*‖

3.4 Rising-falling intonation (ˆ)

A rising-falling intonation is characterized by a movement from relatively low to relatively high and then back to low. The rise-fall is indicated by ˆ . The rise and fall is normally confined within one syllable. When this pattern has two nuclei, which is rare, it is labelled rise-plus-fall and is indicated by ´+`. The symbol ˆ stands before the nucleus or ´ and ` stand before the two nuclei. ' stands before the stressed syllables.

Examples:
‖ ˆ *Yes.*‖, ‖ ˆ *No.*‖, ‖ *In* ˆ *deed.*‖
‖*It was* ˆ *yesterday.*‖, ‖('*Have you* ↗ *heard?*) '*Jill is* ˆ *pregnant.*‖

3.5 Level intonation (→)

A level intonation refers to a nuclear tone which has neither a falling nor a rising component. It is a mid level tone. The level tone is indicated by → and stands before the nucleus. ' stands before the stressed syllables.

Examples:
‖→*Yes.*‖, ‖→*No.*‖, ‖→*Really.*‖
‖*On my way to*→*work* | (*it started to pour*). ‖, ‖ *The other* →*day* | *when I saw the* →*man* | *I was totally unimpressed.* ‖

4. Frequencies of intonation patterns

As far as the frequencies of the different intonational patterns are concerned, the following analysis of three spoken BrE corpora of conversation can give a first impression of their distribution. It clearly shows that a falling intonation is predominant in the speech of English people. It should be added that the figures are not recent and that there is now a tendency especially among young speakers to use a rising intonation even for statements. Consequently, the figures may have to be adjusted.
- Falling intonation: 51.2% (52.5%; 58.7%)
- Rising intonation: 20.8% (24.7%; 16.1%)

- Falling-rising intonation: 16.2%, ie fall-rise: 8.5% and fall-plus-rise: 7.7% (16.2%; 12.5%)
- Rising-falling intonation: 6.9%, ie rise-fall: 5.2% and rise-plus-fall: 1.7% (4.5%; 4.6%)
- Level intonation: 4.9% (2.1%; 8.0%)
(cf. Crystal 1969: 225)

5. Functions of intonation

The functions of intonation in English are manifold. Intonation primarily fulfils a **grammatical and attitudinal (emotional) role**. Thus, it supports the grammatical structure in speech, where it is similar to punctuation. Clauses and sentences are often marked by intonation as well as several specific contrasts like questions and statements. Examples of the **grammatical** role are as follows:
You ↘ *heard her.* (statement) - *You* ↗ *heard her*? (question)
Hasn't she been ↗ *clever*? (question) - *Hasn't she been* ↘ *clever*! (exclamation)

In addition to its purely grammatical role, it has an overwhelmingly emotional role, ie it expresses attitudinal meaning such as anger, surprise, shock, sympathy, delight, impatience, interest and boredom. Examples of the **attitudinal** role are as follows:
She is ↘ *beautiful.* (neutral statement) - *She is* ˇ*beautiful.* (expression of doubt or reservation)
Don't ↘ *lie.* (order) - *Don't* ↗ *lie.* (persuasive attitude, plea)
What's ↘ *wrong*? (neutral question) - *What's* ↗ *wrong*? (showing special interest or sympathy)

Further functions are **informational**, where points of attention are stressed and new information is given. Examples are as follows:
I got the ↘ *job.* (neutral statement) - *I* ↘ *got the job.* (special emphasis, as the outcome was doubtful)
Have my papers been ↗ *destroyed*? (neutral question) - *Have my* ↗ *papers been destroyed*? (special emphasis on *papers*, as other things were destroyed as well)
Finally, the functions of intonation can also be **textual** (contrasts, coherence) and **indexical** (marker of personal and social identity). It should be clear that the meaning of an utterance must always be interpreted within a co-text and context. (cf. Crystal 1995: 249).

Because of the different and often overlapping functions of intonation, it is extremely difficult for students to acquire a native-like intonation. Thus, students should start by familiarizing themselves with typical patterns which can be heard in so-called neutral speech, ie business-like or routine-like speech, where the grammatical pattern is dominant. But as neutral speech is usually perceived as quite unfriendly, it is equally important for students to acquire the appropriate emotional patterns of intonation. The following guidelines can only give an incomplete picture of intonational patterns, as the different functions of intonation - grammatical, attitudinal, informational, textual and indexical functions - are normally intertwined.

Broadly speaking, the falling nuclear tone communicates an impression of completeness, and the rising nuclear tone indicates incompleteness. The falling and rising intonational patterns can be categorized further into low-falling and high-falling (or mid-falling) nuclei and low-rising and high-rising nuclei. Here the main difference is between neutral speech, where one predominantly uses a low-falling and low-rising nucleus, and emphatic speech, where one uses a high-falling and high-rising nucleus. If the normal falling tone is used for a rising tone and vice versa, then this unexpected change of intonation has an attitudinal function.

Whereas falling and rising intonation can express either a neutral attitude or an emotional attitude, the fall-rise, the rise-fall and the level intonation are generally restricted to an emotional attitude thus lacking the neutral aspect. The fall-rise is often used to express a variety of attitudes such as a warning, reservation, contradiction and contrast. The rise-fall usually indicates an indignant or even sarcastic attitude. It is also used for remarks conveying gossip. The level intonation is a tone which is used to show boredom or sarcasm.

5.1 In so-called neutral speech the following patterns are used

Falling intonation

1. Statements
They cheated the ＼ children.

2. Certain questions
a) X-questions or (w)h-questions
Who cheated the ＼ children?
How did they cheat the ＼ children?
b) Rhetoric questions
How dare/can they cheat the ＼ children.

c) Tag questions (with reverse polarity) where the other person is expected to agree
They deliberately cheated the children, ↘ *didn't they?*
The children weren't cheated, ↘ *were they?*

3. Orders or imperatives
Just talk to the ↘ *children.*

4. Requests
Please talk to the ↘ *children.*

5. Exclamations
What lovely ↘ *children!*

6. Greetings
Good ↘ *evening.*

Rising intonation
1. Unfinished parts of sentences
a) Clauses and (longer) phrases
Last ↗ *summer, I met your sister.*
To ↗ *us, this seems to be his best achievement.*
When the people felt ↗ *cheated, they started to rebel.*
In spite of the ↗ *promises, the people felt cheated.*
Making a lot of money in his ↗ *country, he decided to stay.*
What we ↗ *need is plenty of money.*
The new ↗ *film, which was released* ↗ *yesterday, has attracted a lot of people.*
Jill is an excellent bilingual ↗ *secretary and Peter a useless boss.*
He opened the ↗ *door and walked straight in.*
The hotel was very ↗ *expensive but rather dirty.*

b) Enumerations
They went to ↗ *Oxford,* ↗ *Cambridge and* ↘ *Warwick.* (only to these three towns)
They went to ↗ *Oxford,* ↗ *Cambridge and* ↗ *Warwick.* (and other towns)

c) Introductory vocatives
↗ *Jane, I'd like to have a word with you.*

2. Certain questions
a) Yes/No questions
Were the children ↗ *cheated?*

b) Statement questions
The children were ↗ cheated? (You can't be serious)

c) Echo questions
Speaker A: *The children were ↘ cheated.* (statement)
Speaker B: *The children were ↗ cheated?* (echo question)

d) Tag questions (with reverse polarity) where the other person's opinion is asked
The children weren't cheated, ↗ were they?

e) Tag questions after commands
Put it down, ↗ will you?

f) X-questions or (w)h-questions (asking for repetition)
Speaker A: *He arrived on 13th.*
Speaker B: *↗ When did he arrive?*

5.2 In non-neutral speech the following patterns are used

Fall-rise (Fall-plus-rise)

1. Statements
a) expressing a warning: *You'll be ˇlate.*
b) expressing reservation: *I like her ˇhusband, even if I don't like her.*
c) expressing contrast and strong feelings: *John didn't pass his exam, but ˇPeter did. It's her `husband who I don't 'like. `She won't 'help.*
d) expressing contradiction: *She is thirty. ˇForty.*

Rise-fall

1. Statements
a) expressing either a genuine or sarcastic attitude: *That's ^ wonderful. Aren't you ^ lucky!*
b) expressing a feeling of surprise or shock: *She is a complete ^ fool.*
c) expressing gossip:
Speaker A: *Have you heard?*
Speaker B: *Peter's in ^ prison.*

Level intonation

1. Statements
a) expressing sarcasm:
Speaker A: *They're bankrupt.*
Speaker B: *→Really.*

b) expressing boredom:
Speaker A: *I'm back in business.* (repetitive remark by speaker A)
Speaker B: →*Sure.*

2. Unfinished parts of speech
expressing lack of interest or boredom: *The other →day, when I saw →Jill, we talked about the weather.*

3. Enumerations
somewhat pompously expressing the predictability of events: *He →drank, he →cheated, he →stole, and in the end was sent to prison.*

6. Examples of the attitudinal (emotional) function of intonation

1. Statements

a) low rise (with high pitch before it) for soothing or encouraging attitude: *I won't be ↗ long.*
b) low rise (with high pitch before it) for patronizing attitude: *There's no point in ↗ rushing.*
c) low rise (with only low pitched syllables before it) for a complaining attitude: *You mustn't go a↗way.*
d) high rise for a grumbling attitude: *She can't possibly do ↗ that.*
e) (high) rise for a polite suggestion that confirmation is welcome: *She was looking ↗ happy.*
f) fall-rise for a doubtful and reserved attitude leading to a following sentence: *He looked at the ˇwoman (and then recognized her at once). He is ˇfriendly (but I don't trust him).*
g) fall rise for a sceptical attitude followed by a correction: *(He's fifty). ˇSixty.*
h) fall-rise for a warning: *You'll get ˇhurt.*

2. Questions

2.1 X-questions or (w)h-questions
a) rise for showing special interest: *How's your ↗ family?*
b) rise for a more tentative attitude:
Speaker A: *We're leaving on Friday.*
Speaker B: *When are you ↗ leaving?*

2.2 Yes/No questions
a) falling tone expressing a brusque and offensive attitude: *Do you a↘gree?*

b) rise-fall for a strong exclamation: (*She did not help*). *Would you be ˆlieve it*!

2.3 Tag questions
low-rise in tag questions (with constant polarity) showing sympathy:
Speaker A: *I think she's going to leave him.*
Speaker B: *So she won't marry him,* ↗ *won't she.*

3. Orders or imperatives

a) rise for a more gentle and persuasive attitude: *Give me another* ↗ *chance.*
b) rise for a polite invitation: *Go and open the* ↗ *door.*
c) fall-rise for pleading requests: *Close the* ˇ *door.* ˋ*Don't make me* ´*angry.*

7. *Yes* pronounced with different types of intonation

In order to summarize the emotional function of intonation, the pronunciation of the word *yes* provides a good example. The basic meaning, ie agreement, does not change, but the different tunes can add emotions. Thus, one can have up to nine different ways of saying *YES*.

Falling intonation
- low fall: *YES*, THAT IS SO (most neutral tone; unemotional statement)
- mid fall: *YES*, THAT SEEMS TO BE SO (still quite neutral; routine, still quite uncommitted)
- high fall: *YES*, OF COURSE IT IS SO (emotionally involved showing excitement, surprise, anger)

Rising intonation
- low rise: *YES*, I AGREE IN GENERAL or THE 'TELEPHONE' YES (I understand what you have said and I basically agree, please continue)
- mid rise: *YES*, IS IT REALLY SO? (emotionally involved; mild query)
- high rise: *YES*, BUT IT'S UNBELIEVABLE (emotionally involved to a great extent; often disbelief or shock)

Level intonation
YES, BUT IT IS UNLIKELY (emotionally involved showing boredom, sarcasm, irony)

Falling-rising intonation
YES, THAT MAY BE SO (strong emotional involvement expressing
either tentativeness and doubt or urgency and encouragement)

Rising-falling intonation
YES, CERTAINLY (strong emotional involvement expressing
delight).
(cf. Crystal 1995:248)

Q12 Transcribe the following conversation phonemically. Divide the
sentences into tone groups and indicate the type of intonation for each
tone group. Put the stress marks (primary stress only) before the
stressed syllables.

A: Can you recommend somewhere for a holiday?
B: What an odd coincidence! I was just going to tell you about our
holiday!
A: Really? Where did you go? To the South of France again?
B: No, this time we went to Ireland!
A: Oh, you went to Ireland, did you? You were thinking about it the
last time we met.
B: Oh yes, I mentioned it to you, didn't I?
A: You were thinking of Belfast, weren't you?
B: Dublin. But we didn't go there in the end.
A: Didn't you? Where did you go?
B: Where? To Galway.
A: That's on the West coast, isn't it? Was the weather good?
B: Reasonably good.
A: Tell me about the prices there, would you?
B: They weren't too bad. You should go there and try it. But you
ought to go soon. Summer's nearly over.
A: It isn't over yet. But thank you very much for your advice.
B: Good luck. Have a good time.
A: Thank you. Goodbye.
(O'Connor 1971:158-159)

Q13 List the typical differences between English and German intonation.

Q14 What's the difference between the following sentences:
a) *What's the* ↘ *matter*? - *What's the* ↗ *matter*?
b) *He's* ↘ *handsome. - He's ˇ handsome.*
c) *Don't* ↘ *cry. - Don't* ↗ *cry.*
d) *Haven't I been* ↗ *clever*? - *Haven't I been* ↘ *clever*!
e) *The doors weren't* ↘ *locked. - The doors weren't* ↗ *locked.*

Q15 Define **tone unit, prehead, head, body, nucleus, tail, pitch, static tone, kinetic tone** and the **attitudinal function of intonation**.

Key to some questions
Q1 In rapid colloquial speech, one can find all these clusters in initial position. The cluster /ps-/ is found in *besides* and nowadays in more and more words beginning with <ps-> like *psychology* and *pseudo*. The cluster /sg-/ can be heard in *let's go*, /fk-/ in *of course*, /fn-/ in *if not*, /ts-/ in *it's only* and sometimes in *tsar* and *tsetsi*, /tsg-/ in *it's good to know* and /zg-/ in *as good as gold*.

Q3 *definition* /ˌde ˇfɪˈnɪ ˇʃən/, *preparation* /ˌpre ˇpəˈreɪ ˇʃən/, *supposition* /ˌsʌ ˇpəˈzɪ ˇʃən/, *confirmation* /ˌkɒn ˇfəˈmeɪ ˇʃən/, *reformation* /ˌre ˇfəˈmeɪ ˇʃən/, *interpretation* / ˇɪn ˌtɜː ˇprəˈteɪ ˇʃən/, *characterization* /ˌkæ ˇrək ˇtə ˇraɪˈzeɪ ˇʃən/, *recommendation* /ˌre ˇkə ˌmenˈdeɪ ˇʃən/, *peculiarity* / ˇpɪ ˌkjuː ˇliˈæ ˇrɪ ˇti/.

Suggested readings

Arnold, G.F./A.C. Gimson (1965/70) *English Pronunciation Practice*. London: University of London Press
Bradford, B. (1988) *Intonation in Context*. Oxford: Oxford University Press
Brazil D./M. Coulthard/C. Johns (1980) *Discourse Intonation and Language teaching*. London: Longman
Chomsky, N./ M. Halle (1968) *The Sound Pattern of English*. New York: Harper and Row
Couper-Kuhlen, E. (1986) *An Introduction to English Prosody*. Niemeyer: Tübingen
Cruttenden, D. (1986) *Intonation*. Cambridge: Cambridge University Press
Crystal, D. (1969) *Prosodic Systems and Intonation in English*. Cambridge: Cambridge University Press
Crystal, D. (1975) *The English Tone of Voice*. London: Edward Arnold
Crystal, D. (1995) *The Cambridge Encyclopedia of the English Language*. Cambridge: Cambridge University Press

Essen, O.v. (1953/79) *Allgemeine und angewandte Phonetik*. Berlin: Akademie-Verlag

Esser, J. (1979) *Englische Prosodie*. Tübingen: Narr

Fudge, E.C. (1984) *English Word Stress*. London: Allen and Unwin

Halliday, M.A.K. (1970) *A Course in Spoken English: Intonation*. London: Oxford University Press

Kingdon, R. (1958) *The Groundwork of English Stress*. London: Longman

Leech, G./J. Svartvik (1976/94) *A Communicative Grammar of English*. London: Longman

O'Connor, J.D. (1967/80) *Better English Pronunciation*. Cambridge: Cambridge University Press

Poldauf, I. (1984) *English Word Stress: A Theory of Word-Stress in English*. Oxford: Pergamon

Postal, P.M. (1968) *Aspects of Phonological Theory*. New York: Harper and Row

Quirk, R./S. Greenbaum/G. Leech/J. Svartvik (1985) *A Comprehensive Grammar of the English Language*. London: Longman

Note on pronunciation

polysyllabic /ˌpɒlɪsɪˈlæbɪk/, intuitive /ɪnˈtjuːətɪv/, sonorous /ˈsɒnərəs/, coda /ˈkəʊdə/, nucleus /ˈnjuːkliəs/, sequential /sɪˈkwentʃəl/, Czech /tʃek/, primary /ˈpraɪməri/, decisive /dɪˈsaɪsɪv/, prominence /ˈprɒmɪnəns/, secondary /ˈsekəndəri/, tertiary /ˈtɜːʃəri/, penultimate /pəˈnʌltɪmət/, morphologically /ˌmɔːfəˈlɒdʒɪkəli/, affixes /ˈæfɪksɪz/, suffix /ˈsʌfɪks/, prefix /ˈpriːfɪks/, phonological /ˌfəʊnəˈlɒdʒɪkəl/, adjectival /ˌædʒɪkˈtaɪvəl/, compound /ˈkɒmpaʊnd/, morpheme /ˈmɔːfiːm/, vacillation /ˌvæsɪˈleɪʃən/, prescriptivist /prɪˈskrɪptɪvɪst/, pseudo /ˈsjuːdəʊ/, demonstrative /dɪˈmɒnstrətɪv/, interrogative /ɪntəˈrɒgətɪv/, conjunction /kənˈdʒʌŋkʃən/, auxiliary /ɔːgˈzɪliəri/, preposition /ˌprepəˈzɪʃən/, tonic /ˈtɒnɪk/, tonicity /təʊˈnɪsəti/, isochronism /aɪˈsɒkrənɪzm/, isochrony /aɪˈsɒkrəni/, macron /ˈmækrɒn/, idiosyncratic /ˌɪdiəʊsɪŋˈkrætɪk/, pretonic /priːˈtɒnɪk/, proclitic /prəʊˈklɪtɪk/, enclitic /ɪnˈklɪtɪk/, static /ˈstætɪk/, kinetic /kaɪˈnetɪk/, obligatory /əˈblɪgətəri/, diagonal /daɪˈægənəl/, circumflex /ˈsɜːkəmfleks/, nuclei /ˈnjuːkliaɪ/, component /kəmˈpəʊnənt/, manifold /ˈmænɪfəʊld/, intertwined /ˌɪntəˈtwaɪnd/, vice versa /ˈvaɪsi ˈvɜːsə/, rhetoric /ˈretərɪk/, imperative /ɪmˈperətɪv/, enumeration /ɪˌnjuːməˈreɪʃən/, echo /ˈekəʊ/, polarity /pəʊˈlærəti/, patronize /ˈpætrənaɪz/, tentative /ˈtentətɪv/, brusque /brʊsk/, query /ˈkwɪəri/.

4.0 CONNECTED SPEECH

The pronunciation of words can vary depending on whether they are spoken in isolation or in connected speech. Words in isolation keep their full quantitative and qualitative pattern, whereas it is normal for words to change their phonetic realizations in connected speech. Word stress, sentence stress, rhythm, linking and intonation can affect the pronunciation of words, which undergo processes of weakening, neutralization, assimilation and elision.

Furthermore, the pronunciation of words can differ in connected speech depending on the speech style used. In very careful speech, nearly every sound is produced accurately and fully, whereas in very rapid colloquial speech, the above mentioned processes occur.

4.1 WEAK FORMS

1. Introduction

In connected speech, **lexical words** (**content words** like nouns, verbs, adjectives, adverbs etc) normally keep the quantitative as well as the qualitative pattern of their isolate form. In contrast to lexical words, **function words** (**grammatical words** like auxiliaries, prepositions, articles, conjunctions, some pronouns etc) have two or more qualitative and quantitative realizations depending on whether they are unstressed, which is the normal case, or whether they are stressed, which happens in special situations and when spoken in isolation. The unstressed realizations are called **weak forms** and the stressed realizations **strong forms** or **citation forms.** Function words are normally weakened and thus they show obscuration of vowel quality towards /ə, ɪ, ʊ/, reductions in the length of sounds, the elision of vowels and consonants and the assimilation of consonants. Strong forms retain the full vowel and consonantal quality and quantity.

It should be clear that function words are normally realized as weak forms. Their correct use is especially important, since the full pronunciation of these words would distort the rhythmic pattern of English and could lead to constant misunderstanding. There are about forty function words, which occur in the first two hundred most common words in connected speech. The most common function words can be found in the following list.

2. List of function words

	unstressed	stressed	examples
a	/ə/	/eɪ/	a day in the country; a good book.
an	/n, ən/	/æn/	an easy journey; I can see an old house.
the	/ðə/+cons.	/ðiː/	the book is boring; the day is fine.
	/ðɪ/([ði])+vowel	/ðiː/	the idea is attractive; the hour is over.
and	/ənd, nd, ən, n/	/ænd/	Tom and Peter; you and I; bread and butter.
as	/əz/	/æz/	as good as gold; as far as I know; it is as well.
but	/bət/	/bʌt/	I have looked for my purse, but I can't find it.
than	/ðən, ðn/	/ðæn/	better than ever; we need more than that.
that	/ðət/	/ðæt/	I admit that I told her; the light that failed.
who	/hʊ, ʊ, uː/+cons.	/huː/	the girl who saw me; the boy who assisted me.
	/hʊ, ʊ/([hu,u])+v.	/huː/	the man who is coming; who are they?
to	/tə/+cons.	/tuː/	give it to Dave; to be or not to be.
	/tʊ/([tu])+vowel	/tuː/	she went to Oxford; I wanted to ask her.
saint	/sənt, snt, sən, sn/	/seɪnt/	St. Martin's church; St. Anthony; Peter St.John.
Sir	/sə/+cons.	/sɜː/	Sir Winston; Sir Peter.
	/sər/+vowel	/sɜːr/	Sir Edward; Sir Albert.
be	/bɪ/([bi])	/biː/	it could be done; you must be joking.

been	/bɪn/([bin])	/biːn/	*it's been a nice evening; it's been done.*
am	/əm, m/	/æm/	*nor am I; I am tired.*
are	/ə/+cons.	/ɑː/	*the girls are beautiful; our friends are Swedish.*
	/ər, r/+vowel	/ɑːr/	*the men are away; Anne and Ali are out.*
is	/z, s/	/ɪz/	*where is the paper?; that is fine.*
would	/wəd, əd, d/	/wʊd/	*Dad would like it; they would rather not.*
was	/wəz/	/wɒz/	*the weather was terrible; one was enough.*
were	/wə/+cons.	/wɜː/	*they were very pleased; we were nervous.*
	/wər/+vowel	/wɜːr/	*our friends were out; they were away.*
will	/l, ɪl/	/wɪl/	*it will come; that will do; I hope Phil will come.*
shall	/ʃəl, ʃl, l/	/ʃæl/	*I shall be cross; I shall take it up.*
should	/ʃəd, ʃd/	/ʃʊd/	*we should do it; I should have thought so.*
has	/həz, əz, z, s/	/hæz/	*George has come; she's done it; Pete's come.*
have	/həv, əv, v/	/hæv/	*what have you done?; the men have gone; I've got it.*
had	/həd, əd, d/	/hæd/	*what had you done?; Ted had gone; you'd done it.*
do	/dʊ ([du]), də, d/	/duː/	*so do all of us; how do you like it?; do you smoke?*
does	/dəz, z, s/	/dʌz/	*when does the train leave?; what does it mean?*
must	/məst, məs/	/mʌst/	*I must answer that letter; I must go now.*
can	/kən, kn/	/kæn/	*how can I help?; we can do it; wherever can it be?*
could	/kəd, kd/	/kʊd/	*we could come tomorrow; he could have told me.*

some	/səm, sm/	/sʌm/	*some paper; would you like some more?*
at	/ət/	/æt/	*be at the station; at ten; at home; look at that.*
from	/frəm, frm/	/frɒm/	*it is a letter from Clara; a long way from London.*
for	/fə/+cons.	/fɔ:/	*I sent for the doctor; it's for Christine.*
	/fər, fr/+vowel	/fɔ:r/	*just for a laugh; shall we go for a walk?*
of	/əv, v, ə/	/ɒv/	*a pound of sugar; a plea of not guilty.*
you	/ju ([ju]), jə/	/ju:/	*see you tomorrow; I'll give you a pound.*
me	/mɪ ([mi])/	/mi:/	*give me some money; tell me again.*
she	/ʃɪ ([ʃi])/	/ʃi:/	*she's left; she asked for it.*
her	/hə, ə/+cons.	/hɜ:/	*I saw her twice; I took her home.*
	/hər, ər/+vowel	/hɜ:r/	*talk to her in private; take her out*
he	/hɪ ([hi]), i/	/hi:/	*he's gone; where is he?*
him	/ɪm/	/hɪm/	*I told him; I saw him once.*
we	/wɪ ([wi])/	/wi:/	*we can't stay; we asked for help.*
them	/ðəm, əm, m/	/ðem/	*I saw them; I sent them a letter.*
us	/əs, s/	/ʌs/	*she took us home; let us do it.*
her	/hə, ə, ɜ:/+cons.	/hɜ:/	*they changed her car; what's her name?*
	/hər, ər, ɜ:r/+vowel	/hɔ:r/	*he took her arm; what's her address?*
his	/ɪz/	/hɪz/	*take his umbrella; I can see his house*

3. Notes on function words

a) Note that there are certain contexts where the strong form is obligatory:
- in isolation: *What's the English word for 'als' in this context? Than* /ðæn/.

- in citations: *Can the word 'but'* /bʌt/ *stand at the beginning of a sentence*?

- forming of contrast: *It's a cheque for* /fɔː/ *Jane, not from* /frɒm/ *Jane.*

- special emphasis: *You must* /mʌst/ *take your medicine regularly.*

- at the end of a phrase or sentence: *He was shot at* /æt/ *by snipers. Where does she come from* /frɒm/? *What's it made of* /ɒv/? *Yes, I have* /hæv/. Further examples are: *Won't you have <u>some</u>? If she <u>can</u>, anyone <u>can</u>. Who wants it? I <u>do</u>. Phil isn't going, but I <u>am</u>. If they can't do it, we <u>must</u>. A much talked <u>of</u> book. I was called <u>for</u> at nine. What an unheard <u>of</u> idea.*

b) Depending on their word class, the following words do not have weak forms:

- *do, does, have, has, had* (main verbs)
- *that* (demonstrative pronoun)
- *there* (adverb of place or demonstrative adverb)
- *some* (indefinite pronoun)

Examples are:
I didn't do my job properly.
She never does a stroke.
We have no time to travel.
He never has a cold.
Well then, let's have it now.
They'd had great experience.
It's not on that list.
That person is evil.
I went there when I was five.
There goes my bus.
Some might like it.
We got some from the shop.

c) The following words do not have weak forms: *when, then, on.*

d) *Be, been, he, she, we, me, you, who*: the strong forms show long quantity, when unstressed the words are often pronounced with weaker vowels than /iː/ and /uː/ of their strong forms, ie they have /i/ and /u/ resulting in /bi, bin, hi, ʃi, wi, mi, ju, hu/.

e) *He, him, his, her, who*: when these words are unstressed, the /h/ is normally dropped, eg *Did he win? Give him two. I like his tie. Take her home. The man who did it.*

At the beginning of a sentence, /h/ is never dropped: *He can't come.*
He likes it. Her face is red.

f) In questions beginning with an auxiliary verb, that verb may either
be stressed (strong form) or unstressed (weak form), if no stressed
word follows, eg
Are they coming? /'ɑː ðeɪ 'kʌmɪŋ/ or /ə ðeɪ 'kʌmɪŋ/
Does it matter? /'dʌz ɪt 'mætə/ or /dəz ɪt 'mætə/
Can I come? /'kæn aɪ 'kʌm/ or /kən aɪ 'kʌm/

Note: Initial *will* and *would* are normally not weakened.

g) In question tags the verb is stressed and the pronoun unstressed, eg
They aren't ready, 'are they?
They are ready, 'aren't they?
I'm not late, 'am I?
I'm late, 'aren't I?
You weren't there, 'were you?

h) *Not:* the strong form is /nɒt/. The weak form /nt/ is used after an
unweakened auxiliary verb as in *they aren't* /ɑːnt/, *she doesn't* /dʌznt/
or *I can't* /kɑːnt/. If the auxiliary verb is weakened, then the negative
is stressed and keeps its strong form /nɒt/, eg

I'm not	*it's not*
they're not	*I was* /wəz/ *not*
we were /wə/ *not*	*they would* /wəd/ *not*
I should /ʃəd/ *not*	*they'd* /d/ *not*
they had /həd/ *not*	*you've not*
they'd /d/ *not*	*he does* /dəz/ *not*
we must /məs/ *not*	*it could* /kəd/ *not*

Note the following contracted forms:
am I not?	=	*aren't I?* /ɑːnt/
will not	=	*won't* /wəʊnt/
shall not	=	*shan't* /ʃɑːnt/
do not	=	*don't* /dəʊnt/
cannot	=	*can't* /kɑːnt/
we are	=	*we're* /wɪə/
you are	=	*you're* /jʊə/
they are	=	*they're* /ðeə/

i) *There* (indefinite adverb): in sentences the word *there* is always
unstressed and is generally weakened to /ðə/.

I think there is one here.	*He told me there wasn't any.*
I think there is one.	*Why were there so many?*
There isn't much time.	*There'll be a lot left.*
I hope there are some.	*He said there'd be plenty.*
There was a tremendous crowd.	*Would there be room?*

Note: As a demonstrative adverb and an adverb of place *there* is stressed, eg *'There is the book* and *I found him 'there.*

4. Neutralization

Neutralization refers to the pronunciation of words when the distinction between phonemes is lost in particular environments. Examples are German *Bund* and *bunt* or *Bug* and *buk*. In English, a sequence of different phonemes can sometimes be neutralized. Examples are /s/ or /z/ for *has, is* and *does* in unstressed positions in connected speech as in *it has* /ɪts/ *been raining, it is* /ɪts/ *cold, what does* /wɒts/ *it mean* or *she has* /ʃɪz/ *been busy, she is* /ʃɪz/ *busy* and *when does* /wenz/ *the train arrive.*

From the students' point of view, it is also important to realize that the pronunciation of different function words can be identical, ie that there is neutralization of weak forms. The following examples regularly occur in rapid, colloquial speech.

- /ə/ for unstressed *a, are, her, of, or*
It's a nice place.
The houses are cheap.
I drove her home.
The queen of Spain.
Do you want nine or ten items?

- /ən/ for unstressed *and, an*
Tom and Peter.
I bought an old house.

- /ər/ for unstressed *are, or* (before following vowel)
The children are excited.
Nine or ten people.

- /əz/ for unstressed *as, has*
As far as I know.
How much has Jane paid?

- /ðə/ for unstressed *the, there*
The house is empty.
There's no doubt about it.

- /d/ for unstressed *had, would*
I had done it.
I would do it.

- /n/ for unstressed *an, and, not*
I can see an owl.
You and I.
I didn't do it.

- /s/ for unstressed *is, has, does* (after a voiceless sound)
What is it made of?
Pat has left England.
What does it mean?

- /z/ for unstressed *is, has, does* (after a voiced sound)
Where is the book?
Joe has arrived.
When does the train leave?

4.2 ASSIMILATION, ELISION AND LINKING

1. Assimilation

Assimilation refers to the influence that one sound has on the articulation of another, so that the sounds become more similar or identical. The word *assimilation* itself is a product of this process (*ad+simulatio*).
Several types of assimilation can be recognized. Assimilation can be classified according to **impact** (*partial assimilation* - *total assimilation*), **direction** (*regressive* or *anticipatory assimilation* - *progressive* or *perseverative assimilation* - *reciprocal* or *coalescent assimilation*)

and **place** (*contact* or *contiguous* or *direct assimilation - distance* or *non-contiguous* or *indirect assimilation*).

a) Impact of assimilation
- **partial assimilation** refers to the process where two sounds become similar, ie only one feature is adopted. Examples are *impossible* (*<in+possible*), *impatient* (*<in+patient*), *impolite* (*< in+polite*), *tenpence* /tempens/, *ten cups* /teŋ kʌps/ and *newspaper* /njuːspeɪpə/.
- **total assimilation** refers to the process where two sounds become identical. Examples are *assimilation* (*ad+simulatio*), *irresponsible* (*<in+responsible*), *illogical* (*<in+logical*), *bless* (Anglo-Saxon *bletsian*), *bad guys* /bæg gaɪz/ and *ten marks* /tem mɑːks/.

b) Direction of assimilation
- **regressive assimilation** refers to the process where a sound changes because of the influence of the following sound. Examples are *ten* /tem/ *boats, bread and* /əm/ *butter, impertinent* (*<in+pertinent*).
- **progressive assimilation** refers to the process where a sound changes because of the influence of the preceding sound. Examples are *happen* /hæpm/, *ribbon* /rɪbm/, *second chance* /sekŋ tʃɑːns/, *not much snow* /mʌtʃ ʃnəʊ/ and *fish slice* /fɪʃ ʃlaɪs/. This kind of progressive assimilation is relatively rare. There is regular progressive assimilation at the morphophonemic level with plural and third-person <s> as well as with the past marker <ed>. Thus <s> is pronounced as /s/ after voiceless sounds as in *tents* /tents/ and *likes* /laɪks/ or as /z/ after voiced sounds as in *shows* /ʃəʊz/ and *hens* /henz/. The past marker <ed> is pronounced as /t/ after voiceless sounds as in *stopped* /stɒpt/ and *dressed* /drest/ or as /d/ after voiced sounds as in *mowed* /məʊd/ and *begged* /begd/.

Note 1: Notice the difference between *tens* /tenz/ and *tense* /tens/ or *sins* /sɪnz/ and *since* /sɪns/.
Note 2: **Morphophonemics** is a branch of linguistics dealing with the phonological factors which affect the appearance of morphemes or the grammatical factors which affect the appearance of phonemes. In other words, morphophonemics refers to the variation in the form of morphemes resulting from phonetic factors.

- **reciprocal assimilation** refers to the process where sounds change because of the mutual influence of the sounds on each other (**fusion**). Examples are *don't you* /dəʊntʃʊ/ (/t/+/j/ fuse to become an affricate), *did you* /dɪdʒʊ/ (/d/ and /j/ fuse to produce /dʒ/) and *casual* /kæʒuəl/ (/z/ and /j/ fuse to become /ʒ/).

c) Place of assimilation

- **contact (contiguous, direct) assimilation** refers to the process where a sound changes because of the influence of the adjacent sound. Examples are *ten boats* /tem bəʊts/, *stands* /stændz/, *impatient* (< *in+patient*).

- **distance (non-contiguous, indirect) assimilation** refers to the process where a sound changes because of the influence of a remote sound, ie a sound that is further away. Synchronic examples are quite rare, but occur in rapid colloquial speech as in *turn* /tɜːm/ *to the ambassador.*

In historical linguistics, one can identify quite a number of words which were affected by distance assimilation because of the Germanic plural marker <i>. Examples are *foot - feet* (German *Fuß - Füße*), *goose - geese* (German *Gans - Gänse*) and *mouse - mice* (German *Maus - Mäuse*). The last example can be explained as follows:

sing. *mus*   - pl. *mus+i* /muːsiː/

           - pl. *mysi* /myːsiː/ (distance assimilation)

           - pl. *mys* /myːs/ (elision)

           - pl. *mis* /miːs/ (sound shift)

           - pl. *mice* /maɪs/ (sound shift)

Note 1: Distance assimilation can be observed with learners of English, who make mistakes such as */weri wel/ for *very well* or */θʌðən/ for *southern.*

Note 2: The opposite of assimilation is **dissimilation**. Dissimilation refers to the process where similar or identical sounds change to become dissimilar or different. The examples are mainly taken from observations in historical linguistics, ie *pilgrim* (Latin *perigrinus),* *purple* (Latin *purpur*), *turtle* (Latin *turtur*), *colonel* (Italian *colonello,* Spanish *coronel).*

Q1 How would one pronounce the following word pairs in rapid colloquial speech?
- *right person, not me, let me, hot bath*
- *sad person, good boy, good man*
- *one pint, gone back, one girl*
- *hot cake, that girl, that boy.*

2. Elision

Elision refers to the omission (deletion) of sounds in words. Typical cases of omission are:

- avoidance of complex consonant clusters, eg *French* /frenʃ/, *arrange* /əreinʒ/, *acts* /æks/, *postman* /pəusmən/, *scripts* /skrips/, *handbag* /hænbæg/ or /hæmbæg/, *old people* /əul piːpl/, *soft peach* /sɒf piːtʃ/, *best man* /bes mæn/, *left knee* /lef niː/ and *kind neighbour* /kain neibə/.
- loss of schwa after aspirated <p>, <t>, and sometimes <k>, eg *potato* /pteitəu/, *perhaps* /phæps/ or even /præps/, *today* /tdei/, *terrific* /trifik/ and *connect* /knekt/. As the /k/ in <kn-> was dropped in the 17th century, the dropping of schwa after /k/ is rare because of phonotactic restrictions. Compare German *Knut*, which changes to English *Canute* having an epenthetic /ə/.
- loss of schwa and formation of the syllabic consonants /n, l, r/, eg *tonight* /tnait/, *believe* /bliːv/ and *career* /kriə/.
- loss of final /v/ in *of* before consonants, eg *cup of tea* /kʌp ə tiː/ and *kind of people* /kaind ə piːpl/.
- reduction of sounds in function words (cf. weak forms).

Note: The opposite of elision is **intrusion**. Intrusion refers to the addition of sounds which have no etymological basis, but which can facilitate pronunciation, eg *drawing* /drɔːriŋ/, *law and order* /lɔːrənɔːdə/ and *film* /filəm/ (cf. chapters 2, 6 and 7).

Q2 Explain the pronunciations /fkɔːs/ for *of course* and /psaidz/ for *besides*.

3. Linking

One of the typical features of spoken English is linking, ie connecting words smoothly. In connected speech, word groups are pronounced in English without pause or hesitation, so that the words are pronounced not as separate units, but as connected units. There is linking between consonants and vowels, vowels and consonants as well as between vowel and vowel. The latter case refers to linking /ʲ/ and /ʷ/ (cf. chapter 2.2 on linking /r/ and semi-vowels).

Note: **fillers**
Because speech is spontaneous and often quite rapid, it is sometimes necessary to use extra pauses. These pauses can either be empty (or silent) pauses (long, short) or filled pauses. As far as filled pauses are concerned, two kinds of fillers can be used, ie non-lexical fillers and

lexical fillers. Typical non-lexical fillers in English are *er, erm, um, mm, hm*. Typical lexical fillers are *I mean, I say, you know, anyway, really, of course, well, look, I suppose, kind of, sort of, as you say, off the record, God knows, obviously, as I said before, what I wanted to say, as a matter of fact, mind you, you see, the trouble is, to put it another way, what's more*.

The branch of linguistics that deals with pauses is called **pausology**.

To summarize, one can say that in rapid colloquial speech, assimilations, linking, elisions, weak forms as well as fillers are commonly used and natural. Consequently, words can be changed phonetically and phonemically without losing their distinctive quality. In other words, the variant pronunciation of words in connected speech is a normal and natural feature of English pronunciation and will be understood perfectly well.

Q3 List typical fillers in German.

Q4 Repeat the terms used for the different types of assimilation and give examples.

Key to some questions

Q1
- *right person* /raɪp pɜːsən/, *not me* /nɒp mi/, *let me* /lem mi/, *hot bath* /hɒp bɑːθ/
- *sad person* /sæb pɜːsən/, *good boy* /gʊb bɔɪ/, *good man* /gʊb mæn/ or /gʊm mæn/
- *one pint* /wʌm paɪnt/, *gone back* /gɒm bæk/, *one girl* /wʌŋ gɜːl/
- *hot cake* /hɒk keɪk/, *that girl* /ðæg gɜːl/, *that boy* /ðæb bɔɪ/.

Q2 The pronunciation /fkɔːs/ for *of course* can be explained as follows:
- strong form: /ɒv kɔːs/
- regressive assimilation: /ɒf kɔːs/
- neutralization: /əf kɔːs/
- elision: /fkɔːs/.

The pronunciation /psaɪdz/ for *besides* can be explained as follows:
- strong form: /bɪsaɪdz/
- elision: /bsaɪdz/
- regressive assimilation: /psaɪdz/.

Suggested Readings

Brown, G. (1977/90) *Listening to Spoken English*. London: Longman

Crystal, D. (1995) *The Cambridge Encyclopedia of the English Language*. Cambridge: Cambridge University Press

Crystal, D. (1984) *Who Cares about English Usage?* Harmondsworth: Penguin

Knowles, G. (1987/93) *Patterns of Spoken English*. London: Longman

O'Connor, J.D. (1967/80) *Better English Pronunciation*. Cambridge: Cambridge University Press

Pring, J.T. (1959/70) *Colloquial English Pronunciation*. London: Longman

Note on pronunciation

affect (v.) /əˈfekt/, neutralization /njuːtrəlaɪˈzeɪʃən/, elision /ɪˈlɪʒən/, quantitative /ˈkwɒntɪtətɪv/, qualitative /ˈkwɒlɪtətɪv/, indefinite /ɪnˈdefənət/, regressive /rɪˈɡresɪv/, anticipatory /ænˈtɪsɪpətəri/, perseverative /pəˈsevərətɪv/, reciprocal /rɪˈsɪprəkəl/, contiguous /kənˈtɪɡjuəs/, coalescent /kəʊəˈlesənt/, process (n.), (v.) /ˈprəʊses/, fusion /ˈfjuːʒən/, synchronic /sɪnˈkrɒnɪk/, deletion /dɪˈliːʃən/, etymological /etɪməˈlɒdʒɪkəl/, morphophonemics /mɔːfəʊfəʊˈniːmɪks/.

5.0 BASICS IN PHONOLOGY

1. Introduction: phonetics and phonology

Human speech sounds can be studied from two major angles. One can study sounds from the point of view of their **production** (**articulatory phonetics**), **transmission** (**acoustic phonetics**) and **perception** (**auditory phonetics**) or from the point of view of their **function** (**phonology**). **Phonetics** is the science dealing with the physical side of human speech sounds and examines all human vocal speech sounds in any language without any special reference to the function of sounds. Phonetics thus describes sounds as physical entities, whereas **phonology** describes the functional aspect of the speech sounds in one particular language. 'Functional' means relevant to the purpose of communication, relevant to the description of one sound system and relevant to the distinctive nature of sounds.

The two approaches can be illustrated by a simple example. If one studies the sound [s] from a phonetic point of view, one can make the following observations:
- If a person produces the sound [s] twice, one should hear two slightly different sounds, which can be verified by exact spectrographic analysis. The reason is that no single sound is produced repeatedly in exactly the same position within the human articulatory apparatus, since there are no totally fixed points of articulation when producing a single sound. The position of the articulatory organs can differ slightly and the sounds can be produced with a difference in air pressure and muscular force. Consequently, a sound produced twice by the same speaker will never have the same physical quality, because there is an infinite number of insignificant, very small differences between any one person's speech on any two occasions.
- If two speakers pronounce the same sound, their realizations will obviously also be different. Apart from the reasons mentioned above, other factors are responsible for the difference, eg difference in voice quality, age, gender and difference in the articulatory organs.

Phonetically, infinite variations of a single sound are possible. Despite these infinite variations, people are still able to identify and discriminate between sounds systematically and learn to communicate. The [s] sound always remains an [s], no matter who pronounces it and no matter when, where or how it is uttered. The task of phonology is to extract out of an infinite range of speech sounds those features which can be understood as the same. Phonology attempts to identify the invariable function of a sound which makes it possible to communicate with ease and to distinguish between the different sounds. Phonology describes the function of sounds and the contrasts between them within the context of one particular language thus establishing the sound system of a language.

The term **phonology** can be used in two ways. On the one hand, it refers to the description of the sound system of a particular language and the rules governing the distribution of the sounds in English, German or French for example. On the other hand, phonology refers to that part of the general theory of human language that deals with the universal features of natural sound systems and the rules governing the distribution of sounds.

Although the aims of phonetics and phonology are different, phonology has to rely on the phonetic description of sounds, which demonstrates the interdependency of phonetics and phonology. In other words, phonological classification depends on phonetic description.

2. Phones, allophones, phonemes and variants

The term **phone** is used in phonetics to refer to the smallest perceptible discrete segment in a language which distinguishes sounds in a stream of speech. It is any physically observed objective speech sound. From the point of view of phonology, phones are the physical realizations of phonemes regardless of how they fit into the system of any given language. Phones are any unclassified sounds.

The term **phoneme** is used in phonology to refer to the smallest unit in the sound system of a language which distinguishes between meanings. The phonemes /b/ and /p/ distinguish the words *bet* and *pet* for example. The phonemes of a language are basically abstractions, since the particular phonetic shape they take depends on many factors such as their position in relation to other sounds and their position within a word itself.

The term **allophone** is used to refer to the positional phonetic realizations of a phoneme. As far as the position of a phoneme in a word is concerned, the phoneme /l/ serves as an example of the difference in allophonic realization. The phoneme /l/ is articulated as a clear [l] before vowels or /j/ and as a dark [ɫ] before consonants or in final position. As far as the position in relation to other sounds is concerned, the phoneme /n/ serves as another example of the difference in allophonic realization. The phoneme /n/ is usually articulated in alveolar position as in *ten* for example, but it can occur in dental position in the word *tenth* because of the influence of the following sound, which is produced in dental position. The phoneme /k/ is usually articulated in velar position as in *cool*, but it is articulated fronted from velar in *keen*.

Allophones that reflect an automatic adjustment of tongue position to facilitate co-articulation with the following sound are sometimes termed **accommodatory** (**intrinsic, co-articulated**) allophones. Allophones that do not reflect an automatic adjustment, but are determined by the phonetic environment alone with its traditional rules, are sometimes termed **non-accommodatory** (**extrinsic**) allophones.

Apart from the different functions of phonemes and allophones, their **distribution**, ie the range of positions in which these two units can occur also varies.
- Phonemes are said to be in **equivalent (contrastive) distribution**, ie they can stand in the same place or environment as other phonemes. They are in **paradigmatic relation**, which refers to the set of substitutional relationships a speech unit has with other units. The phonemes /k/ and /m/ are in paradigmatic relation in the words *cat-mat, taking - taming* and *hack - ham*. Words which differ in meaning when only one phoneme is changed are referred to as **minimal pairs**.
- Allophones are said to be in **complementary distribution**, ie they cannot stand in the same place or environment, but always occur in a different place or environment. In other words, complementary distribution refers to the mutual exclusiveness of related sounds in a certain phonetic environment. Allophones are in **syntagmatic relation**, which refers to the sequential characteristics of speech in linear order. The aspirated and unaspirated allophones of the phoneme /p/ can never occur in the same environment and can therefore never form a contrast, ie unaspirated [p] occurs after /s/ as in *spin,* whereas aspirated [pʰ] as in *pin* occurs in initial positions. If [p] and [pʰ] could occur in the same environment, they would have phonemic status. In

Hindi, for example, the feature of aspiration functions distinctively in voiceless plosives and consequently /p/ and /pʰ/ have phonemic status. In some Asian languages, [l] and [r] are allophones, but have phonemic status in English and other European languages.

It is also possible for two phonemes to be in **partially complementary distribution**, ie they are in complementary distribution in some positions or environments, but in equivalent distribution in others. Examples are /h/ and /ŋ/ in English. The phoneme /h/ appears initially, but not finally, where /ŋ/ can occur. In these positions the two phonemes are in complementary distribution. Both phonemes occur in medial position (*anyhow* and *singer*), but no minimal pairs exist in medial positions. Because of the partially complementary distribution and the complete lack of **phonetic similarity**, /h/ and /ŋ/ are clearly interpreted as two different phonemes.

The term **variant** or **variable** refers to linguistic items which have various forms. In phonology it refers to the substitutability of one sound for another in a given environment. The substituted sounds can have either phonetic or phonemic status. There is no change in the word's meaning, not even in the latter case. These different realizations of a phoneme are also called **free variants**. Examples are *very* or *while*, where /r/ in *very* can be realized as a tap [ɾ] and where /w/ can also be pronounced as [hw] or [ʍ]. In the cases of the words *economic* or *data,* /iː/ can be sustituted by /e/ in *e̠conomic* and /eɪ/ can be replaced by /ɑː/ or /æ/ in *data.* Normally /iː, e, eɪ, ɑː, æ/ have phonemic status and distinguish between the meanings of words, but in the case of free variation their distinctive function is neutralized.

Q1 List typical allophones and variants in English.

3. Some definitions of the term 'phoneme'

Various linguistic schools have viewed the term 'phoneme' differently. Some linguists interpret the term as a 'psychological unit', others as a 'concrete physical unit' and yet others as an 'abstract unit'.

Q2 Comment on the following definitions of a phoneme.
 - "A phoneme is a family of sounds in a given language which are related in character and are used in such a way that no one member

ever occurs in a word in the same phonetic context as any other member (Jones 1950)."

- "The phonemes of a language are...the elements which stand in contrast with each other in the phonological system of the language... A phoneme is defined, not as a sound produced in such-and-such a manner, but as a point of reference in an interlocking network of contrasts (Hockett 1958)."

- "... a minimum unit of distinctive sound feature, a phoneme...The phonemes of a language are not sounds, but merely features of sounds ... (Bloomfield 1933)."

- "Oppositions of sound capable of differentiating the lexical meaning of two words in a particular language are *phonological* or *phonologically distinctive* or *distinctive oppositions*..."
"...the phoneme is the smallest distinctive unit of a given language."
"...the phoneme is *the sum of the phonologically relevant properties of a sound unit* (Trubetzkoy 1939)."

- "The distinctive features combined into one simultaneous or...concurrent bundle form a *phoneme* (Jakobson, Fant, Halle 1952)."

4. The phoneme as a bundle of features

The above listed definitions indicate that phonemes are functional units which are defined by their distribution and opposition. They also show that a phoneme, which so far has been said to be the smallest distinctive unit, can be divided into smaller units, ie features. The difference between *pet* and *bet* is recognized, because the two words are distinguished from each other by certain characteristics. The features which are required to distinguish one word from another are said to be **distinctive**. In the case of *pet* and *bet*, the features of the phoneme /b/ are bilabial, plosive and voice and the features of the phoneme /p/ are bilabial, plosive and voicelessness. The distinctive feature is **voicing**. It follows that any phoneme can be further analyzed into features. Trubetzkoy, for example, takes traditional articulatory terms as the main basis for his description stating that every sound contains several acoustic-articulatory properties and is differentiated from any other sound by one or more of these properties. In other words, phonemes differ from each other in respect of at least one of these features and the particular properties or characteristics which distinguish one phoneme from another are **distinctive features**. The phoneme can be seen as a bundle of distinctive features. These minimal contrastive units are used to explain how the sound system of a language or languages is organized. Features that are not relevant for the classification of a sound system are **redundant features**. The contrast between /p/ and /b/ can be defined in terms of voicing, muscular tension and aspiration. But only one of these features is necessary to specify the contrast between the phonemes, ie voicing. The other two features are redundant for the classification.

The necessity to describe phonetic processes and define rules in one language or in languages in general led to the development of the distinctive feature theories of phonology. The concept of the phoneme as the smallest linguistic unit was abandoned and was replaced by features, which can be seen as an alternative to the notion of the phoneme. Nevertheless the term 'phoneme' is still used as a convenient abbreviation for particular sets of features and the description of certain phonological relations. With the help of features as the minimal units of phonological analysis, it has become easier to make generalizations about the relationship of sounds, to make intralingual as well as interlingual comparisons and to make statements about phonological universals (properties which are common to all languages in the world).

5. Feature Theories

There are a number of distinctive-feature systems. One of the earliest systems was devised by Jakobson, Fant and Halle. They set up 12 features in pairs and defined them primarily in acoustic terms, but with some reference to articulatory criteria. The features are **vocalic/non-vocalic, consonantal/non-consonantal, nasal/oral, compact/diffuse, interrupted/continuant, strident/mellow, checked/unchecked, voice/voiceless, tense/lax, grave/acute, flat/plain (non-flat)** and **sharp/plain (non-sharp)**. In the Chomsky and Halle approach, more attention is paid to the phonetic realizations and a different system of classification is devised. They also use a **binary system**, which means that a feature is used in terms of two mutually exclusive possibilities such as [+voice] or [-voice] and [+tense] or [-tense]. In an attempt to establish a universal set of features, Chomsky and Halle have come up with the following suggestions. The features listed below are not complete, but are sufficient for a description of the English phonological system.

5.1 Some Chomsky/Halle features

major class features:
sonorant
syllabic
consonantal

cavity features:
coronal
anterior
high
low
back
round
nasal
lateral

manner of articulation features:
continuant
delayed release
tense

source features:
voice
strident

The above features can be described as follows:

sonorant: Sonorant sounds are produced with a vocal tract cavity in which spontaneous voicing is possible. The vocal tract is not constricted to such an extent that the airflow is inhibited. Vowels, glides, liquids and nasals arc [+sonorant]. Obstruents (plosives, affricates, fricatives) are [-sonorant].

syllabic: Syllabic sounds are produced without obstruction, but with varying positions of the jaw and tongue which alter the shape of the oral cavity. A sound is syllabic, if the position of the tongue is not higher than for /iː/ or /uː/. Vowels and liquids are [+syllabic]. Glides, nasals and obstruents are [-syllabic].

consonantal: Consonantal sounds are produced with a major obstruction involving contact or near-contact at the point of articulation. Obstruents, nasals and liquids are [+consonantal]. Vowels and glides are [-consonantal].

coronal: Coronal sounds are produced with the blade of the tongue raised from its neutral position. The tongue either touches the teeth or the alveolar ridge. Dental, alveolar, retroflex, rolled and palato-alveolar sounds are [+coronal]. Bilabial, labiodental, palatal, velar, uvular, pharyngeal and glottal sounds are [-coronal].

anterior: Anterior sounds are produced with an obstruction that is located in front of the palato-alveolar region of the mouth. Bilabial, labiodental, dental and alveolar sounds are [+anterior]. Retroflex, post-alveolar, palato-alveolar, palatal, velar, uvular, pharyngeal and glottal sounds are [-anterior].

high: High sounds are produced by raising the body of the tongue above the level that it occupies in the neutral position. High vowels, glides, retroflex, palato-alveolar, palatal and velar sounds are [+high].

low: Low sounds are produced by lowering the body of the tongue below the level that it occupies in the neutral position. Low vowels, pharyngeal and glottal sounds are [+low].

back: Back sounds are produced by retracting the body of the tongue from the rest position (quiet breathing position). Back vowels, velar, uvular, pharyngeal and glottal sounds are [+back].

round: Rounded sounds are articulated with lip-rounding. English back vowels, English /r/ and the glide /w/ are [+round].

nasal: Nasal sounds are produced with a lowered velum, and the air flowing through the nasal cavity only. The three English nasals /m/, /n/ and /ŋ/ are [+nasal].

lateral: Lateral sounds are produced by lowering the mid-section of the tongue at both sides or at one side only, thereby allowing the air to flow out of the mouth near the molar teeth. English /l/ is [+lateral].

continuant: Continuant sounds are made in such a way that the oral cavity is not blocked off completely. There is a continuous air flow through the oral cavity. English vowels, glides, liquids and fricatives are [+continuant]. Stops, affricates and nasals are [-continuant].

delayed release: The plosive articulation is released slowly with friction. Affricates are [+delayed release]. Plosives are [-delayed release].

tense: Tense sounds are produced with a deliberate tension in the articulatory organs. In English, all long vowels, diphthongs and fortis consonants are [+tense].

voice: Voiced sounds are made with vibration of the vocal cords. In English, all vowels and voiced consonants are [+voice].

strident: Strident sounds are characterized by the high-frequency turbulent noise in the production of English affricates and all fricatives with the exception of /ð/ and /θ/.

5.2 Chomsky/Halle's binary features for place of articulation.

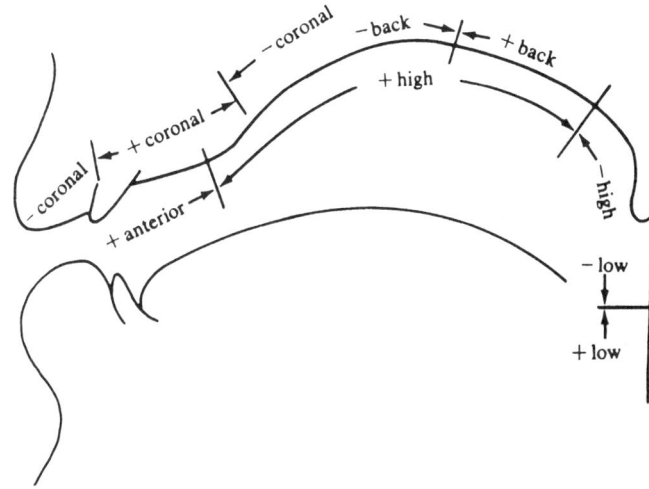

(Ladefoged 1975/94: 243)

5.3 Some Chomsky/Halle features of place of articulation and their equivalent traditional terms

	anterior	coronal	high	back	low
bilabial	+	-	-	-	-
labiodental	+	-	-	-	-
dental	+	+	-	-	-
alveolar	+	+	-	-	-
retroflex	-	+	+	-	-
palato-alv.	-	+	+	-	-
palatal	-	-	+	-	-
velar	-	-	+	+	-
uvular	-	-	-	+	-
phraryngeal	-	-	-	+	+
glottal	-	-	-	+	+

5.4 Some Chomsky/Halle features of manner of articulation and their equivalent traditional terms

traditional phonetic description   **feature specifications**

voiced	consonants	symbol	nasal	con-tinuant	delayed release	strident	lateral
bilabial	nasal	**m**	+	-		-	-
dental	fricative	**ð**	-	+		-	-
alveolar	plosive	**d**	-	-	-	-	-
alveolar	fricative	**z**	-	+		+	-
alveolar	lateral	**l**	-	+		-	+
pal.-alv.	affricate	**dʒ**	-	-	+	+	-

5.5 Chomsky/Halle features of various vowels

vowel	iː	ɪ	æ	e	uː	ɔː	eɪ
syllabic	+	+	+	+	+	+	+
high	+	+	-	-	+	-	-
low	-	-	+	-	-	+	-
back	-	-	-	-	+	+	-
round	-	-	-	-	+	+	-
tense	+	-	-	-	+	+	+

Q3 Repeat the definitions of the following terms: **equivalent (contrastive) distribution, complementary distribution, partially complementary distribution, paradigmatic relation of sounds, syntagmatic relation of sounds, phonetic similarity, distinctive features, redundant features, universals.**

Q4 Repeat the definitions of Chomsky/Halle's features.

Q 5 List the features of the word *spend, height, thought* and *freak* using the traditional approach and the Chomsky/Halle approach.

Suggested readings

Akmajian, A./R. A. Demers/A. K. Farmer/R. M. Harnish (1995) *Linguistics.* Cambridge, Mass.: M.I.T. Press
Atkinson, M./D. Kilby/I. Roca (1982) *Foundations of General Linguistics.* London: George Allen and Unwin
Chomsky, N./M. Halle (1968) *The Sound Pattern of English.* New York: Harper and Row
Fischer-Jørgensen, E. (1975) *Trends in Phonological Theory.* Copenhagen: Akademisk Forlag
Giegerich, H.J. (1992) *English Phonology.* Cambridge: Cambridge University Press
Hawkins, P. (1984/92) *Introducing Phonology.* London: Routledge
Hyman, L.M. (1975) *Phonology, Theory and Analysis.* New York: Holt, Rinehart and Winston
Jakobson, R./C.G.M. Fant/M. Halle (1951/72) *Preliminaries to Speech Analysis.* Cambridge, Mass.: M.I.T. Press
Jones, D. (1976) *The Phoneme: its Nature and Use.* Cambridge: Cambridge University Press

Katamba, F. (1989) *An Introduction to Phonology*. London: Longman
Ladefoged, P. (1975/94) *A Course in Phonetics*. New York: Harcourt Brace Jovanovich
Lass, R. (1984) *Phonology*. Cambridge: Cambridge University Press
Schane, S.A. (1973) *Generative Phonology*. Englewood Cliffs, New Jersey: Prentice-Hall
Sommerstein, A.H. (1977) *Modern Phonology*. London: Edward Arnold
Wolfram, W./R. Johnson (1982) *Phonological Analysis: Focus on American English*. Washington: Center for Applied Linguistics

Note on pronunciation

spectrographic /spektrəʊˈgræfɪk/, muscular /ˈmʌskjʊlə/, insignificant /ɪnsɪgˈnɪfɪkənt/, infinite /ˈɪnfɪnət/, invariable /ɪnˈveəriəbəl/, interdependency /ɪntədɪˈpendənsi/, presuppose /priːsəˈpəʊz/, phonemic /fəʊˈniːmɪk/, allophone /ˈæləfəʊn/, allophonic /æləˈfɒnɪk/, accommodatory /əˈkɒmədeɪtəri/, equivalent /ɪˈkwɪvələnt/, paradigmatic /pærədɪgˈmætɪk/, complementary /kɒmplɪˈmentəri/, environment /ɪnˈvaɪərənmənt/, variant /ˈveəriənt/, variable /ˈveəriəbəl/, substitutability /sʌbstɪtjuːtəˈbɪləti/, redundant /rɪˈdʌndənt/, feature /ˈfiːtʃə/, abandon /əˈbændən/, muscular /ˈmʌskjʊlə/, abbreviation /əbriːviˈeɪʃən/, analysis /əˈnæləsɪs/, sonorant /ˈsɒnərənt/, syllabic /sɪˈlæbɪk/, consonantal /kɒnsəˈnæntəl/, coronal /ˈkɒrənəl/, anterior /ænˈtɪəriə/, continuant /kənˈtɪnjuənt/, strident /ˈstraɪdənt/.

6.0 TRANSCRIPTION

6.1 TYPES OF TRANSCRIPTION

1. Introduction

Every student of English is well aware of the discrepancy between spelling and pronunciation in the English language. Words like *dough, bough, cough, enough, thorough, through* and *rough* or *horizon, Haitian, trophy, fuchsia, measles, Sioux, sew* and *dessert* always present learners with great cognitive difficulties. The reason is that the graphic notation is no longer phonetic, ie the graphic representation no longer gives unambiguous information as to how to pronounce English words. To overcome these difficulties for foreign learners, it was necessary to devise a method of describing speech sounds systematically and consistently. Thus, a system of **transcription** (**notation** or **script**) was created to represent sounds and sound sequences in written form. One of the most commonly used and most successful systems is that of the *International Phonetic Association* (**IPA**), which was founded in France in 1886. It was first called *The Phonetic Teachers' Association* and then renamed *Association Phonétique Internationale (International Phonetic Association or Weltlautschriftverein).* Their journal was called *The Phonetic Teacher* and then *Le Maître Phonétique.* All articles published up to 1969 were written in phonetic/phonemic transcription only. The present name of the periodical is *Journal of the International Phonetic Association (JIPA).*

Q1 What is the role of the IPA these days?

2. Broad and narrow transcription

Two main types of transcription are recognized: **phonemic** (broad) and **phonetic** (narrow) transcription. A phonemic transcription is intended to contain only as many symbols as are necessary to represent the particular language system without ambiguity, ie it only represents the distinctive sounds (phonemes) of a language. Consequently, a phonemic transcription does not show the finer points of pronunciation and certain conventions still have to be learnt, eg the distribution of dark [ɫ] and clear [l] or the different degrees of aspiration with voiceless plosives. Aspiration refers to the little puff of air that follows a speech sound. Oblique lines (slanted lines) enclose phonemic transcription. An example is /pɪn/.

A phonetic (narrow) transcription uses symbols for each individual sound, including detailed symbols and diacritrical marks to show exactly how a sound is pronounced. Phonetic transcription uses square brackets. The word *pin* is transcribed phonetically as [pʰɪˑ°n̥] with the raised *h* showing the aspirated nature of the [p]. The dot after the vowel shows that the vowel is slightly lengthened (half-length), which is based on the rule that any final voiced consonant lengthens the preceding vowel. The raised *ə* indicates slight diphthongization and the little circle underneath [n̥] refers to devoicing.

Q2 How is the word *titles* transcribed phonemically and phonetically?

3. What is understood by qualitative and quantitative phonemic transcription?

In a qualitative transcription, the difference between the vowels in for example *pool* and *pull* is mainly seen in the distinguishing quality of the two vowels, and thus two different symbols /u/ and /ʊ/ are used. The difference in quantity can be inferred. In a quantitative transcription, the different length of the two vowels is decisive leaving the difference in quality to be inferred. From a scientific point of view, the qualitative approach seems to be superior, since the difference between the two vowels can easily be explained with the help of an articulatory, acoustic and auditory analysis. The main advantage of a quantitative notation lies in the fact that it has fewer symbols and thus can be learned more easily than a qualitative transcription.

As quantitative and qualitative transcriptions are equally well-founded phonemically, both approaches represent the sound system correctly. It should also be clear to students that in any phonemic transcription system, they have to learn about conventions and about the different realizations of sounds. If one compares English, Spanish, French and German /r/ or /p, t, k/, one will realize that on the phonemic level the linguistic units are the same, whereas on the phonetic level the differences are rather striking. As far as the representation of short and long English vowels is concerned, the quantitative approach might obscure the fact that the difference between the vowels is not primarily in length, but in quality. Modern pronouncing dictionaries thus favour the qualitative approach.

4. Vowel length

A comparison of the length of the vowels in the words *bit - beat - bid - bead* illustrates the significance of length in English pronunciation. Measurements have shown that the so-called long vowel in *beat* is normally shorter than the so-called short vowel in *bid*. The reason is that vowels in RP are always lengthened before final voiced consonants. In an experiment, the actual length of the vowel in *bit, bid, beat* and *bead* was measured accurately and the results were as follows: the vowel in *bit* had a length of 7 centiseconds, the vowel in *bid* 14 centiseconds, the vowel in *beat* 12 centiseconds and the vowel in *bead* 28 centiseconds. Despite these findings, one can justify the division between long and short vowels in English, because in identical surroundings the short vowel is always shorter than the long vowel, ie /ɪ/ between /b/ and /t/ is shorter than /iː/ between /b/ and /t/.

It seems obvious that the length of any vowel varies according to its **environment**, ie to its place in a word or in an utterance. The following rules apply in RP:

- In identical distribution, a stressed vowel is always longer than an unstressed one, eg *heˈllo* vs *ˈhallow*.
- In identical distribution, a vowel is longest in **free position**, ie if it is not followed by a consonant. It is also very long, when followed by a lenis consonant. It is shortest, when followed by a fortis consonant. Thus the vowel /iː/ is longest in *bee*, followed by *beam* and shortest in *beat*.

Note: In AmE, the second rule only applies to a certain degree, since stressed vowels can be lengthened regardless of the environment (cf. American drawl). This phenomenon is reflected in a variety of American transcription systems, which generally do not use length marks.

Q3 Why does Gimson in the 14th edition (1977) and why do Roach and Hartman in the 15th edition (1997) of the *English Pronouncing Dictionary* still use length marks?

Q4 How do the *English Pronouncing Dictionary* (14th ed., 1977 and 15th ed., 1997) and the *Pronunciation Dictionary* (1990) differ?

5. Various transcription systems

A number of transcription systems have been devised to represent the sound system of English. As far as British English (RP) is concerned, the systems are based on the recommendations made by the IPA (Jones, Gimson, Wells), whereas systems dealing with American English are more independent of these recommendations (Trager/Smith, Kenyon/Knott). The following table is a comparison of some of the most common transcription systems.

Vowels

EXAMPLE	JONES	GIMSON	WELLS	TRAGER/ SMITH	KENYON/ KNOTT
1. *seat*	iː	iː	iː	iy	i
2. *sit*	ɪ	ɪ	ɪ	ɪ	ɪ
3. *set*	e	e	e	e	ɛ
4. *sat*	æ	æ	æ	æ	æ
5. *calm*	ɑː	ɑː	ɑː	ah	a/ɑ
6. *not*	ɔ	ɒ	ɒ	ɔ	ɒ
7. *saw*	ɔː	ɔː	ɔː	ɔh	ɔ
8. *put*	u	ʊ	ʊ	u	ʊ/ə
9. *moon*	uː	uː	uː	uw	u
10. *sun*	ʌ	ʌ	ʌ	ə	ʌ
11. *turn*	əː	ɜː	ɜː	ər	ɝ
12. *ago*	ə	ə	ə	ə	ə
13. *happy*	i	ɪ	i	ɪ	ɪ
14. *punctual*	u	ʊ	u	u	ʊ
15. *tame*	ei	eɪ	eɪ	ey	e
16. *time*	ai	aɪ	aɪ	ay	aɪ
17. *toy*	ɔi	ɔɪ	ɔɪ	ɔy	ɔɪ
18. *tone*	ou	əʊ	əʊ	ow	o
19. *town*	au	aʊ	aʊ	aw	aʊ
20. *fear*	iə	ɪə	ɪə		
21. *fair*	ɛə	eə	eə		
22. *tour*	uə	ʊə	ʊə		

Semi-Vowels

IPA American Notation

1. **w**
2. **j**   y

Consonants

IPA American Notation
1. **p**
2. **b**
3. **t**
4. **d**
5. **k**
6. **g**
7. **tʃ**   č
8. **dʒ**   ǰ
9. **θ**
10. **ð**
11. **f**
12. **v**
13. **s**
14. **z**
15. **ʃ**   š
16. **ʒ**   ž
17. **h**
18. **m**
19. **n**
20. **ŋ**
21. **r**
22. **l**

Some additional phonetic symbols

1. r
2. ɹ
3. ɾ
4. ɻ
5. ʁ
6. ç
7. x
8. ʍ
9. ʔ
10. ɬ
11. ɫ
12. l̥

More symbols and diacritical marks

1. / /   phonemic notation
2. [ ]   phonetic notation
3. :   length, eg /biːd/
4. ·   half length, eg [bɪ·d]
5. ̥   loss of voice, eg [sn̥əʊ], [hænd̥]
6. ̩   syllabic consonant, eg [neɪʃn̩], [æpl̩]

Q5 Find words with /w/, /j/, /tʃ/, /dʒ/, /ʃ/, /ʒ/, /θ/, /ð/ and /ŋ/.

Note: Wells and Roach/Hartman use additional /i/ and /u/. The reason is that the pronunciation of unstressed /ɪ/ and /ʊ/ have changed from lax vowels to tense and short vowels in certain positions. Therefore, the new symbols represent the phonetic realities better than the old ones. The tense and short /i/ usually appears at the end of a word as in *happy* (and in derivations such as *happiness*) and in an unstressed syllable in medial position when the following sound is a vowel as in *obvious*. The /u/ occurs in an unstressed syllable in medial position when the following sound is a vowel as in *situation* and *punctual*.

Q6 What are the recommendations of the IPA and what are the general principles of an efficient notation?

Q7 Explain the following pronunciations: /aɪˈdɪərəvɪt/, /ˈlɔːrənˈɔːdə/, /ˈdrɔːrɪŋ/ and /ˈʃʌˈrʌp/.

6. Phonetic symbols

The following symbols are often used in a phonetic transcription: [ɹ, ɻ, ɾ, r, ʁ, ç, x, ɫ, ɫ̩, l̥, ʔ]
- [ɹ] = postalveolar frictionless continuant as in *round*
- [ɻ] = retroflex frictionless continuant as in AmE *card*
- [ɾ] = alveolar tap as sometimes used in English *very*
- [r] = alveolar roll as sometimes used in Scottish English *borough*
- [ʁ] = uvular fricative as in German *reden*
- [ç] = palatal fricative as in German *echt*
- [x] = velar fricative as in German *buchen*
- [ɫ] = velarized alveolar lateral as in *peel*
- [ɫ̩] = syllabic velarized alveolar lateral as in *kettle*
- [l̥] = devoiced alveolar lateral as in *play*
- [ʔ] = glottal plosive as in German *vereisen*
- [ʍ] = voiceless labio-velar fricative as in *whine* (sometimes)

Q8 Which of the above mentioned sounds occur in British English and in German?

7. Notation of stress

' primary stress
ˌ secondary stress
ˣ weak stress (unstressed)

8. Notation of intonation

As far as the notation of intonation is concerned, the model in this book is basically an **accentual type (tonetic stress type)** and is as follows:

↘	falling intonation
'	high-pitched stress
ˌ	low-pitched stress
↗	rising intonation
ˇ	falling-rising intonation
ˆ	rising-falling intonation
→	level intonation

Other conventions include the **scale type, level type, frequency type** (= numerical types), **dot type, dash type, dot-and-dash type, line type, musical notation** (= linear types) and the **head-nucleus type** (=accentual type) (cf. Mackey 1965/71: 58ff).

6.2 THE INTERNATIONAL PHONETIC ALPHABET (1996)

THE INTERNATIONAL PHONETIC ALPHABET (revised to 1993, corrected 1996)

CONSONANTS (PULMONIC)

	Bilabial	Labiodental	Dental	Alveolar	Postalveolar	Retroflex	Palatal	Velar	Uvular	Pharyngeal	Glottal
Plosive	p b			t d		ʈ ɖ	c ɟ	k g	q ɢ		ʔ
Nasal	m	ɱ		n		ɳ	ɲ	ŋ	N		
Trill	B			r					R		
Tap or Flap				ɾ		ɽ					
Fricative	ɸ β	f v	θ ð	s z	ʃ ʒ	ʂ ʐ	ç ʝ	x ɣ	χ ʁ	ħ ʕ	h ɦ
Lateral fricative				ɬ ɮ							
Approximant		ʋ		ɹ		ɻ	j	ɰ			
Lateral approximant				l		ɭ	ʎ	L			

Where symbols appear in pairs, the one to the right represents a voiced consonant. Shaded areas denote articulations judged impossible.

CONSONANTS (NON-PULMONIC)

Clicks		Voiced implosives		Ejectives	
ʘ	Bilabial	ɓ	Bilabial	'	Examples:
ǀ	Dental	ɗ	Dental/alveolar	p'	Bilabial
ǃ	(Post)alveolar	ʄ	Palatal	t'	Dental/alveolar
ǂ	Palatoalveolar	ɠ	Velar	k'	Velar
ǁ	Alveolar lateral	ʛ	Uvular	s'	Alveolar fricative

OTHER SYMBOLS

ʍ Voiceless labial-velar fricative

w Voiced labial-velar approximant

ɥ Voiced labial-palatal approximant

ʜ Voiceless epiglottal fricative

ʢ Voiced epiglottal fricative

ʡ Epiglottal plosive

ɕ ʑ Alveolo-palatal fricatives

ɺ Alveolar lateral flap

ɧ Simultaneous ʃ and x

Affricates and double articulations can be represented by two symbols joined by a tie bar if necessary.

k͡p t͡s

VOWELS

Front Central Back

Close i•y ——— ɨ•ʉ ——— ɯ•u

ɪ ʏ ʊ

Close-mid e•ø ——— ɘ•ɵ ——— ɤ•o

ə

Open-mid ɛ•œ — ɜ•ɞ — ʌ•ɔ

æ ɐ

Open a•ɶ ———————— ɑ•ɒ

Where symbols appear in pairs, the one to the right represents a rounded vowel.

SUPRASEGMENTALS

ˈ Primary stress

ˌ Secondary stress

ˌfoʊnəˈtɪʃən

ː Long eː

ˑ Half-long eˑ

˘ Extra-short ĕ

| Minor (foot) group

‖ Major (intonation) group

. Syllable break ɹi.ækt

‿ Linking (absence of a break)

DIACRITICS Diacritics may be placed above a symbol with a descender, e.g. ŋ̊

̥	Voiceless	n̥ d̥	̤	Breathy voiced	b̤ a̤	̪	Dental	t̪ d̪
̬	Voiced	s̬ t̬	̰	Creaky voiced	b̰ a̰	̺	Apical	t̺ d̺
ʰ	Aspirated	tʰ dʰ	̼	Linguolabial	t̼ d̼	̻	Laminal	t̻ d̻
̹	More rounded	ɔ̹	ʷ	Labialized	tʷ dʷ	̃	Nasalized	ẽ
̜	Less rounded	ɔ̜	ʲ	Palatalized	tʲ dʲ	ⁿ	Nasal release	dⁿ
̟	Advanced	u̟	ˠ	Velarized	tˠ dˠ	ˡ	Lateral release	dˡ
̠	Retracted	e̠	ˤ	Pharyngealized	tˤ dˤ	̚	No audible release	d̚
̈	Centralized	ë	̴	Velarized or pharyngealized	ɫ			
̽	Mid-centralized	ɤ̽	̝	Raised	e̝ (ɹ̝ = voiced alveolar fricative)			
̩	Syllabic	n̩	̞	Lowered	e̞ (β̞ = voiced bilabial approximant)			
̯	Non-syllabic	e̯	̘	Advanced Tongue Root	e̘			
˞	Rhoticity	ɚ a˞	̙	Retracted Tongue Root	e̙			

TONES AND WORD ACCENTS

LEVEL			CONTOUR		
e̋ or	˥	Extra high	ě or	˩˥	Rising
é	˦	High	ê	˥˩	Falling
ē	˧	Mid	e᷄	˦˥	High rising
è	˨	Low	e᷅	˩˨	Low rising
ȅ	˩	Extra low	e᷈	˧˩˧	Rising-falling
↓		Downstep	↗		Global rise
↑		Upstep	↘		Global fall

Key to some questions

Q2 This word is transcribed phonemically as /taɪtlz/ and phonetically as [tˢʰä̈ëtɫz̥]. The raised *s* (superscript *s*) after the *t* indicates that the [t] behaves as it would in the first part of an affricate, ie the plosive is produced with a slow, fricative release. The raised *h* (superscript *h*) denotes aspiration, the two dots above the *a* show a more centralized articulation of the first element of the diphthong. The dot after the *a* indicates half-length. The more centralized articulation of *e* is also indicated by the two dots above this symbol. The *l* is a 'dark l' which is devoiced in its first stage (see the circle underneath) and which is voiced in its second stage. The final voiced consonant is devoiced which is shown by the circle under the *z* (cf. Gimson 1962/94: 48).

Q3 "It can reasonably be argued that to show features of both quality and quantity entails redundancy of notation, since either is predictable by rule from the other. The redundancy involved in the retention of the length mark (:) has, however, seemed justifiable both for the sake of greater explicitness in a large number of oppositions and also in order to provide an additional differentiating cue between /i/ and /ɪ/, /u/ and /ʊ/, which may be confused in small print (1977: xiii)."

Q4 The *Pronunciation Dictionary* (1990) by John Wells is quite revolutionary in that it approaches the whole subject of English pronunciation in a very liberal way. The following are noteworthy:
- The number of variants within RP has been increased considerably.
- Educated pronunciations outside RP are listed.
- American English pronunciations are given.
- The problem of syllable division is approached in a new way.
- Additional pages deal with problems of pronunciation.
- The different colours in print (black and blue) are user-friendly.
- The symbols /i/ and /u/ have been added to the transcription system.

The *English Pronouncing Dictionary* (1977) by A.C. Gimson also includes variant pronunciations, but remains quite conservative as far as the other aspects mentioned above are concerned. The *English Pronouncing Dictionary* (1997) by Peter Roach and John Hartman follows Wells' practice in a number of cases and thus includes more variants, American English pronunciations and the symbols /i/ and /u/. The *English Pronouncing Dictionary* also takes modern research on syllable division into consideration.

Q6 Consult the recommendations of the IPA. Mackey's guidelines are as follows: "First, *analytical adequacy*; the notation must be able to represent the results of the analysis. Secondly, *clarity*; the relation between the parts must be self-evident, for example, the relation between syllable, tone and stress. Third, *legibility*; it should be easily read and not have to be deciphered. Fourth, *produceability*; it should be easy to write, type, or print. Fifth, *concision*; there should be economy in the use of configurations. Sixth, *visual suggestion*; the forms should suggest what they stand for. Seventh, *range*; while expressing the analytical minimum, the notation should be capable of recording the perceptible maximum, for example, the regional variations needed for the description [of] dialects. And finally, *synthesis*; although each level may be noted separately in analysis it should be capable of appearing again in a synthesis which constitutes a reflection of the utterance as a whole; for example, it should be possible to read the whole utterance at once, not one level at a time, starting with the phonemes, then adding the stress, then the intonation, then the features of catenation [ie linking] (1965/71: 52)."

Q7 All the listed pronunciations are examples of the so-called intrusive /r/ (cf. chapter 2.2) The pronunciation /'ʃʌ'rʌp/ can be explained as follows: the /t/ in /ʃʌt/ is replaced by a glottal stop, which is then weakened and finally elided resulting in /'ʃʌ'ʌp/. The hiatus is avoided by adding an intrusive /r/.

Q8 All the sounds occur in British English. The first symbol [ɹ] represents the typical RP /r/, ie a postalveolar frictionless continuant. The uvular [ʁ] can be found in the North East of England. It is the so-called *Northumbrian burr.* The rolled [r] is typical of a Scottish English pronunciation, the tapped [ɾ] can be heard intervocalically in RP and the retroflex [ɻ] in the South West of England. The symbol [ç] ('*ich*-sound') can be used in RP to replace /hj/ in words such as *huge, hue, human* and the symbol [x] ('*ach*-sound') is used in Scottish English (*och, Tough*). The following symbols represent realizations of the /l/ phoneme: [ɫ] is the dark *l* as in *bill, bulk, pull*, [ɫ̩] is the syllabic dark *l* as in *Bible, apple, rattle* and the devoiced [l̥] appears after /p/ or /k/ as in *plough, clean, clown*. The glottal stop [ʔ] can be used in RP before a stressed vowel (*awful, easy*) and in socioregional varieties such as Cockney and Glaswegian English to replace /t/ for example (*water, little, butter*).
As far as German is concerned, all the sounds with the exception of the retroflex [ɻ] occur either in Standard German (*hochdeutsch*) or in

regional German. Typical examples of regional pronunciations are the 'dark l' in the Ruhr area, the tapped [ɾ] in Northern Germany and the 'typical English [ɹ]' in the very restricted area of Westerwald.

Suggested Readings

Abercrombie, D. (1967/74) *Elements of General Phonetics.* Edinburgh: Edinburgh University Press

Catford, J.C. (1977) *Fundamental Problems in Phonetics.* Edinburgh: Edinburgh University Press

International Phonetic Association (1949) *The Principles of the International Phonetic Association.* London: Department of Phonetics, University College

Mackey, W. F. (1965/71) *Language Teaching Analysis.* London: Longman

Nolan, F. (1995) "Preview of the IPA Handbook", *Journal of the International Phonetic Association,* 25, 1, 3-47

Pullum, G. K./W. A. Ladusaw (1986/96) *Phonetic Symbol Guide.* Chicago: The University of Chicago Press

Trager, G.L./H.L. Smith (1951) *An Outline of English Structure.* Norman, Oklahoma: Battenburg Press

Note on pronunciation

discrepancy /dɪsˈkrepənsi/, dough /dəʊ/, bough /baʊ/, cough /kɒf/, thorough /ˈθʌrə/, horizon /həˈraɪzən/, Haitian /ˈheɪʃən/, trophy /ˈtrəʊfi/, fuchsia /ˈfjuːʃə/, measles /ˈmiːzəlz/, Sioux /suː/, sew /səʊ/, dessert /dɪˈzɜːt/, graphic /ˈgræfɪk/, notation /nəʊˈteɪʃən/, unambiguous /ʌnæmˈbɪɡjuəs/, association /əsəʊsiˈeɪʃən/, periodical /pɪəriˈɒdɪkəl/, ambiguity /æmbiˈɡjuːəti/, plosive /ˈpləʊsɪv/, oblique /əˈbliːk/, slanted /ˈslɑːntɪd/, decisive /dɪˈsaɪsɪv/, representation /reprɪzenˈteɪʃən/, centisecond /ˈsentɪsekənd/, distribution /dɪstrɪˈbjuːʃən/, fortis /ˈfɔːtɪs/, recommendation /rekəmenˈdeɪʃən/, comparison /kəmˈpærɪsən/, derivation /derɪˈveɪʃən/, medial /ˈmiːdiəl/, accentual /əkˈsentʃuəl/, tonetic /təʊˈnetɪk/, nucleus /ˈnjuːkliəs/, fricative /ˈfrɪkətɪv/, redundancy /rɪˈdʌndənsi/, catenation /kætɪˈneɪʃən/, elide /ɪˈlaɪd/, adequacy /ˈædɪkwəsi/, clarity /ˈklærɪti/, legibility /ledʒəˈbɪləti/, decipher /dɪˈsaɪfə/, produceability /prɒdjuːsəˈbɪləti/, concision /kənˈsɪʒən/, synthesis /ˈsɪnθəsɪs/, represent /ˈreprɪzent/, retroflex /ˈretrəʊfleks/, uvular /ˈjuːvjʊlə/, velarized /ˈviːləraɪzd/, Northumbrian /nɔːˈθʌmbriən/, intervocalically /ɪntəvəʊˈkælɪkli/, Glaswegian /glɑːzˈwiːdʒən/.

7.0 SPELLING AND PRONUNCIATION

1. Discrepancy between spelling and pronunciation

The main vehicle used by natural languages for communication is the spoken word. The other main medium is the written word. An ideal relationship between the spoken and the written word is achieved, when one phoneme is represented by one **grapheme**. A grapheme is the smallest unit in a writing system of a language. The English spelling system is far removed from this ideal. The combination of several conflicting spelling traditions, ie Anglo-Saxon, French, Latin and Greek, which have to be integrated into one spelling system, and the relatively rapid changes in pronunciation are major obstacles in the establishment of a successful and simple spelling system. It should also be remembered that today's orthography dates back to the 18th century, when it was fixed in Samuel Johnson's *Dictionary of the English Language* (1755). Only few alterations have been made since. The present spelling system is therefore a historical one. It is also a hybrid system, since it is based on various traditions and therefore represents the result of many compromises.
The following examples can illustrate the dilemma:
- *trough, brougham, chough, slough* (= *swamp*), *slough* (= *cast-off skin*), *Peterborough.*
- *brooch, fuchsia, plaid, mosaic, chamois, choir, prestige.*
- *Warwick, Worcester, Hawick, Edinburgh, Beauchamp, St.John, Prestige.*

Q1 Read and transcribe the above words.

Q2 Read the following passage and transcribe the last verse.

I take it you already know
Of tough and bough and cough and dough?
Others may stumble but not you,
On hiccough, thorough, laugh and through.
Well done! And now you wish, perhaps,
To learn of less familiar traps?

Beware of heard, a dreadful word
That looks like beard and sounds like bird,
And dead: it's said like bed, not bead -
For goodness' sake don't call it 'deed'!
Watch out for meat and great and threat
(They rhyme with suite and straight and debt).

A moth is not a moth in mother
Nor both in bother, broth in brother,
And here is not a match for there
Nor dear and fear for bear and pear,
And then there's dose and rose and lose -
Just look them up - and goose and choose,
And cork and work and card and ward,
And font and front and word and sword,
And do and go and thwart and cart -
Come, come, I've hardly made a start!
A dreadful language? Man alive!
I'd mastered it when I was five!
(From *The Times*)

Q3 Read the following poem.

The Chaos

Dearest creature in Creation,
Studying English pronunciation,
I will teach you in my verse
Sounds like corpse, corps, horse and worse.

It will keep you, Susy, busy,
Make your head with heat grow dizzy;
Tear in eye your dress you'll tear.
So shall I! Oh, hear my prayer.

Pray, console your loving poet,
Make my coat look new, dear, sew it!
Just compare heart, beard and heard,
Dies and diet, lord and word,

Sword and sward, retain and Britain,
(Mind the latter, how it's written!)
Made has not the sound of bad,
Say-said, pay-paid, laid but plaid.

Now I surely will not plague you
With such words as vague and ague,
But be careful how you speak,
Say break, steak, but bleak and streak.

Previous, precious, fuchsia, via;
Pipe, snipe, recipe and choir,
Cloven, oven; how and low;
Script, receipt; shoe, poem, toe.

Hear me say, devoid of trickery:
Daughter, laughter and Terpsichore,
Typhoid, measles, topsails, aisles,
Exiles, similes, reviles;

Wholly, holly; signal, signing;
Thames; examining, combining;
Scholar, vicar and cigar,
Solar, mica, war and far.
(George N. Trenité)

Note: The complete version of the poem can be found at the end of the book (Part II, 3.0).

2. Written realizations of English sounds

2.1 Vowels in stressed position (also unstressed /ɪ/, /ə/)

/iː/		/ɪ/		/e/		/æ/	
e	*be*	i	*list*	e	*bet*	a	*bat*
ea	*tea*	ie	*sieve*	ea	*sweat*	ai	*plait*
ee	*tree*	y	*symbol*	er	*severity*	ar	*narrow*
ei	*seize*	e	*pretty*	a	*any*		
ey	*key*	o	*women*	ai	*said*		
eo	*people*	u	*busy*	ay	*says*		
i	*police*	ui	*guinea*	eo	*leopard*		
ie	*field*	---------------		ei	*heifer*		
ae	*Caesar*	unstressed		ie	*friend*		
oe	*Phoebe*	a	*senate*	u	*bury*		
ay	*quay*	ai	*mountain*				
		e	*enough*				
		ey	*money*				
		i	*profit*				
		u	*minute*				

/ɑː/		/ɒ/		/ɔː/		/ʊ/	
a	class	**o**	clock	**or**	horse	**u**	put
ar	far	**ou**	cough	**oa**	broad	**o**	woman
ear	heart	**ow**	knowledge	**oar**	board	**oo**	wool
er	clerk	**a**	want	**oor**	floor	**ou**	could
au	aunt	**ar**	quarrel	**ou**	fought		
		au	because	**our**	course		
				a	call		
				ar	war		
				au	daughter		
				aw	saw		

/uː/		/ʌ/		/ɜː/		/ə/	
o	do	**u**	sun	**er**	term	unstressed	
oo	food	**o**	wonder	**ir**	stir	**a**	ago
ou	group	**oo**	flood	**yr**	myrtle	**ai**	villain
u	rude	**ou**	country	**ur**	turn	**e**	the
eu	neuter			**ear**	earn	**ei**	foreign
ew	new			**our**	journey	**er**	perform
oe	shoe			**or**	word	**i**	possible
ui	fruit					**o**	polite
						ou	anxious
						u	minus
						ure	figure
						ay	always

/eɪ/		/aɪ/		/ɔɪ/		/əʊ/		/aʊ/	
a	late	**i**	time	**oi**	voice	**o**	so	**ou**	house
ai	aim	**y**	dry	**oy**	boy	**oa**	coal	**ow**	town
ay	day	**ie**	lie	**uoy**	buoy	**oe**	toe	**ough**	plough
ei	eight	**ye**	dye			**ou**	soul		
ey	prey	**ei**	either			**ow**	know		
ea	great	**ey**	eye			**au**	chauffeur		
é	café	**ay**	aye			**eau**	beau		
et	ballet					**oo**	brooch		
						ew	sew		
						eo	yeoman		

/ɪə/		/eə/		/ʊə/	
eer	beer	**are**	care	**ure**	sure
ear	dear	**air**	fair	**oor**	boor
ere	here	**aer**	aeroplane	**our**	tour
eir	weird	**ear**	bear	**eur**	liqueur
ier	fierce	**ere**	there	**ewr**	Jewry
		eir	heir		

2.2 Consonants

\<b\>	/b/	*beauty, robbing, rub*
	/Ø/	*climb, plumber, bombing, debt, subtle*
\<c\>	/k/	*catch, sceptic, cold, cut*
	/s/	*cynic, centre, civil*
	/tʃ/	*cello, Cenci, concerto*
	/Ø/	*victuals, indict, scythe*
\<ch\>	/tʃ/	*church, marching, rich*
	/k/	*echo, stomach, archangel, chaos, ache*
	/ʃ/	*Chicago, machine, champagne*
	/dʒ/ or /tʃ/	*Harwich, Greenwich, sandwich*
	/Ø/	*yacht*
\<d\>	/d/	*do, hiding, hand, begged*
	/t/	*asked, passed*
	/Ø/	*handkerchief, sandwich*
\<f\>	/f/	*for, before, leaf*
	/v/	*of*
\<ff\>	/f/	*off*
\<g\>	/g/	*Gertrude, gulf, gander, goal, phlegmatic, bug*
	/dʒ/	*general, agent, gaol*
	/ʒ/	*prestige, rouge*
	/Ø/	*gnu, foreigner, phlegm, resign*
\<gg\>	/g/	*leggings, egg*
	/dʒ/	*suggest, exaggerate*
\<gh\>	/g/	*ghost*
	/Ø/	*high, through, sight*
	/f/	*enough, rough*
\<gu\>	/g/	*guess, vague*
	/gw/	*language, linguistics*

\<h\>	/h/	*hot, herbs* (BrE), *ahead*
	/Ø/	*Graham, take her back, honour, hour, heir, ah, oh, herbs* (AmE)
	/Ø/ or /h/	*hotel, historical, horizon, hysterical*
\<k\>	/k/	*kennel, akin, ark*
	/Ø/	*knife, knee, knave, Knorr, Knirps*
\<l\>	/l/	*love, peeling, pool*
	/Ø/	*calm, half, palm, yolk, salmon, would*
\<mn\>	/m/	*autumn, solemn*
	/mn/	*autumnal, solemnity*
\<n\>	/n/	*no, anew, hen*
	/Ø/	*autumn*
	/ŋ/	*anchor, uncle, thanks*
\<ng\>	/ŋg/	*hunger, linger, longer, single*
	/ŋ/	*singer, singing, slangy, long*
	/ŋ/ or /ŋg/	*longish, youngish*
	/ndʒ/	*danger, manger*
\<p\>	/p/	*pen, open, hop*
	/Ø/	*pneumonia, receipt, corps*
	/p/ or /Ø/	*psychology, pseudo*
\<ph\>	/f/	*phase, photograph*
	/f/ or /p/	*diphthong, diphtheria*
	/v/	*Stephen*
\<qu\>	/kw/	*queen, quiet*
	/k/	*quay, picturesque*
\<r\>	/r/	*rain, daring, farm* (AmE), *bar* (AmE)
	/Ø/	*bar* (BrE), *garter* (BrE), *farm* (BrE)

\<s\>	/s/	*so, crisis, loss, cease, hiss, taste, tents*
	/z/	*easy, desert, gooseberry, his, husband, bands*
	/Ø/	*aisle, isle, island*
	/ʃ/	*sugar, sure*
	/ʒ/	*leisure, pleasure*
\<sc\>	/s/	*scissors, scent, scene*
	/sk/	*sceptic, scan, scone*
\<sch\>	/sk/	*school, schooner*
	/ʃ/	*schwa, schmaltz, schlep*
	/ʃ/ or /sk/	*schedule*
	/s/ or /sk/	*schism*
\<ss\>	/s/	*lesson, dress*
	/z/	*dessert, scissors, dissolve*
	/ʃ/	*mission, pressure*
\<t\>	/t/	*tone, acting, bet*
	/Ø/	*castle, listen, ballet, action, patient*
	/tʃ/	*nature, mature*
	/ʃ/	*nation, ration*
\<th\>	/t/	*thyme, Esther, Thames*
	/θ/	*thin, anthem, bath*
	/ð/	*the, this, though, smooth*
	/Ø/ or /θ/	*asthma, isthmus*
	/Ø/ or /ð/	*clothes*
\<w\>	/w/	*wan, wizard, aware*
	/Ø/	*write, wrong, two, sword, answer*
\<wh\>	/w/	*which, where, when*
	/h/	*who, whore, whole*
\<x\>	/z/	*xylophone, xerox, anxiety, Xerxes*
	/gz/	*exhibit, exhaust*
	/ks/	*exhibition, vexation*

Q4 How does one pronounce *bomber, paths, Anthony, exit, relaxation, thumb, viva voce, oesophagus, leotard, leonine, Geoffrey, Beowulf, ayes, noes, yeas, nays, thyme, Annie, manifold, hover, Thames, Ouse, mouths*?

Q5 Would a spelling reform be worthwhile? After a spelling reform, how would one spell
a) *awe, or, ore, oar*?
b) *photograph - photographer - photographic, infer - inference - inferential, telephone - telephonic - telephonist, demon - demonic - demonology, refer - reference -referee*?
c) *car, afternoon, lieutenant, porter* (RP and GenAmE)?
d) *poor, fire, tone* (conservative, general and advanced RP)?

Q6 Explain the following terms: **homophones**, **homonyms**, **homographs**.

3. Phonetic spelling and spelling pronunciation

Phonetic spelling and spelling pronunciation are two terms which are used to show the impact of pronunciation on spelling on the one hand and the impact of spelling on pronunciation on the other. Thus phonetic spelling refers to the influence of pronunciation on spelling and spelling pronunciation to the influence of spelling on pronunciation.

Q7 Explain the pronunciation and the spelling of the following sets of words.
a) *Ralph, nephew, forehead.*
b) *alive, heaven, ten o'clock, ancient, passenger, sound, nightingale* (cf. German **ebend, namentlich, niemand*).
c) *psychology.*
d) *phlegm, sign, paradigm, malign, solemn, autumn, diaphragm.*
e) *divide - division, decide - decision.*
f) *electric - electricity - electrician.*

4. Specific changes in pronunciation

One can explain some changes in the pronunciation of words by the phenomena of **epenthesis**, **prothesis** and **paragoge**.
Epenthesis is a term used to refer to the intrusion of an extra sound in initial, medial or final position in order to facilitate the pronunciation of a word. This term is normally used as a general (superordinate) term, but is sometimes used only with reference to the medial position of a word. Examples are *chamber* (Latin *camera*), *nightingale* (German *Nachtigall*), *thunder* (Anglo-Saxon *θunor,* German *Donner*), *idea(r) of it* ('intrusive /r/'), German *namentlich* (*namen+lich*), French *vas-y* (*va+y*).
Prothesis refers to the intrusion of an extra sound in the initial position of a word. Examples are *especial* (Latin *specialis), esprit* (Latin *spiritus*), French *étoile* or Spanish *estrella* (Latin *stella*), *espionage* (Old High German *spehon,* Italian *spione*), French *Etienne* (English *Stephen* and German *Stefan*), Spanish *espray* (English *spray*).
Paragoge refers to the intrusion of an extra sound in the final position of a word. Examples are *sound* (French *son*), *ancient* (French *ancien*), *whilst* (Anglo-Saxon *hwile*), German *niemand* (Middle High German *nie+man*).

Note: lamb (German *Lamm*) and *dumb* (German *dumm*) have lost their final /b/ in the pronunciation, but not in their spelling. Interesting in this context is the pronunciation /nəʊp/ for *no* in emphatic speech (cf. also /jep/ for *yes*).

Key to some questions

Q1 trough /trɒf/, brougham /'bruːəm/, chough /tʃʌf/, slough (= swamp) /slaʊ/, slough (= cast-off skin) /slʌf/, Peterborough /'piːtəbərə/, brooch /brəʊtʃ/, fuchsia /'fjuːʃə/, plaid /plæd/, mosaic /məʊ'zeɪɪk/, chamois /'ʃæmwɑː/ (/'ʃæmi/), choir /'kwaɪə/, prestige /pre'stiːʒ/, Warwick /'wɒrɪk/, /'wɔːwɪk/, Worcester /'wʊstə/, Hawick /'hɔɪk/, Edinburgh /'edɪnbərə/, Beauchamp /'biːtʃəm/, St.John /sənt'dʒɒn/, (/'sɪndʒɪn/), Prestige /'prestɪdʒ/.

Q2 A moth is not a moth in mother
Nor both in bother, broth in brother,
And here is not a match for there
Nor dear and fear for bear and pear,
And then there's dose and rose and lose -
Just look them up - and goose and choose,
And cork and work and card and ward,
And font and front and word and sword,
And do and go and thwart and cart -
Come, come, I've hardly made a start!
A dreadful language? Man alive!
I'd mastered it when I was five!

/ə 'mɒθ ɪz 'nɒt ə 'mɒθ ɪn 'mʌðə/
/nɔ: 'bəʊθ ɪn 'bɒðə 'brɒθ ɪn 'brʌðə/
/ənd 'hɪər ɪz 'nɒt ə 'mætʃ fə 'ðeə/
/nɔ: 'dɪər ən 'fɪə fə 'beər ən 'peə/
/ən 'ðen ðəz 'dəʊs ən 'rəʊz ən 'luːz/
/dʒəst 'lʊk ðəm 'ʌp ən 'guːs ən 'tʃuːz/
/ən 'kɔːk ən 'wɜːk ən 'kɑːd ən 'wɔːd/
/ən 'fɒnt ən 'frʌnt ən 'wɜːd ən 'sɔːd/
/ən 'duː ən 'gəʊ ən 'θwɔːt ən 'kɑːt/
/'kʌm 'kʌm aɪv 'hɑːdli 'meɪd ə 'stɑːt/
/ə 'dredfəl 'læŋgwɪdʒ 'mæn ə'laɪv/
/aɪd 'mɑːstəd ɪt wen aɪ wəz 'faɪv/

Q4 bomber /'bɒmə/, paths /pɑːðz/, Anthony /'æntəni/, exit /'eksɪt/, relaxation /riːlæ'kseɪʃən/, thumb /θʌm/, viva voce /vaɪvə 'vəʊtʃi/, oesophagus /iː'sɒfəgəs/, leotard /'liːətɑːd/, leonine /'liːəʊnaɪn/, Geoffrey /'dʒefri/, Beowulf /'beɪəʊwʊlf/, ayes /aɪz/, noes /nəʊz/, yeas /jeɪz/, nays /neɪz/, thyme /taɪm/, Annie /'æni/, manifold /'mænɪfəʊld/, hover /'hɒvə/, Thames /temz/, Ouse /uːz/, mouths /maʊðz/.

Q5 A spelling reform which would normally attempt to avoid unnecessary discrepancies between pronunciation and spelling seems impossible for a number of reasons. Although there are certain 'sensational' spellings such as *lite, thru, tho, Xing* (*crossing*) and *sox,* the arguments against a spelling reform seem rather solid. First of all, one should note that the English spelling system is the result of a mixture of several, basically incompatible traditions, ie Anglo-Saxon, French, classical Latin and classical Greek. Furthermore, a spelling reform could lead to an increase of homophones in the language, which is not always desirable (cf. a) *awe, or, ore, oar*). Semantically and etymologically related words where one has different pronunciations of one and the same letter would lose their graphic similarity (cf. b) *photograph - photographer - photographic, infer - inference - inferential, telephone - telephonic - telephonist, demon - demonic - demonology, refer - reference -referee*). The different national standard varieties like AmE, AustrE, NZE, SAfrE, CanE, IrE and BrE would drift apart even more quickly if words were spelled according to the pronunciation (cf. c) *car*, BrE possibly *kah* and AmE *kar*; *afternoon*, BrE possibly *ahftenoon* and AmE *afternoon; lieutenant,* BrE possibly *léfténent* and AmE *looténent*; *porter,* BrE possibly *pohte* and AmE *pohrder*). Because of the relatively rapid changes in the pronunciation of BrE (RP) alone, a spelling reform would have to be repeated regularly after a short period of time (cf. d) *poor, fire, tone* which are pronounced differently in conservative, general and advanced RP). Last but not least, tradition will always play a very important role as far as a spelling system is concerned. Consequently, the aim of a simplified spelling system, let alone of a one-to-one relation between sound and letter would prove impossible to achieve in the English language.

Q6 Homophones are words which sound alike, but have a different spelling and meaning, eg *alms - arms, aye - eye - I, farther - father, no - know.*
Homonyms are words which have the same spelling and the same pronunciation, but which have different meanings, eg *lie* (= *not tell the truth*) *- lie* (= *to be in a horizontal position*)*, bear* (= *animal*) *- bear* (= *carry*)*, ear* (= *part of the body*) *- ear* (= *of corn*).
Homographs are words which have the same spelling, but which are pronounced differently and which may have different meanings, eg *(to) lead - lead* (n.)*, (to) live - live* (adj.)*, (to) tear - tear* (n.).

Note: The terms homophone and homonym are not always used consistently. Homophones are sometimes called homonyms.

Q7
a) *Ralph* (/reɪf/ - /rælf/) , *nephew* (/-v-/ - /-f-/), *forehead* (/fɒrɪd/ - /fɔːhed/). The second pronunciations are typical examples of spelling pronunciation.
b) *alive, heaven* (Anglo-Saxon *an life* and *heofan*; intervocalic <f> is always pronounced /v/ in Anglo-Saxon), *ten o'clock* ('*ten of the*

clock'), ancient, passenger, sound (French *ancien, passager* and *son*), *nightingale* (German *Nachtigall*). Cf. German **ebend, namentlich, niemand.* All the words are typical examples of phonetic spelling.

c) *psychology* /ps-/ or /s-/. A new example of spelling pronunciation.

d) *phlegm, sign, paradigm, malign, solemn, autumn, diaphragm.* It seems that the <g> and <n> are redundant, but they would be needed in derivations such as *phlegmatic, malignant* or *solemnity* for instance. Again, a spelling reform could not solve these problems convincingly.

e) *divide - division, decide - decision* and f) *electric - electricity - electrician.* The words are related and the different phonetic realizations are the result of the different environments. A change in the spelling would conceal this fundamental relationship.

Suggested readings

Baugh, A.C./Th. Cable (1951/93) *A History of the English Language.* London: Routledge

Berndt, R. (1980/89) *A History of the English Language.* Leipzig: Verlag Enzyklopädie

Crystal, D. (1995) *The Cambridge Encyclopedia of the English Language.* Cambridge: Cambridge University Press

Lass, R. (1987) *The Shape of English.* London: Dent

McArthur, T., ed. (1992) *The Oxford Companion to the English Language.* Oxford: Oxford University Press

Note on pronunciation

homophone /'hɒməfəʊn/, homonym /'hɒmənɪm/, homograph /'hɒməgrɑːf/, phenomena /fə'nɒmɪnə/, prothesis /'prɒθəsɪs/, epenthesis /e'penθəsɪs/, paragoge /pærə'gəʊdʒi/, intrusion /ɪn'truːʒən/, superordinate /suːpər'ɔːdənət/, orthography /ɔː'θɒgrəfi/, semantically /sə'mæntɪkli/, etymologically /etɪmə'lɒdʒɪkli/, lose /luːz/, photograph /'fəʊtəgrɑːf/, photographer /fə'tɒgrəfə/, photographic /fəʊtə'græfɪk/, infer /ɪn'fɜː/, inference /'ɪnfərəns/, inferential /ɪnfə'rentʃəl/, telephone /'telɪfəʊn/, telephonic /telɪ'fɒnɪk/, telephonist /tə'lefənɪst/, demon /'diːmən/, demonic /dɪ'mɒnɪk/, demonology /diːmə'nɒlədʒi/, refer /rɪ'fɜː/, reference /'refərəns/, referee /refə'riː/, car (RP and GenAmE) /kɑː/ ‖ /kɑːr/, afternoon (RP and GenAmE) /ɑːftə'nuːn/ ‖ /æftər'nuːn/, lieutenant (RP and GenAmE) /lef'tenənt/ ‖ /luː'tenənt/, porter (RP and GenAmE) /'pɔːtə/ ‖ /'pɔːrDər/.

8.0 VARIOUS MODELS OF PRONUNCIATION

8.1 BRITISH ENGLISH

8.1.1 RECEIVED PRONUNCIATION AND VARIATION WITHIN RP

1. Received Pronunciation

Received Pronunciation is a type of pronunciation that has the status of standard. Received in this context means 'socially accepted as good' or 'accepted as an authority'. Traditionally, it has been taught in private schools in all parts of the country and is therefore non-regional or supra-regional, although its origin lies in the South East of England. Until relatively recently, an RP accent was required of all BBC announcers. It is spoken by three to five per cent of the population. RP is usually associated with people like doctors, politicians, academics, the clergy, higher civil servants, officers and business executives and therefore enjoys very high social prestige. RP speakers are also viewed as more competent, intelligent, self-confident, industrious and more successful in their argumentation than speakers who have a mild or broad socioregional accent. Women with an RP accent share the same prestige as men with an RP accent and are consequently stereotyped as more competent, independent and enterprising than their counterparts with a socioregional accent.

The following definitions of RP have been given:

- A. J. Ellis (1869): "In the present day we may...recognize a received pronunciation all over the country, not widely differing in any particular locality, and admitting a certain degree of variety. It may be especially considered as the educated pronunciation of the metropolis, of the court, the pulpit, and the bar."

- D. Jones (1917): A pronunciation recorded as "that most usually heard in everyday speech in the families of Southern English persons whose menfolk have been educated at the great public [ie private] boarding-schools."

- D. Jones (1956) "I take the view that people should be allowed to speak as they like... I do not believe in the feasibility of imposing one particular form of pronunciation on the English-speaking world ... RP means merely 'widely understood pronunciation', and... I do not hold it up as a standard which everyone is recommended to adopt."
English Pronouncing Dictionary

- P. Roach/J. Hartman (1997): "The time has come to abandon the archaic name Received Pronunciation. The model used ...is what is referred to as BBC English; this is the pronunciation of professional speakers employed by the BBC ..."
English Pronouncing Dictionary

There are a number of different terms for RP: **English Standard Pronunciation** (Trim), **Educated Southern British English** (Gimson), **Southern British Standard** (Wells) or **BBC English** (Roach/Hartman).

Q1 Explain the following terms: **Standard English, Queen's English** or **King's English, BBC English, Oxford English, Modified Standard, Educated Regional, Affected RP, Conservative RP, General RP, Advanced RP, Modified RP, Mainstream RP, Upper-Crust RP ('U-RP'), Adoptive RP, Near RP**.

2. Variation within RP

2.1 Some vowel changes in RP

Examples	conservative RP	general (mainstream) RP	advanced RP
pore	[ɔə]	[ɔː]	[ɔː]
poor	[ʊə]	[ʊə]	[ɔː]
there	[ɛə]	[ɛə] or [ɛː]	[ɛː]
fire	[aɪə]	[aɪə] or [aə]	[aː]
power	[aʊə]	[aʊə] or [aə]	[aː]
off	[ɔː]	[ɒ]	[ɒ]
tone	[ou]	[əu]	[ɛʊ]

Furthermore, RP /æ/ is often realized with a more open quality approaching the cardinal vowel [a] and the diphthongs /aʊ/ and /aɪ/ have the same centrally open starting point.

Unstressed /ɪ/ and /ʊ/ change into [i] and [u] in certain positions:

The sound [i] nowadays occurs in unstressed word-final position in words spelled <y>, <ey> or <ay> (*happy, money, Saturday*) and in derivations (*happiness, happier*) as well as in an unstressed syllable in medial position when the following sound is a vowel (*obvious*). It also occurs in prefixes like <re->, <de-> or <pre-> if they are unstressed and precede a vowel (*react, preeminent, deactivate*), in the suffixes <-iate> and <-ious> if the two syllables are pronounced (*appreciate, furious*) and in unstressed *he, she, we, me* and *be*. The word *the* is also pronounced with [i] when it precedes a vowel.

The sound [u] nowadays occurs in an unstressed syllable in medial position when the following sound is a vowel (*situation, influenza*). It is also found in unstressed *you, to, into* and *who* when they precede a vowel.

2.2 Segmental variation within individual words

new variant - established variant
accomplish /əˈkʌmplɪʃ/ - /əˈkɒmplɪʃ/   (92%-8%)
acoustic /əˈkʊstɪk/ - /əˈkuːstɪk/
aesthetic /esˈθetɪk/, /ɪs- /, /eɪs-/ - /iːsˈθetɪk/
again /əˈgeɪn/ - /əˈgen/   (20%-80%)
an historical - a historical /ən ɪsˈtɒrɪkl/ - /ə hɪsˈtɒrɪkl/
an hotel - a hotel /ən ə(ʊ)ˈtel/ - /ə hə(ʊ)ˈtel/
Anthony /ˈænθəni/ - /ˈæntəni/
anti- /ˈæntaɪ/ - /ˈænti/
apparatus /ˌæpəˈrætəs/, /-ˈrɑː-/ - /ˌæpəˈreɪtəs/
armada /ɑːˈmɑːdə/ - /ɑːˈmeɪdə/ (old-fashioned)
assume /əˈʃuːm/ - /əˈsuːm/ - /əˈsjuːm/ (5%-11%-84%)
ate /eɪt/ - /et/   (45%-55%)
auction /ˈɒkʃən/ - /ˈɔːkʃən/   (13%-87%)

baths /bɑːθs/ - /bɑːðz/   (50%-50%)
bedroom /ˈbedruːm/ - /ˈbedrʊm/ (63%-37%)
been (stressed) /bɪn/ - /biːn/   (8%-92%)
bequeath /bəˈkwiːθ/ - /bəˈkwiːð/ (42%-58%)
booth /buːθ/ - /buːð/
booths /buːθs/ - /buːðz/
breeches /ˈbriːtʃəz/ - /ˈbrɪtʃəz/
broom /bruːm/ - /brʊm/ (92%-8%)

casual /'kæʒuəl/ - /'kæzjuəl/ (77%-23%)
centenary /sen'tenəri/ - /sen'tiːnəri/, /sən-/
chrysanthemum /krɪ'zænθəməm/ - /krɪ'sænθəməm/ (39%-61%)
clothes /kləuz/ - /kləuðz/
composite (adj.) /'kɒmpəzaɪt/, /-saɪt/ - /-zɪt/, /-sɪt/
crescent /'kresənt/ - /'krezənt/ (45%-55%)
cyclical /'saɪklɪkl/ - /'sɪklɪkl/ (42%-58%)

data /'dætə/, /'dɑːtə/ - /'deɪtə/ (2%-6%-92%)
debut /'debjuː/ - /'deɪbjuː/ (31%-69%)
deity /'deɪəti/ - /'diːəti/ (80%-20%)
delirious /dɪ'lɪəriəs/ - /dɪ'lɪrəs/ (46%-54%)
derisive /dɪ'r(a)ɪzɪv/ - /dɪ'raɪsɪv/
digest (v.) /daɪ'dʒest/ - /dɪ'dʒest/, /də-/
dilemma /daɪ'lemə/ - /dɪ'lemə/
dinghy /'dɪŋɪ/ - /'dɪŋgɪ/
diphtheria /dɪp'θɪəriə/ - /dɪf'θɪəriə/
dissect /daɪ'sekt/ - /dɪ'sekt/, /də-/
dour /dauə/ - /duə/
drastic /'drɑːstɪk/ - /'dræstɪk/ (12%-88%)

earthen /'ɜːðən/ - /'ɜːθən/
economic /ˌekə'nɒmɪk/ - /ˌiːkə'nɒmɪk/ (38%-62%)
economics /ˌekə'nɒmɪks/ - /ˌiːkə'nɒmɪks/ (38%-62%)
either /'iːðə/ - /'aɪðə/ (13%-88%!)
England /'ɪŋlənd/ - /'ɪŋglənd/
envelope /'ɒnvələup/ - /'envələup/ (22%-78%)
etcetera /ek'tset(ə)rə/ - /et'set(ə)rə/
exasperate /ɪg'zæspəreɪt/ - /ɪg'zɑːspəreɪt/ (54%-46%)
exit /'egzɪt/ - /'eksɪt/ (45%-55%)
February /'februri/, /-rəɪ-/, /-jur-/, /-jər-/ - /'februəri/
fetid /'fiːtɪd/ - /'fetɪd/
forehead /'fɔːhed/ - /'fɒrəd/

Glasgow /'glɑːzgəu/, /-æ-/ - /'glɑːsgəu/, /-æ-/ (85%-15%)
graph /grɑːf/ - /græf/ (59%-41%)
guerilla /ge'rɪlə/ - /gə'rɪlə/

half-past /ˌhɑː'pɑːst/, /ˌhʌ-/ - /ˌhɑːf 'pɑːst/
hectare /'hekteə/ - /'hektɑː/
homogeneous /ˌhɒmə(u)'dʒiːniəs/ - /ˌhəumə(u)'dʒiːniəs/
homogenous /hɒ'mɒdʒənəs/ - /hə'mɒdʒənəs/
homosexual /ˌhɒmə(u)'sekʃuəl/ - /ˌhəumə(u)'sekʃuəl/ (41%-59%)
hotel /(h)ə(u)'tel/, /əu-/ - /ˌhəu'tel/

idea of it /aɪˈdɪərəvɪt/ - /aɪˈdɪəəvɪt/
inherent /ɪnˈherənt/ - /ɪnˈhɪərənt/ (66%-34%)
inveigle /ɪnˈveɪgl/ - /ɪnˈviːgl/
involve /ɪnˈvəʊlv/ - /ɪnˈvɒlv/ (14%-86%)
issue /ˈɪʃjuː/ - /ˈɪʃuː/ - /ˈɪsjuː/ (21%-49%-30%)

January /ˈdʒænjʊri/ - /ˈdʒænjuəri/
jewellery /ˈdʒuːlri/ - /ˈdʒuːəlri/

kilogram /ˈkiːləgræm/ - /ˈkɪləgræm/

lather /ˈlæðə/ - /lɑːðə/ (28%-72%)
longitude /ˈlɒŋgɪtjuːd/ - /ˈlɒn(d)ʒɪtjuːd/
luxury /ˈlʌgʒəri/ - /ˈlʌkʃəri/ (4%-96%)

maintain /meɪnˈteɪn/ - /menˈteɪn/ - /mənˈteɪn/ (90%-6%-4%)
masquerade /mɑːskəˈreɪd/ - /mæskəˈreɪd/ (39%-62%!)
medicine /ˈmedɪsɪn/ - /ˈmedsɪn/
migraine /ˈmaɪgreɪn/ - /ˈmiːgreɪn/, /ˈmɪ-/ (39%-61%)
months /mʌns/ - /mʌnθs/

Nazi /ˈnɑːzi/, /ˈnætsi/ - /ˈnɑːtsiː/, /ˈnɑːtsi/
nephew /ˈnefjuː/ - /ˈnevjuː/ (79%-21%)
niche /niːʃ/ - /nɪtʃ/, /nɪʃ/
nuclei /ˈnjuːkliiː/ - /ˈnjuːkliaɪ/

oaths /əʊθs/ - /əʊðz/
often /ˈɒftən/ - /ˈɒfən/ - /ˈɔːfən/ (rarely) (27%-72%-1%)
ophthalmic /ɒpˈθælmɪk/ - /ɒfˈθælmɪk/
opposite /ˈɒpəsɪt/ - /ˈɒpəzɪt/ (33%-67%)
opus /ˈɒpəs/ - /ˈəʊpəs/

Parliament /ˈpɑːljəmənt/, /-lɪəmənt/ - /ˈpɑːləmənt/
patriotic /ˌpeɪtriˈɒtɪk/ - /ˌpætriˈɒtɪk/ (21%-79%)
plaque /plæk/ - /plɑːk/ (61%-39%)
plastic /ˈplɑːstɪk/ - /ˈplæstɪk/ (9%-92%!)
poor /pɔː/ - /pʊə/ (57%-43%)
presume /prɪˈʒuːm/ - /prɪˈzuːm/ - /prɪˈzjuːm/ (8%-16%-77%!)
privacy /ˈprɪvəsi/ - /ˈpraɪvəsi/ (88%-12%)
pseudo /ˈpsjuːdəʊ/, /ˈpsuː-/ - /ˈsjuːdəʊ/, /ˈsuː-/
psychology /psaɪˈkɒlədʒi/ - /saɪˈkɒlədʒi/

rabies /ˈreɪbɪz/ - /ˈreɪbiːz/
record (n.) /ˈrekəd/ - /ˈrekɔːd/
room /ruːm/ - /rʊm/ (82%-19%!)

salt /sɒlt/ - /sɔːlt/ (57%-43%)
sandwich /ˈsænwɪtʃ/ - /ˈsænwɪdʒ/ (47%-54%!)
scenario /sɪˈneəriəʊ/, /se-/ - /səˈnɑːriəʊ/
schedule /ˈskedjuːl/, /-duːl/ - /ˈʃedjuːl/, /-duːl/
schism /ˈskɪzm/ - /ˈsɪzm/ (71%-29%)
sheik /ʃiːk/ - /ʃeɪk/ - /ʃek/
Soviet /ˈsɒvjet/ - /ˈsəʊvjet/ (27%-73%)
spinach /ˈspɪnɪtʃ/ - /ˈspɪnɪdʒ/
spontaneity /ˌspɒntəˈneɪti/ - /ˌspɒntəˈniːəti/
status /ˈstætəs/ - /ˈsteɪtəs/
stereo /ˈstɪəriəʊ/ - /ˈsteriəʊ/ (10%-90%)
substantial /səbˈstɑːnʃl/ - /səbˈstænʃl/ (7%-93%)
suit /suːt/ - /sjuːt/ (72%-28%)
surveillance /səˈveɪləns/ - /sɜːˈveɪləns/
syndrome /ˈsɪndrəm/ - /ˈsɪndrəʊm/

trait /treɪt/ - /treɪ/
trans- /trɑːns/ - /træns/
transistor /trɑːnˈzɪstə/ - /trænˈzɪstə/ (14%-86%), /-ˈsɪs-/ - /-ˈzɪs-/ (37%-63%)
transition /trɑːnˈzɪʃn/ - /trænˈsɪʃn/ - /trænˈzɪʃn/ (9%-16%-75%)
truths /truːθs/ - /truːðz/

unprecedented /ʌnˈpriːsɪdentɪd/ - /ʌnˈpresɪdentɪd/
usage /ˈjuːsɪdʒ/ - /ˈjuːzɪdʒ/ (72%-28%)

vitamin /ˈvɪtəmɪn/ - /ˈvaɪtəmɪn/

with /wɪθ/ - /wɪð/

xylophone /ˈgzaɪləfəʊn/, /ˈzɪl-/ - /ˈzaɪləfəʊn/

year /jɪə/ - /jɜː/ (80%-20%)
youngish /ˈjʌŋgɪʃ/ - /ˈjʌŋɪʃ/
youths /juːθs/ - /juːðz/

zebra /ˈzebrə/ - /ˈziːbrə/ (83%-17%)
zoology /zuˈɒlədʒi/ - /zəʊˈɒlədʒi/

Note on percentages given: The percentages given refer to Wells'
study where RP speakers were asked about their preferred pronunciations. The additional exclamation marks indicate that the percentages were rounded up by Wells resulting in 101%.

2.3 Suprasegmental variation (stress variation) within individual words

new variant - established variant
'abdomen - ab'domen
'acumen - a'cumen
ad'mirable - 'admirable
'adult - a'dult /'ædʌlt/ - /ə'dʌlt/
'allies (n.) - a'llies (n.) /'ælaɪz/ - /ə'laɪz/
'anchovy - an'chovy
a'pplicable - 'applicable /ə'plɪkəbl/ - /'æplɪkəbl/ (77%-23%)
a'ristocrat - 'aristocrat /æ'rɪstəkræt/, /ə'r-/ - /'ærɪstəkræt/
articu'latory - ar'ticulatory

'bitumen - bi'tumen
bou'quet - 'bouquet /bʊ'keɪ/, /bəʊ-/ - /'buːkeɪ/ (83%-17%)
'brochure - bro'chure /'brəʊʃə/, /-ʊə/ - /brɒ'ʃʊə/, /brə-/ (90%-10%)

ca'pitalist - 'capitalist /kə'pɪtəlɪst/, /kæ'-/ - /'kæpɪtəlɪst/
Ca'ribbean - Cari'bbean
cavi'ar - 'caviar /ˌkæ'vɑː/ - /'kævɑː/ (23%-77%)
cen'trifugal - centri'fugal /sen'trɪfjʊgl/ - /ˌsentrɪ'fjuːgl/
centri'petal - cen'tripetal /ˌsentrə'piːtl/ - /sen'trɪpɪtl/
cer'vical - 'cervical /sə'vaɪkl/, /sɜː-/ - /'sɜːvɪkl/
'cigarette - ciga'rette /'sɪgəret/ - /ˌsɪgə'ret/ (15%-85%)
'clandestine - clan'destine /'klændestaɪn/ - /klæn'destɪn/ (39%-61%)
climac'teric - cli'macteric
com'munal - 'communal /kəm'juːnəl/ - /'kɒmjʊnəl/, /-jən-/ (32%-68%)
com'parable - 'comparable /kəm'pærəbl/, /-'peər-/ - /'kɒmp(ə)rəbl/
con'gratulatory - congratu'latory /kən'grætjʊlətəri/ - /kən ˌgrætʊ'leɪtəri/, /-tjʊ-/
'consummate (adj.) - con'summate (adj.) /'kɒnsəmət/, /-sjʊm-/, /-sjuːm-/ - /kən'sʌmət/
con'template - 'contemplate
'contribute - con'tribute /'kɒntrɪbjuːt/ - /kən'trɪbjuːt/ (27% -73%)
con'troversy - 'controversy /kən'trɒvəsi/ - /'kɒntrəvɜːsi/ (56%-44%)
con'tumely - 'contumely /kən'tjuːmli/, /-mɪli/ - /'kɒntjuːmli/, /-tjʊmli/
con'versant - 'conversant
co'vert - 'covert /kəʊ'vɜːt/, /'kəʊvɜːt/ - /'kʌvət/ (9%-37%-54%)

de'cade - 'decade /dɪ'keɪd/, /de-/ - /'dekeɪd/ (14%-86%)
(/'dekəd/ is used in a religious sense, part of the rosary)

de'cadent - 'decadent
'defect (n.) - de'fect (n.) /'diːfekt/ - /dɪ'fekt/ (86%-14%)
de'ficit - 'deficit /dɪ'fɪsɪt/ - /'defɪsɪt/
de'monstrable - 'demonstrable /də'mɒnstrəbl/ - /'demənstrəbl/ (63%-37%)
de'spicable - 'despicable /dɪ'spɪkəbl/ - /'despɪkəbl/
di'rigible - 'dirigible
'disputable - dis'putable /'dɪspjʊtəbl/ - /dɪs'pjuːtəbl/
'dispute (n.) - dis'pute (n.) /'dɪspjuːt/ - /dɪs'pjuːt/ (38%-62%)
'distribute - di'stribute /'dɪstrɪbjuːt/ - /dɪ'strɪbjuːt/ (26%-74%)
doc'trinal - 'doctrinal

e'querry - 'equerry
'etiquette - eti'quette
e'xigency - 'exigency
'expletive - ex'pletive
ex'plicable - 'explicable
ex'quisite - 'exquisite /ɪks'kwɪzɪt/, /ek-/, /ək-/ - /'ekskwɪzɪt/ (69%-31%)

for'midable - 'formidable /fə'mɪdəbl/, /fɔː-/ - /'fɔːmɪdəbl/ (54%-46%)
frag'mentary - 'fragmentary

gla'diolus - gladi'olus

ha'rass - 'harass /hə'ræs/ - /'hærəs/ (32%-68%)
'hegemony - he'gemony /'hegəməni/, /'hedʒ-/, /-dʒem-/ - /hɪ'geməni/, /hiː-/
hos'pitable - 'hospitable /həs'pɪtəbl/, /hɒs-/ - /'hɒspɪtəbl/ (81%-19%)

'ice cream - ice 'cream /'aɪskriːm/ - /ˌaɪs'kriːm/ (34%-66%)
impor'tunc - im'portune
i'llustrative - 'illustrative
in'crease (n.) - 'increase (n.) /ɪn'kriːs/ - /'ɪŋkriːs/, /'ɪn-/ (15%-85%)
in'culcate - 'inculcate
inde'corous - in'decorous
inex'plicable - in'explicable
inex'tricable - in'extricable
in'tegral - 'integral /ɪn'tegrəl/ - /'ɪntəgrəl/
in'tricacy - 'intricacy /ɪn'trɪkəsi/ - /'ɪntrɪkəsi/
irre'vocable - i'rrevocable /ˌɪrə'vɒkəbl/ - /ɪ'revəkəbl/

jubi'lee - 'jubilee

ki'lometre - 'kilometre /kɪ'lɒmɪtə/ - /'kɪləmiːtə/ (48%-52%)

la'mentable - 'lamentable / lə'mentəbl/ - /'læməntəbl/

'magazine - maga'zine /'mægəziːn/ - /ˌmægə'ziːn/
man'datory - 'mandatory /mæn'deɪtəri/ - /'mændət(ə)ri/
me'tallurgy - 'metallurgy /me'tælədʒi/ - /'metələːdʒi/
mi'scellany - 'miscellany
mis'chievous - 'mischievous
mo'lybdenum - molyb'denum
momen'tarily - 'momentarily /ˌməʊmən'terɪli/ - /'məʊməntərəli/
muni'cipal - mu'nicipal /ˌmjuːnɪ'sɪpl/ - /mjʊ'nɪsɪpl/

nece'ssarily - 'necessarily /ˌnesə'serəli/ - /'nesəsərəli/
no'menclature - 'nomenclature

obscu'rantist - ob'scurantist
o'vert - 'overt /ə(ʊ)'vɜːt/ - /'əʊvɜːt/

pa'riah - 'pariah /pə'raɪə/ - /'pærɪə/, /'peə-/
pe'jorative - 'pejorative /pɪ'dʒɒrətɪv/ - /'piːdʒərətɪv/
'peremptory - pe'remptory /'perəm(p)t(ə)ri/ - /pə'rem(p)t(ə)ri/
'precedence - pre'cedence
pre'fer(r)able - 'preferable /prɪ'fɜːrəbl/ - /'prefərəbl/
'premature - prema'ture
pri'marily - 'primarily /praɪ'merəli/ - /'praɪmərəli/ (51%-49%)
pro'missory - 'promissory
'protest (v.) - pro'test (v.) /'prəʊtest/ - /prə'test/, /prəʊ-/

quan'dary - 'quandary

'recondite - re'condite /'rekəndaɪt/ - /rɪ'kɒndaɪt/, /rə-/
'research (v.) - re'search (v.) /'riːsɜːtʃ/ - /rɪ'sɜːtʃ/ (20%-80%)
'remonstrate - re'monstrate
re'plica - 'replica
'resource - re'source /'rɪzɔːs/ - /rɪ'zɔːs/ - /rɪ'sɔːs/ (6%-50%-45%!)

'secretive - se'cretive
'sonorous - so'norous
'spectator - spec'tator /'spekteɪtə/ - /spek'teɪtə/ (9%-91%)
sub'stantive (adj.) - 'substantive (adj.)
sub'marine - 'submarine /sʌbmə'riːn/ - /'sʌbməriːn/ (58%-42%)
sub'sidence - 'subsidence /səb'saɪdəns/ - /'sʌbsɪdəns/ (47%-53%)

'television - tele'vision
tempo'rarily - 'temporarily /ˌtempə'rerəli/ - /'tempərərəli/

'trachea - tra'chea
trans'ference - 'transference

'Ulysses - U'lysses
U'ranus - 'Uranus
u'rinal - 'urinal

'vagary - va'gary

Q2 Transcribe those words where the transcription is not given. Then translate all the words into German.

8.1.2 RP and Socioregional Varieties

1. British English socioregional varieties
Socioregional varieties are dialects, which differ from the standard language in grammar, lexis and pronunciation. The term 'accent' refers to the pronunciation only. There are sixteen major dialects in England, which are as follows:
- NORTH
Northern: Northeast, Central North, Central Lancashire, Humberside.
Central: Merseyside, Northwest Midlands, West Midlands, Central Midlands, Northeast Midlands, East Midlands.
- SOUTH
South East: South Midlands, East Anglia, Home Counties.
South West: Upper Southwest, Central Southwest, Lower Southwest.
(cf. Crystal 1995: 325)

Q3 What is understood by mild accent, mixed accent, and broad accent?

2. RP and local accent pronunciation of home

Edinburgh	Newcastle	Liverpool	Bradford	Dudley	Norwich	London	
həʊm	həʊm	həʊm	həʊm	həʊm	həʊm	həʊm	**RP**
hoːm	hoːm	houm	houm	hɒum	huːm	hʌum	**Interme-**
hoːm	hʊom	hoːm	hɔːm	ɒum	hum	ʌum	**diate**
heːm	hɪem	oːm	ɔːm	wʊm	ʊm	æʊm	**Most lo-**
	jem						**calised**

(Trudgill 1974/95: 42)

3. Accents and prestige

3.1 General attitudes towards different accents.

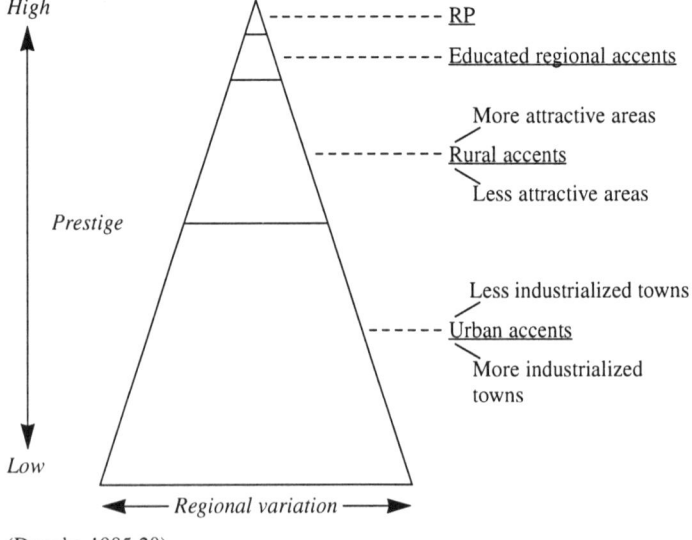

(Dretzke 1985:20)

3.2 Generalised structure of three dimensions of accent evaluation in rank order from conceptual stimuli
- Giles (1970:218)

Aesthetic content	Communicative content	Status content
1. R.P. (2.5)*	1. "accent identical to your own" (1.5)*	1. R.P. (1.9)
2. "accent identical to your own" (2.9)*	2. R.P. (2.3)	2. French* & "accent identical to your own"* (3.3)
3. French (3.0)*	3. French (3.5)	
4. Scottish (3.4)	4. Irish, S. Welsh & N. American (3.8)	4. N. American & Scottish (3.8)
5. Irish (3.7)		
6. N. English & Somerset (4.0)		6. German (3.9)*
	7. N. England & Scottish (3.9)	7. Irish (4.2)
8. Italian & German (4.1)		8. S. Welsh, N. England & Somerset (4.3)
	9. Somerset (4.0)	
10. S. Welsh (4.2)	10. Liverpool, German & Italian (4.4)	
11. W. Indies (4.3)		11. Italian (4.7)
12. N. America [sic] (4.5)		12. W. Indies & Liverpool (5.0)
13. Indian (4.6)	13. W. Indies (4,5)	
14. Birmingham & Liverpool (4.7)	14. Cockney, Indian & Birmingham (4.7)	14. Indian & Cockney (5.1)
16. Cockney (4.8)		16. Birmingham (5.2)

*indicates age differences in rating; 17/18yr. attitude presented.

Note: The highest mark is 1 (positive), the lowest mark 7 (negative).

- Dretzke (1985:108)

Akzente	I. *Pleasant-ness*	II. *Intelligi-bility*	III. *Social Prestige*	*Gesamt-eindruck*
RP	4,5	6,3	6,5	5,8
Cockney	2,8	2,8	2,3	2,6
Yorkshire	4,2	4,1	3,5	3,9
Am. English	3,4	5,0	4,5	4,3
Austr. English	3,4	4,1	3,8	3,8
Indian English	2,5	2,5	2,4	2,5
French English	5,1	4,3	4,6	4,7
German English	4,2	4,2	4,6	4,3

Note: The highest mark is 7 (positive), the lowest mark 1 (negative).

4. The inherent norm hypothesis and the imposed norm hypothesis

The inherent norm hypothesis "...maintains that some linguistic varieties are inherently more attractive and pleasant than others, and that
these varieties have become accepted as standards or have acquired
prestige simply because they are the most attractive. According to this
view, for example, British R.P. is the most prestigious British accent
because it has, as it were, risen to the top - or...been elevated to this
position by a socially powerful group - as a result of its inherent outstanding attractiveness (Trudgill/Giles 1976:7)."
According to the imposed norm hypothesis, "...different varieties of
the same language are objectively as pleasant as each other, but are
perceived positively or negatively because of particular cultural pressures operating in each language community. Standard dialects and
prestige accents acquire their high status directly from the high status
social groups that happen to speak them, and it is because of their
high status that they are perceived as 'good' and therefore as 'pleasant'...The argument ...is that evaluations of language varieties...are
the *direct* result of cultural pressures (ibid.: 10)."

5. Accents with overt and covert prestige

It seems that accents are still the class markers par excellence in England, so that some linguists talk of an 'accent bar'. G.B. Shaw remarked: "...it is impossible for an Englishman to open his mouth without making some other Englishman despise him." The 'wrong accent' may still be an obstacle to social recognition or advancement. Whereas RP has overt prestige in England and is said to be 'nice', 'pure', 'pleasant', 'correct' and 'sophisticated', all the other accents are rated more unfavourably than RP. As far as the prestige of accents is concerned, RP is followed by Modified RP or educated regional and then by rural accents, which are often rated as 'quaint' and 'genuine', but also as 'not proper', 'not polite' and 'socially unacceptable'. Right at the bottom of the scale are the urban accents having the lowest prestige. They are often regarded as 'unpleasant', 'not proper', 'ugly', 'degenerate', 'wrong', 'corrupt', 'harsh' and 'slovenly'. Nevertheless, low-class accents also have a kind of prestige, which can be described as covert prestige, because attitudes of this type are not usually overtly expressed and deviate sharply from the mainstream societal values. This appreciation of low-class accents is the direct result of group solidarity and personal identity. In this case, the community norm (ie solidarity and identity), which is usually deeply rooted in the language behaviour of people, is stronger than the social norm (ie status). Status-stressing signals are linked to values such as 'intelligence', 'wealth', 'education' and 'success', whereas solidarity-stressing values include 'kindness', 'trustworthiness', 'integrity' and 'reliability'. Group solidarity and identity can be seen in national, regional, social, ethnic, age, gender and religious groups. It seems obvious that the different group interests can overlap and that certain values will be predominant.

In England, working class accents often have connotations of masculinity (ie toughness), honesty and integrity and thus have covert prestige. The standard RP accent is sometimes downgraded by working class people and ridiculed as 'a cut-glass accent', 'posh English', 'effeminate English', 'talking posh' or 'talking la-di-da'.

The expression 'dropping one's aitches' is sometimes used by RP speakers to discriminate against non-RP speakers. 'Dropping one's aitches' literally means that people do not pronounce /h/ where it is normally pronounced. The connotation is that people who 'drop their aitches' are less educated and less intelligent than speakers who pronounce /h/ correctly.

Q4 Explain the terms **acrolect, basilect** and **mesolect**.

6. Linguistic convergence and linguistic divergence

Linguistic convergence refers to the processes whereby individuals change their speech styles and accent to become more like the language of the person with whom they are communicating. Upward convergence means a shift in the direction of a language style or accent that has high prestige, whereas downward convergence means a shift in the direction of a language style or accent that has low prestige. Generally, a shift is undertaken to reduce embarrassment between people of differing social status and to prepare a common basis for the communication of ideas and feelings. It reflects a speaker's desire for his or her listener's social approval.

Linguistic divergence is the opposite of linguistic convergence. Speakers deliberately diverge in the direction of a low-status language style or accent or in the direction of a high-status language style or accent to make a certain point. It is a means of establishing a certain degree of distinctiveness.

Q5 Explain the terms **hypercorrection, overgeneralization** and **rhotic accents.**

7. Cockney

Cockney is the socioregional variety spoken in and around London. Some typical features in the pronunciation of Cockney are as follows:
- consonants:
a) /t/ is replaced intervocalically and before pause by /ʔ/ (*butter, wet*).
b) /θ/ is generally replaced by /f/ (*thin, Cathy, both*).
c) /ð/ is replaced medially and finally by /v/ (*together, bathe*) and initially often by a zero or /d/ (*the, they*).
d) /l/ after a vowel in final position, before a consonant in the same syllable or as a syllable in itself is pronounced as /ʊ/ (*well, milk, apple*).
e) <-ing> is usually /ɪn/, it is /ɪŋk/ in *nothing, something*.
f) /h/ is usually not pronounced (*hammer, hat*).

- vowels:
a) /æ/ is often realized as [ɛ] or [ɛɪ] (*bag, rat*).
b) /iː/ is usually [ɪi] or [əi] (*tea, see*).
c) /eɪ/ is usually [æɪ] (*paper, wait*).
d) /əʊ/ is usually [æʊ] (*home, soaked*).

e) /aɪ/ is usually [ɒɪ] (*time, inside*).
f) /aʊ/ is usually [æə] (*now, town*).

Note: There are also different grammatical and lexical features in Cockney. One typical lexical feature is worth quoting, ie Cockney rhyming slang. Rhyming slang refers to words or phrases that rhyme with the words that are really meant: *apples and pears* for *stairs*, *God forbids* for *kids*, *struggle and strife* for *wife*, *Molly Malone* or *dog and bone* for *telephone*, *jam jar* or *la-di-da* for *car*. Non-natives have the greatest difficulties with 'clipped rhyming slang', where the rhyming word is left out: *boat* for *face* (ie *boat race*), *porkies* for *lies* (ie *pork pies*), *loaf* for *head* (ie *loaf of bread*) or *titfer* for *hat* (ie *tit for tat*).

8. Estuary English

Estuary English is a socioregional variety which has spread from London to the areas of the Thames estuary and beyond. As far as the accent of this variety is concerned, it can roughly be placed on a continuum between Cockney and RP. An important fact is that, from a social point of view, the development of Estuary English works from both ends of the social spectrum. On the one hand, there is upward mobility with Londoners who feel the need to modify their Cockney accent. On the other, some RP speakers want to identify more with their social environment and consequently exhibit downward convergence.

Q6 Why have low-class accents survived for such a long time?

8.2 AMERICAN ENGLISH

1. Introduction

There is no recognized standard pronunciation for the whole of the United States as there is for England. American English pronunciation can roughly be divided into three major areas, ie eastern, southern and the rest of the country. The pronunciation in the rest of the country is particularly uniform. The following description concentrates on what is labelled **General American English** (**GenAmE**), which as a concept refers to non-eastern and non-southern accents. This kind of English pronunciation is also known as **Network English**, which is most frequently heard from professional speakers on national network news and informative programmes thus covering the whole of the United States. Network English is the variety which is most acceptable on radio and television. Although professional speakers show a great deal of conformity, their pronunciation is not altogether monolithic. Network English also shows a certain degree of variability.

One of the most striking features of GenAmE is the fact that <r> is pronounced in all environments. The pronunciation of postvocalic /r/ before consonants and in final position makes GenAmE a **rhotic accent**. All vowels followed by /r/ are affected by a so-called **r-colouring**, which is due to the production of the vowel where the tongue curls slightly and is pulled back in the mouth (**retroflex /r/**). This combination of vowel and retroflex /r/ often results in a retroflex vowel as in *bird* /bɜˑd/. In contrast to BrE, where *law-lore, paw-pore, bawd-bored* and *saw-sore* are homophones, GenAmE distinguishes these pairs through the pronunciation of postvocalic /r/.

Two general features which are often said to be typically American, ie the **American drawl** and the **nasal twang** require some explanation. The **American drawl** (**lengthening**) is the best-known characteristic of a mainly southern pronunciation. It refers to a general lengthening and sometimes diphthongization of vowels in stressed syllables. In other words, the length of a vowel is not determined by its environment, but solely by the fact that the vowel is stressed. Consequently one has lengthened vowels in words such as *stop, fast, can't, not* and *talk*. General American, on the other hand, normally follows the British English rule, where stressed vowels in open syllables and vowels before voiced consonants are longer than before voiceless consonants. American transcription systems are usually qualitative, ie they do not have length marks. The **nasal twang** (**nasalization**) which describes the nasalized pronunciation of vowels can mostly be heard in southern areas. Vowels become nasalized before nasals (sometimes after nasals and after initial /kw/) in words such as *man, glance, drink, camp, time, song, small* and *quite.*

2. Inventory of phonemes

vowels: monopththongs

iː   as in feet
ɪ   as in *fit*
e   (also /ɛ/) as in *bet*
æ   as in *bat*
ɑː   as in *father* and in *lot*
ɔː   as in *caught* (in some dialects), *born, corn*
ʊ   as in *put*
uː   as in *pool*
ʌ   (also /ə/) as in *hut*
ɜː   as in *bird*
ə   as in *ago*

vowels: diphthongs

eɪ   as in *tame*
oʊ   as in *tone*
aɪ   as in *time*
aʊ   as in *town*
ɔɪ   as in *boy*

semivowels

j   as in *yes*
w   as in *wine* (also **GenAmE /wh/** or /ʍ/ as in *whine)*

consonants

p	as in *pan*	dʒ	as in *gin*	ʃ	as in *shin*
b	as in *ban*	f	as in *fin*	ʒ	as in *genre*
t	as in *tan*	v	as in *van*	h	as in *hen*
d	as in *den*	θ	as in *thin*	m	as in *man*
k	as in *can*	ð	as in *than*	n	as in *no*
g	as in *gun*	s	as in *sin*	ŋ	as in *sing*
tʃ	as in *chin*	z	as in *zone*	r	as in *rot*
				l	as in *lot*

3. Specific features of General American English in contrast to BrE (RP)

Segmentals: vowels and consonants

1. Raising: BrE /ɑː/ - GenAmE /æ/ in certain environments

GenAmE has /æ/ before /n/+consonant, before /m/+consonant, before the voiceless fricatives /f/, /s/ as well as /θ/ and before the voiced fricative /v/, where BrE has /ɑː/.

Examples are *can't, dance, aunt, example, sample, half, behalf, laugh, staff, halve, glass, basket, past, bath, path*.

Note 1: In a number of words spelled with /n/ or /f/ or /s/+consonant, GenAmE and BrE have /æ/ as in *ant, pant, gaffe, daffodil, gas, passage*.

Note 2: In certain environments, GenAmE retains /ɑː/, ie in final syllable (*shah, ma, pa*), before <-lm> (*palm, calm, balm*), in words spelled with <ar> (*bar, barring, farm, park*) and in the words *father* as well as *sergeant*.

2. Mergers: BrE /ɒ/ - GenAmE /ɑː/, also /ɔː/; BrE /ɔː/ - GenAmE /ɔː/, also /ɑː/

BrE /ɒ/ is regularly replaced by **GenAmE /ɑː/** (also/ɔː/) and BrE /ɔː/ is usually replaced by GenAmE /ɔː/ or /ɑː/. The different realizations depend on regional factors.

Examples are *whopper, mob, rod, pot, hot, sorry, borrow, novel, lock, rod, conflict, Hollywood, doll, ton, long, song, thought, water, lawn*.

Note 1: There is usually free variation between /ɑː/ and /ɔː/ in words spelled with <qua> or <wa> (*quarrel, quarantine, wallet, water*) and with words spelled with <o> before /n/ and /m/ (*on, common, gone*), before /g/ (*fog, log, clog, jog*), before /ŋ/, /s/, /f/, /θ/ (*gong, glossary, office, Gothic*) and before intervocalic /r/ (*foreign, sorry, tomorrow, orange*).
A large number of Americans retain /ɔː/ in open stressed syllables (*law, saw*) and in words spelled with <aun> (*laundry, gaunt*), but especially when a vowel is followed by /r/+consonant (*born, bored, force, morgue, morph, north, war*).

Note 2: Whereas BrE distinguishes the vowels in *hot - heart, lock - lark* and *pot - part*, the pronunciations of the GenAmE vowels are usually identical. The difference in pronunciation is to be found in the articulation of postvocalic /r/ in GenAmE.

Note 3: BrE distinguishes the vowels in *caller - collar, dawn - don, taught - tot* and *caught - cot*, where the GenAmE pronunciations are usually homophonous.

3. Yod dropping: BrE /juː/ - GenAmE /uː/

- After /t, d, l, n, s, z, θ/ GenAmE uses /uː/ in stressed syllables. Examples are *attitude, adieu, dew, due, duke, Luke, student, new, assume, resume, tune, enthusiasm*.

- After /b, f, h, k, m, m, p, sp, sk, v/ GenAmE and BrE have /juː/, eg *beauty, future, fume, hue, cube, Cuba, skew, music, computer, punitive, spew, view*.

Note: GenAmE has /j/ in *figure* /fɪɡjər/.

4. Smoothing: tendency towards monophthongization in GenAmE with /eɪ/ and /oʊ/

Examples are *fail, nation, name, home, stone, load*.

Note: In some American transcription systems, /eɪ/ and /oʊ/ are transcribed as /e/ and /o/.

5. Vowels before /r/

5.1. BrE diphthongs /ɪə/, /ʊə/ and /eə/ are realized in GenAmE as /ɪr/, /ʊr/ and /er/.

Examples are *fear, sheer, tour, sure, fair, bare*.

Note: Since General American English is a rhotic accent, the following pronunciations can be interpreted as a combination of vowel+/r/, eg *here, fair, tour*, where British English has diphthongs. One also has *bird, bar* or *bored* and *mother* as a combination of vowel and /r/ for example. The transcription of words containing vowel+/r/ varies, reflecting the range of pronunciations heard in GenAmE. Thus one can find the following transcriptions for *here* /hɪˤr, hɪɚ, hɪr, hir/, for *fair* /feˤr, fæˤr, feɚ, fer, fær, fer/ and for *tour* /tʊˤr, tʊɚ, tʊr, tur/. Similarly, different transcriptions of *bird* or *mother* can be found, eg /bɝd/, /bɜːrd/, /bɻd/ and /mʌðɚ/, /mʌðˤr/, /mʌðər/.

5.2 BrE /ɑː/ is replaced in some words in GenAmE by /ɜːr/.

Examples are *Derby, clerk, Berkeley*.

5.3 BrE has /ʌr/ in some words, where GenAmE has /ɜːr/.

Examples are *worry, hurry, hurricane, furrow, nourish, courage, current, curry*.

6. Rhoticity: BrE is non-rhotic and GenAmE is rhotic (/r/ is pronounced in all environments).

Examples are *cart, board, farther, car, stir, burr.*

7. Velarization of /l/: dark [ɫ] can be found in any environment, ie also in prevocalic position, depending on regional factors.

Examples are *love, leave, follow, bully, fill it, peel it.*

8. Tapping: the flapped [D]

The so-called flapped [D] is similar to /d/ in so far as it is a voiced sound and is articulated at the alveolar ridge. However, it is much shorter than a /d/. The tip/blade of the tongue touches the alveolar ridge and is rapidly pulled back. In other words, it is articulated by quickly tapping the tip/blade of the tongue against the tooth ridge. Both /t/ and /d/ change into a [D] in certain environments. The process is called tapping or flapping. The transcription of the flap varies, one finds [D] and [ṭ].

8.1 Tapping of /t/ in GenAmE between vowels when the preceding vowel is stressed resulting in [D] (flap or tap).

Examples are *writer, atom, bitter, better, latter, united, waiting.*

Note 1: Furthermore a word ending in a <t> is pronounced as a flap if the following word begins with a vowel, eg *out of Africa, they shot at him, get out of here, not alone.*

Note 2: Flapping also occurs in the combination of stressed vowel+ /l/ or /r/ or /n/ + /t/ + stressed vowel or stressed vowel + /t/ + syllabic /l/, eg in *malted, hearty, party, porter, winter* and *little, bottle, dental, subtle, startle.*

Note 3: In rapid colloquial speech, /t/ is elided after /n/, eg *center* /'senər/, *winter* /'wɪnər/, *county* /'kaʊni/, *intercity* /'ɪnərsɪDi/.

Note 4: The weakening rule, ie weakening of *fortis* consonants, is sometimes applied in the case of /p/ and rarely /k/ resulting in a [b]-like and [g]-like pronunciation, eg *capital* /'kæBɪDəl/ and *rickety* /'rɪGəDi/.

8.2 Tapping of /d/ in GenAmE between vowels and in the sequences vowel+/r/+/d/+vowel as well as vowel+/d/+/l/, when the preceding vowel is stressed.

Examples are *heading, ladder, wading, rider, harder, border, middle.*

Note 1: Furthermore, a word ending in <d> is sometimes pronounced as a flap if the following word begins with a vowel, eg *she hid it, he had it, good enough.*

Note 2: /d/ is not flapped after vowel+/n/ or /l/+/d/+vowel, eg in *finding, kinder, shoulder.*

Note 3: The weakening rule makes words like *writer - rider, atom - Adam, bitter - bidder, latter - ladder* homophonous. If a distinction is made at all, it is made on the basis of the preceding vowel, which may be longer before <d> (<dd>).

Q7 In which of the following words does flapping occur?
Adore, adder, atom, atomic, attain, attempt, biting, erotic, natal, nativity, nutty, riding, united, fighting, fighter, hotter, button.

9. Glide cluster retention: in GenAmE, words beginning with <wh> frequently have the pronunciation /hw/ (/ʍ/) in content words. Function words have /hw/ when used emphatically.

Examples are *wheat, whet* (in contrast to *wet*), *whether* (in contrast to *weather*), *whine* (in contrast to *wine*), *whale* (in contrast to *wail*) as well as emphatic *what, where, when.*

10. Variation: different priorities in words ending in <-ersion> and <-sia>, where BrE has /ʃ/ or /ʒ/ and GenAmE /ʒ/ or /ʃ/.

Examples are *conversion, immersion, inversion, diversion, Asia, Persia.*

11. Yod assimilation: GenAmE prefers assimilated forms.
- BrE /tj/ or /tʃ/ - GenAmE predominantly has /tʃ/: *virtue, statue, righteous.*
- BrE /dj/ or /dʒ/ - GenAmE predominantly has /dʒ/: *educate, graduate, did you.*

- BrE /sj/ or /ʃ/ - GenAmE predominantly has /ʃ/: *issue, miss you, sensual.*
- BrE /ʒ/ or /zj/ - GenAmE /ʒ/: *azure, glazier.*

12. Certain words have final /s/ in GenAmE and /z/ in BrE.

Examples are *blouse, erase.*

Note: *houses* is sometimes pronounced /'haʊsəz/ in GenAmE.

13. In certain prefixes ending in <-i>, GenAmE predominantly has /aɪ/, where BrE has /ɪ/ only (sometimes /ɪ/ or /aɪ/).

Examples are *semi* and *anti.*

Note: The word *demi* has /ɪ/ only in both BrE and GenAmE.

14. Some non-systematic differences between BrE and GenAmE in individual words

word	BrE	GenAmE
again, against	/ə'gen(st)/ or /ə'geın(st)/	/ə'gen(st)/
albino	/æl'bi:nəʊ/	/æl'baınoʊ/
aluminium	/ælə'mınjəm/	*aluminum* /ə'lu:mınəm/
apricot	/'eıprıkɒt/	/'æprıkɑ:t/ or /'eıprıkɑ:t/
ate	/et/ or /eıt/	/eıt/
borough	/'bʌrə/	/'bɜːroʊ/
brassiere	/'bræzıə/ or /'bræsıə/	/brə'zır/
brooch	/brəʊtʃ/	/broʊtʃ/ or /bru:tʃ/
buoy	/bɔı/	/'bu:i/ or /bɔı/
charade	/ʃə'rɑ:d/	/ʃə'reıd/
creek	/kri:k/	/krık/
herb	/hɜːb/	/ɜːrb/ (not the name *Herb*)
khaki	/'kɑ:ki/	/'kæki/
leisure	/'leʒə/	/'li:ʒər/
lever	/'li:və/	/'levər/ or /'li:vər/
lieutenant	/lef'tenənt/	/lu:'tenənt/
morale	/mə'rɑ:l/ or /mɒ'rɑ:l/	/mə'ræl/
nephew	/'nevju:/ or /'nefju:/	/'nefju:/
penalize	/'pi:nəlaız/	/'penəlaız/ or /'pi:nəlaız/
plait	/plæt/	/pleıt/ or /plæt/
rather	/'rɑ:ðə/	/'ræðər/
route	/ru:t/	/raʊt/ or /ru:t/
schedule	/'ʃedju:l/ or /'skedju:l/	/'skedju:l/
shone	/ʃɒn/	/ʃoʊn/
tomato	/tə'mɑ:təʊ/	/tə'meıDoʊ/
vase	/vɑ:z/	/veıs/ or /veız/
wrath	/rɔ:θ/	/ræθ/
z	/zed/	/zi:/
zenith	/'zenıθ/	/'zi:nıθ/

Q8 Transcribe the following words (RP and GenAmE): *Anthony, aton-al, Bernard, caffeine, dahlia, depot, deuce, epoch, frustrate, genuine, halfpenny, harem, Hellenic, hilarious, impious, internecine, mimosa, moustache, pyjamas (pajamas), paprika, pecan, perfume, phalanx, philistine, placate, plaque, plaza, premature, premier, produce, progress, quinine, raccoon, rodeo, Sahara, short-lived, sojourn, solder, tiara, trachea, trespass, trombone, vermouth, volition, waft, wont, weir.*

4. Suprasegmentals: stress

4.1 In words of French origin, BrE often moves the main stress one syllable forward, GenAmE keeps the French stress pattern, ie stress on the last syllable.

Examples are *attaché* /ə'tæʃeɪ/ - /ætə'ʃeɪ/, *ballet* /'bæleɪ/- /bæ'leɪ/, *baton* /'bætən/ - /bə'tɑːn/, *beret* /'beri/, /'bereɪ/ (also /bə'reɪ/, cf. American English influence on BrE) - /bə'reɪ/, *café* /'kæfeɪ/ (also /kæ'feɪ/) - /kæ'feɪ/, /kə'feɪ/, *chagrin* /'ʃægrɪn/ - /ʃə'grɪn/, *debris* /'debriː, 'deɪbriː/ - /də'briː/, *premier* /'premiə/ - /prɪ'mɪr, priː'mjɪr, priː'mɪːr/, *précis* /'preɪsiː/ - /preɪ'siː/.

Q9 Transcribe the following words (RP and GenAmE): *adieu, cabaret, chamois, cliché, coupé, croquet, cul-de-sac, detail, fiancé, frontier, mirage, nuance, parquet, ragout, ricochet, résumé, soufflé, tableau.*

4.2 Various words usually have the main stress on the first syllable in GenAmE, where BrE has stress on the second or third syllable.

- words ending in <-ate>, where the first part is not a prefix, eg BrE *dic'tate, do'nate, mi'grate, ro'tate, va'cate, vi'brate* vs. GenAmE *'dictate, 'donate, 'migrate, 'rotate, 'vacate, 'vibrate.*

Note: Prefixed verbs are pronounced the same in BrE and GenAmE, eg *be'rate, de'bate, e'late.*

- BrE *inquiry* /ɪn'kwaɪəri/, *laboratory* /lə'bɒrətəri/, *corollary* /kə'rɒləri/, *capillary* /kə'pɪləri/ and *ancillary* /æn'sɪləri/ vs. GenAmE *inquiry* /'ɪŋkwəri/, *laboratory* /'læbərətɔːri/, *corollary* /'kɔːrəleri/, *capillary* /'kæpəleri/ and *ancillary* /'ænsəleri/.

- BrE *maga'zine* and *marga'rine* vs. GenAmE *'magazine* and *'margarine*.

Note: The word *advertisement* is BrE /əd'vɜːtɪsmənt/ or /əd'vɜːtɪzmənt/ and GenAmE /ædvər'taɪzmənt/.

4.3 Various words usually have the main stress on the first syllable in GenAmE, where BrE has variable stress.

BrE *arti'san* and *'artisan, prin'cess* and *'princess, doc'trinal* and *'doctrinal, else'where* and *'elsewhere, further'more* and *'furthermore, ice-'cream* and *'ice-cream, week'end* and *'weekend* vs. GenAmE *'artisan, 'princess, 'doctrinal, 'elsewhere, 'furthermore, 'ice-cream, 'weekend* .

4.4 Word endings such as <-ary>, <-ery>, <-ony>, <-ory>, <-ative> have a secondary stress in GenAmE resulting in a full vowel.

Examples where the main stress is the same in BrE and GenAmE are *adversary, arbitrary, commentary, dictionary, secretary, temporary, cemetery, monastery, stationery, alimony, ceremony, matrimony, testimony, auditory, category, inventory, territory, administrative, authoritative, speculative* /-eɪDɪv/.

4.5 Secondary stress in BrE but not in GenAmE in words ending in -ile: BrE /aɪl/ and GenAmE /əl/, /ɪl/ or /l/.

Examples are *agile, docile, fertile, fissile, fragile, futile, hostile, missile, mobile, sterile, tactile, versatile, virile.*

Note: The word *docile* is BrE /'dəʊsaɪl/ and GenAmE /'dɑːsəl/.

4.6 Geographical names ending in <-burgh>, <-bury>, <-ham>, <-mouth>, <-folk>, <-shire>, <-wich> are weakened in BrE, but have a secondary stress in GenAmE.

Examples are *Edinburgh, Canterbury, Birmingham, Cunningham, Portsmouth, Norfolk, Devonshire, Norwich.*

Q10 Transcribe the above place names (BrE and GenAmE).

5. Suprasegmentals: intonation

The intonation of BrE and GenAmE is very similar, but certain small differences can be identified. The most striking difference between BrE and GenAmE is the pitch range, which is smaller in GenAmE than in BrE. Consequently, the high pitch at the beginning of a sentence (high heads), the high falls, the high rises and the rise-falls are higher in BrE than in GenAmE. BrE has a high head and the rest of the syllables form a gradually falling contour, whereas GenAmE has a medium head with the rest of the syllables more or less on the same level as the medium head. Thus, the gradual fall after the first stressed syllable to the end of a sentence is unknown in GenAmE. GenAmE prefers a more level melody avoiding high pitch. Falls are realized more on a level in GenAmE, whereas in BrE (RP) downglides are very common. Because of the smaller pitch range, there are also fewer high rises in GenAmE. Generally speaking, the melody in GenAmE centres more around the middle and sounds more monotonous than in BrE.

6. Influence of American English pronunciation on British English (RP)

GenAmE has influenced BrE and added variation in the pronunciation of BrE (RP). The following words are typical of this influence:
aesthetic, anti-, apparatus, arbitrarily, assume, baths, booth, charade, cigarette, data, economic, either, evolution, issue, presume, record, schedule, status, truths, vitamin, youths, zebra, zenith;
adult, communal, comparable, demonstrable, formidable, harass, hospitable, magazine, miscellany, momentarily, necessarily, temporarily (cf. variation within RP).

Q11 BrE is often preferred to AmE by the majority of Germans. They often claim that BrE (RP) is clearer, purer, better and more attractive than an AmE pronunciation. Discuss this attitude and its implications.

Q12 Read and transcribe the following text (GenAmE).
The car was a dark blue seven-passenger sedan, a Packard of the latest model, custom-built. It was the kind of car you wear rope pearls in. It was parked by a fire-hydrant and a dark foreign-looking chauffeur with a face of carved wood was behind the wheel. The interior was upholstered in quilted grey chenille. The Indian put me in the back. Sitting there alone I felt like a high-class corpse, laid out by an undertaker with a lot of good taste.

The Indian got in beside the chauffeur and the car turned in the middle of the block and a cop across the street said: 'Hey', weakly, as if he didn't mean it, and then bent down quickly to tie his shoe.

We went west, dropped over to Sunset and slid fast and noiseless along that. The Indian sat motionless beside the chauffeur. An occasional whiff of his personality drifted back to me. The driver looked as if he was half asleep but he passed the fast boys in the convertible sedans as though they were being towed. They turned on all the green lights for him. Some drivers are like that. He never missed one.

It had been a warm afternoon, but the heat was gone. We whipped past a distant cluster of lighted buildings and an endless series of lighted mansions, not too close to the road. We dipped down to skirt a huge green polo field with another equally huge practice field beside it, soared again to the top of the hill of clean concrete that passed orange groves, some rich man's pet because this is not orange country, and then little by little the lighted windows of the millionaires' homes were gone and the road narrowed and this was Stillwood Heights. (Fletcher 1990:72, 98)

Key to some questions

Q1 Consult Gimson (1962/94), Leisi (1969/85), Trudgill (1974/95) and Wells (1982).

Q5 a) hypercorrection refers to the native speakers' over-extension and overgeneralization of a rule beyond the point set by the standard variety of the language in question. In pronunciation, speakers of a variety who do not distinguish between /ʊ/ and /ʌ/ and only use /ʊ/ in words like *put* and *putt* might say "Put */pʌt/ the pussy */pʌsi/ on the cushion */kʌʃən/."

b) overgeneralization also refers to the over-extension and overgeneralization of a rule beyond the point set by the standard variety of the language in question. The term is mainly used in language acquisition studies referring to children and foreign language learners.

c) rhotic accent refers to accents of English where /r/ is pronounced in all environments, ie also in final position and before consonants (*car, cart, parts*). Accents like RP, which do not have this feature, are non-rhotic.

Q8 Transcribe the following words (RP and GenAmE). Anthony /ˈæntəni/ ‖ /ˈænθəni/, atonal /eɪˈtəʊnəl/ ‖ eɪˈtoʊnəl/, Bernard /ˈbɜːnəd/ (/bəˈnɑːd/) ‖ /ˈbɜːrnərd/ (/bərˈnɑːrd/), caffeine /ˈkæfiːn/

‖ /kæˈfiːn/, dahlia /ˈdeɪlɪə/ ‖ /ˈdæljə/ (/ˈdɑːljə/), depot /ˈdepəʊ/ ‖ /ˈdepoʊ/ (/ˈdiːpoʊ/), deuce /ˈdjuːs/ ‖ /ˈduːs/, epoch /ˈiːppk/ ‖ /ˈepək/, frustrate /frʌˈstreɪt/ ‖ /ˈfrʌstreɪt/, genuine /ˈdʒenjuɪn/ ‖ /ˈdʒenjuɪn/ (/ˈdʒenjuaɪn/), halfpenny /hɑːfˈpeni/ (/ˈheɪpni/) ‖ /hæfˈpeni/, harem /ˈhɑːriːm/ ‖ /ˈhærəm/, Hellenic /heˈliːnɪk/ ‖ /heˈlenɪk/, hilarious /hɪˈleərɪəs/ ‖ /hɪˈlerɪəs/, impious /ˈɪmpɪəs/ ‖ /ˈɪmpiːəs/ (/ɪmˈpaɪəs/), internecine /ɪntəˈniːsaɪn/ ‖ /ɪnDərˈniːsən/, mimosa /mɪˈməʊzə/ ‖ /mɪˈmoʊsə/ (/maɪˈmoʊsə/), moustache /məˈstɑːʃ/ ‖ /ˈmʌstæʃ/, pyjamas /pəˈdʒɑːməz/ ‖ pajamas /pəˈdʒæməz/, paprika /ˈpæprɪkə/ ‖ /pəˈpriːkə/, pecan /pɪˈkæn/ ‖ /pɪˈkɑːn/, perfume /ˈpɜːfjuːm/ ‖ /ˈpɜːrfjuːm/ (/pɜːrˈfjuːm/), phalanx /ˈfælæŋks/ ‖ /ˈfeɪlæŋks/, philistine /ˈfɪlɪstaɪn/ ‖ /ˈfɪlɪstiːn/, placate /pləˈkeɪt/ ‖ /ˈpleɪkeɪt/, plaque /plæk/ (/plɑːk/) ‖ /plæk/, plaza /ˈplɑːzə/ ‖ /ˈplæzə/, premature /ˈpremətʃə/ ‖ /priːməˈtʊr/, premier /ˈpremɪə/ ‖ /prɪˈmɪr/, produce (v.) /prəˈdjuːs/ ‖ /prəˈduːs/, progress /ˈprəʊgres/, (/ˈprɒgres/) ‖ /ˈprɑːgrəs/, quinine /kwɪˈniːn/ ‖ /ˈkwaɪnaɪn/, raccoon /rəˈkuːn/ ‖ /ræˈkuːn/, rodeo /rəʊˈdeɪəʊ/ ‖ /roʊˈdeɪoʊ/, Sahara /səˈhɑːrə/ ‖ /səˈhærə/, short-lived /ʃɔːtˈlɪvd/ ‖ /ʃɔːrtˈlaɪvd/, sojourn /ˈsɒdʒən/ ‖ /ˈsoʊdʒɜːrn/, solder /ˈsɒldə/ (/ˈsəʊldə/) ‖ /ˈsɑːdər/, tiara /tiˈɑːrə/ ‖ /tiˈærə/, trachea /trəˈkiːə/ ‖ /ˈtreɪkɪə/, trespass /ˈtrespəs/ ‖ /ˈtrespæs/, trombone /trɒmˈbəʊn/ ‖ /trɑːmˈboʊn/, vermouth /ˈvɜːməθ/ ‖ /vərˈmuːθ/, volition /vəʊˈlɪʃən/ ‖ voʊˈlɪʃən/, waft /wɑːft/ (/wɒft/) ‖ /wæft/, wont /wəʊnt/ (/wɒnt/) ‖ /wɑːnt/, weir /wɪə/ ‖ /wɪr/.

Suggested readings

Barltrop, R./J. Wolveridge (1980) *The Muvver Tongue.* London: The Journeyman Press

Bauer, L. (1994) *Watching English Change.* London: Longman

Dretzke, B. (1985) *Fehlerbewertung im Aussprachebereich.* Hamburg: Buske

Chambers, J.K. (1995) *Sociolinguistic Theory.* Oxford: Blackwell

Coggle, P. (1993) *Do you speak Estuary?* London: Bloomsbury

Crystal, D. (1995) *The Cambridge Encyclopedia of the English Language.* Cambridge: Cambridge University Press

Ellis, A.J. (1869) *On early English pronunciation.* London. Early English Text Society

Fletcher, C. (1990) *Pronunciation Dictionary. Study Guide.* London: Longman`

Giles, H. (1970) "Evaluative Reactions to Accent", *Educational Review* 22, 211-227

Giles, H./N. Coupland/J. Coupland, eds. (1991) *Contexts of Accommodation: Developments in Applied Sociolinguistics.* Cambridge: Cambridge University Press

Giles, H./P.F. Powesland (1975) *Speech Style and Social Evaluation*. London: Academic Press

Giles, H./ R. StClair (1979) *Language and Social Psychology*. Oxford: Blackwell

Honey, J. (1989) *Does Accent Matter? The Pygmalion Factor*. London: Faber and Faber

Hudson, R.A. (1980/96) *Sociolinguistics*. Cambridge: Cambridge University Press

Hughes, A./ P. Trudgill (1979/96) *English Accents and Dialects*. London: Arnold

Leisi, E. (1969/85) *Das heutige Englisch*. Heidelberg: Carl Winter

Michaelis, H./D. Jones (1913) *A Phonetic Dictionary of the English Language*. Hannover: Carl Meyer

Jones, D. (1937) *An English Pronouncing Dictionary*. London: J.M. Dent

Milroy, J./L. Milroy (1985) *Authority in Language*. London: Routledge & Kegan Paul

Ramsaran, S., ed. (1990) *Studies in the pronunciation of English. A commemorative volume in honour of A.C. Gimson*. London: Routledge

Scherer, K.R./H. Giles, eds. (1979) *Social Markers in Speech*. Cambridge: Cambridge University Press

Trudgill, P. (1974/95) *Sociolinguistics*. Harmondsworth: Penguin

Trudgill, P./H. Giles (1976 "Sociolinguistics and Linguistic Value Judgements: Correctness, Adequacy and Aesthetics", (Series B. Paper No. 10, reproduced by *Linguistic Agency University of Trier)*, 1-19

Trudgill, P./J. Hannah (1982/94) *International English*. London: Edward Arnold

Note on pronunciation

academics /ˌækə'demɪks/, clergy /klɜː'dʒi/, executives /ɪg'zekjutɪvz/, stereotyped /'steriətaɪpt/, locality /ləu'kæləti/, metropolis /mə'trɒpəlɪs/, feasibility /fiːzə'bɪləti/, abandon /ə'bændən/, archaic /aː'keɪk/, derivation /deɪɪ'veɪʃən/, precede /prɪ'sɪːd/, Mersey /'mɜːzi/, Anglia /'ængliə/, rural /'ruərəl/, urban /'ɜːbən/, hypothesis /haɪ'pɒθəsɪs/, sophisticated /sə'fɪstɪkeɪtɪd/, genuine /'dʒenjuɪn/, slovenly /'slʌvənli/, societal /sə'saɪətəl/, integrity /ɪn'tegrəti/, reliability /rɪlaɪə'bɪləti/, predominant /prɪ'dɒmɪnənt/, connotation /kɒnə'teɪʃən/, dialect /'daɪəlekt/, masculinity /mæskju'lɪnɪti/, effeminate /ɪ'femɪnət/, la-di-da /lɑːdiː'dɑː/, acrolect /'ækrəulekt/, basilect /'bæzɪlekt/, mesolect /'mesəulekt/, convergence /kən'vɜːdʒəns/, embarrassment /ɪm'bærəsmənt/, hypercorrection /haɪpəkə'rekʃən/, rhotic /'rəutɪk/, estuary /'estjuri/, informative /ɪn'fɔːmətɪv/, monolithic /mɒnə'lɪθɪk/, area /'eərɪə/, homophonous /hə'mɒfənəs/, emphatic /ɪm'fætɪk/, monotonous /mə'nɒtənəs/.

9.0 CONTRASTIVE ANALYSIS AND ERROR ANALYSIS

1. Introduction

Contrastive analysis is used in linguistics to refer to differences between units in two languages. In phonetics and phonology, contrastive analysis is used to compare the phonemic systems, the phonetic features, the distribution of sounds, the combination of sounds and the relative frequency of sounds. As the speech apparatus is universal in humans, a contrastive approach to phonetic features is extremely useful and reliable.

The goals of contrastive analysis are quite often pedagogical. The **strong version** of contrastive analysis claims to be predictive as far as errors are concerned. In other words, a contrastive analysis of two languages can be used to predict the errors that speakers of the first language will make in learning the second. Consequently, the predictions can be of use in the development of teaching methodology and materials. The **weak version** of contrastive analysis approaches the problem from a different angle. It takes into account the observed errors by starting with classroom data and using the differences between the two linguistic systems to explain the errors. On the basis of the comparison, contrastive analysis predicts or simply registers difficulties in foreign language learning with zero items and different items, whereas identical and similar items in the two languages are described as being easy to learn. As far as errors are concerned, they are seen as **interlingual mistakes**, which are errors resulting from negative language transfer and which are due to the learner's native language. Language transfer is the effect of one language upon the learning of another and **negative transfer** or **interference** is the use of a native-tongue pattern or rule which leads to an unacceptable or inappropriate form in the target language. The mispronunciations */sɪn/ for *thin,* */vel/ for *well* or */pɪk/ for *pig* are typical interlingual mistakes. Interlingual mistakes can also be the result of interference from a further foreign language. **Positive transfer** is likely to occur when both the native language and the target language have the same form. The three nasals /m, n, ŋ/ are identical in German and English and basically do not cause any mispronunciations.

Neither the strong nor the weak version of contrastive analysis can be expected to account for all errors in language learning. Because not all the predictions resulting from the contrastive approach have proved to be correct, **error analysis** has developed as a complementary approach to contrastive analysis. Error analysis deals with all the mistakes made by people who learn a language. Its starting point is the systematic collection of raw data. Error analysis identifies mistakes, describes and classifies mistakes, evaluates mistakes and attempts to eliminate mistakes. Evidence suggests that many errors are due to faulty or partial application of target-language rules. These errors, which are caused by the influence of one target-language item upon another, are termed **intralingual errors**. The mispronunciations */wɪlɪdʒ/ for *village,* */tʃɒp/ for *shop* and */ræd/ for *red* are typical examples of intralingual mistakes. There is further evidence that the cause of errors is manifold. Errors can have psychomotoric causes (ie difficulties in articulation) or cognitive causes (ie lack of knowledge of how to pronounce a word). They can also be induced by the classroom situation in general, by other students and even the teachers themselves, by the media (presenting 'German English' on TV and the radio for example), by random guessing, by total lack of knowledge etc. One's personality including intelligence, motivation and attitude, certain learning strategies and communicative strategies as well as one's particular physical and psychological state of mind can also play a dominant role in the production of errors. The type of language produced by foreign-language learners is called **interlanguage**. Detailed **interlanguage studies** complement error analysis in the attempt to understand and categorize the linguistic and psycholinguistic processes involved in the learners' attempts to master a foreign language.

2. Contrastive analysis

Contrastive analysis should comprise the following five steps:

Step 1: **Comparison of the phonemic systems of the two languages.**

Step 2: **Comparison of the (distinctive as well as the redundant) features of sounds.**

Step 3: **Comparison of the distribution of sounds.**

Step 4: **Comparison of the combination of sounds.**

Step 5: **Comparison of the relative frequency of sounds in the two languages.**

2.1 Comparison of the phonemic systems of English and German

consonants

British English (RP)	German
/p, b, t, d, k, g, tʃ, dʒ/	/p, b, t, d, k, g, (pf, ts)/
/f, v, θ, ð, s, z, ʃ, ʒ, h/	/f, v, s, z, ʃ, ʒ, x ([ç], [x], [x]), h/
/m, n, ŋ/	/m, n, ŋ/
/r, l/	/r, l/
/j, w/	/j/

vowels: monophthongs and diphthongs

British English (RP)	German
/iː, ɪ, e, æ/	/iː, ɪ, yː, ʏ, eː, ɛː, ɛ, øː, œ/
/ə, ɜː, ʌ/	/ə, a/
/ɑː, ɒ, ɔː, ʊ, uː/	/aː, ɔ, oː, ʊ, uː/
/eɪ, əʊ, aɪ, aʊ, ɔɪ/	/aɪ, aʊ, ɔɪ/
/ɪə, eə, ʊə/	Ø

Q1 Identify differences between German and English and state what insights one can gain from a comparison of the two phonemic systems.

2.2 Comparison of the features of sounds

From a comparison of the German and English phonemic systems, one can draw the conclusion that there are quite a lot of identical phonemes in both languages such as /v/, /p/, /r/, /uː/, /e/ and /aʊ/. This means that the phonemic systems are partially similar, but it does not necessarily follow that the various realizations of one and the same phoneme are identical. The realizations of English and German /r/, for example, are completely different. English /r/ is realized initially as a consonant with the features voice, post-alveolar, frictionless and continuant, whereas initial German /r/ is often realized as a voiced uvular fricative. English /v/ is usually a labiodental voiced fricative, whereas German /v/ is a labiodental frictionless continuant. English /v/ may be realized in medial intervocalic position as a labiodental frictionless continuant as in *avid* and *moving*. The realizations of German and English /p/ are basically identical, but there is some difference in the degree of aspiration.

Q2 Compare the features of English and German /l/, /s/, /p/, /uː/ and /aʊ/.

2.3 Distribution of English sounds compared to German sounds

consonants and semivowels

British English (RP)			German		
initial	**medial**	**final**	**initial**	**medial**	**final**
/p/ pin	hopping	tap	Panne	Oper	knapp
/b/ bin	mobbing	tab	Boot	Ober	Ø
/t/ tin	letter	cat	Ton	Bote	rot
/d/ din	meadow	mad	Dach	Ader	Ø
/k/ kin	vicar	back	Kinn	Acker	Lack
/g/ gone	eager	bag	Gans	mager	Ø
/tʃ/ chin	matches	batch	(Tschechin)	rutschen	Matsch
/dʒ/ gin	bridges	badge	...		
/f/ fin	offer	half			
/v/ vine	saver	have			
/θ/ thorn	ether	lath			
/ð/ they	either	smooth			
/s/ seal	racing	bus			
/z/ zeal	raising	buzz			
/ʃ/ shelf	rasher	bush			
/ʒ/ (genre)	illusion	rouge			
/m/ mince	hammer	swim			
/n/ nail	sinner	tan			
/ŋ/ Ø	singer	song			
/h/ hot	ahead	Ø			
/r/ rot	around	Ø			
/l/ lot	alone	till			
/j/ yacht	beyond	Ø			
/w/ wine	away	Ø			

Q3 Complete the above list.

vowels: monophthongs and diphthongs

British English (RP)			German		
initial	medial	final	initial	medial	final
/iː/ eel	peeling	fee	ihn	Sieb	die
/ɪ/ ill	mill	[i] happy	in	Sitz	Ø
/e/ elk	letter	Ø	/ɛ/ essen	Bett	Ø
/æ/ add	shadow	Ø			
/ɑː/ art	father	car	Aal	Vater	da
/ɒ/ odd	rotten	Ø	/ɔ/ offen	Sonne	Ø
/ɔː/ ought	border	saw	/oː/ Ofen	Sohn	so
/ʊ/ Ø	bush	Ø	unten	Trunk	Ø
/uː/ ooze	food	shoe	U̲hu	Ruhm	Kuh
/ʌ/ other	mother	Ø	/a/ alle	kann	Ø
/ɜː/ earn	turn	fir			
/ə/ ago	melo̲n	reader	Ø	haben	Rose
/eɪ/ eight	racing	bay			
/aɪ/ ice	lighter	fry	Eimer	nein	Blei
/ɔɪ/ oyster	boiler	boy	Eule	neun	neu
/əʊ/ old	tone	low			
/aʊ/ out	pout	cow	aus	bauen	blau
/ɪə/ ear	fearful	beer			
/eə/ air	faring	share			
/ʊə/ Ø	assurance	sure			

Q4 Complete the German examples.

2.4 Some typical combinations of sounds

1. Initial consonant clusters: /br/, /dw/, /kw/, /sm/, /sn/, /sp/, /spr/, /skw/, /st/, /str/, /sw/, /θr/, /θw/, /tr/, /tw/.

2. Medial consonant clusters: /mbl/, /ŋg/, /ŋgr/, /ŋkʃ/, /ŋst/, /ndl/, /nθ/, /ŋz/.

3. Final consonant clusters: /bd/, /bz/, /dz/, /dθ/ or /tθ/, /dθs/ or /tθs/, /fθ/, /fθs/, /gz/, /ksθ/, /ksθs/, /ldʒd/, /lfθ/, /lfθs/, /ðd/, /ðz/, /ðmz/, /ts/, /tθs/, /ndz/, /nθ/, /nθs/.

Typical examples are
- *brown, dwell, queen, small, snow, sport, spring, squire, steal, stroll, swallow, three, thwart, tree, tweed.*
- *mumbling, hunger, hungry, anxious, youngster, handling, anthem, anxiety.*
- *stabbed, rubs, heads, width, widths, fifth, fifths, gags, sixth, sixths, bulged, twelfth, twelfths, breathed, clothes, rhythms, hats, eighths, hands, month, months.*

Q5 Which combinations of English sounds are difficult for German learners? Which are the most difficult? Give reasons.

2.5 Relative frequency of English and German sounds in percentages

British English (RP) vowels and consonants		German vowels and consonants	
1. /ə/ = 10.7	23. /əʊ/ = 1.5	1. /n/ = 9.1	23. /z/ = 1.6
2. /ɪ/ = 8.3	24. /h/ = 1.5	2. /t/ = 8.9	24. /ɔ/ = 1.5
3. /n/ = 7.6	25. /æ/ = 1.5	3. /ə/ = 8.2	25. /h/ = 1.3
4. /t/ = 6.4	26. /ɒ/ = 1.4	4. /r/ = 7.4	26. /p/ = 1.1
5. /d/ = 5.1	27. /ɔː/ = 1.2	5. /a/ = 7.0	27. /oː/ = 1.0
6. /s/ = 4.8	28. /ŋ/ = 1.2	6. /ɪ/ = 6.4	28. /uː/ = 0.9
7. /l/ = 3.7	29. /uː/ = 1.1	7. /s/ = 5.2	29. /ŋ/ = 0.8
8. /ð/ = 3.6	30. /g/ = 1.1	8. /d/ = 5.0	30. /ɣ/ = 0.7
9. /r/ = 3.5	31. /ʃ/ = 1.0	9. /l/ = 3.6	31. /yː/ = 0.5
10. /m/ = 3.2	32. /j/ = 0.9	10. /ɛ/ = 3.5	32. /j/ = 0.5
11. /k/ = 3.1	33. /ʊ/ = 0.9	11. /ʊ/ = 3.0	33. /ɛː/ = 0.3
12. /e/ = 3.0	34. /ɑː/ = 0.8	12. /f/ = 2.9	34. /øː/ = 0.2
13. /w/ = 2.8	35. /aʊ/ = 0.6	13. /iː/ = 2.4	35. /œ/ = 0.1
14. /z/ = 2.5	36. /dʒ/ = 0.6	14. /m/ = 2.3	
15. /v/ = 2.0	37. /ɜː/ = 0.5	15. /x/ = 2.1	
16. /b/ = 2.0	38. /tʃ/ = 0.4	16. /aː/ = 2.0	
17. /aɪ/ = 1.8	39. /θ/ = 0.4	17. /eː/ = 2.0	
18. /f/ = 1.8	40. /eə/ = 0.3	18. /b/ = 1.9	
19. /p/ = 1.8	41. /ɪə/ = 0.2	19. /k/ = 1.8	
20. /ʌ/ = 1.8	42. /ɔɪ/ = 0.1	20. /g/ = 1.7	
21. /eɪ/ = 1.7	43. /ʒ/ = 0.1	21. /ʃ/ = 1.6	
22. /iː/ = 1.7	44. /ʊə/ = 0.06	22. /v/ = 1.6	

(cf. Gimson 1962/94:136, 196 and Meinhold/Stock 1980/82: 99, 145)

Note: The German diphthongs, which make up 3.9% of all sounds, are counted as separate vowels in the above statistics.

3. Relative functional load of some consonant contrasts in English

The functional load refers to the relative importance of linguistic contrasts in a language. Not all the distinctions or contrasts within the structure of a language are of the same importance. In phonology, for example, some phonemes have a high functional load, because of the relatively high number of possible contrasts. For instance, in initial position a multitude of words can be distinguished by the contrasts between /k/ and /h/ as in *kit - hit, cot - hot* and *cat - hat*, whereas in final position no words can be contrasted, since /h/ cannot occur finally in English.

consonants	initial	final	vowels	any position
/k/ - /h/	100	Ø	/ɪ/-/æ/ *bit-bat*	100
/p/ - /b/	98	14	/iː/-/ɪ/ *beet-bit*	95
/m/ - /n/	59	42	/ɪ/-/e/ *bit-bet*	54
/k/ - /g/	50	29	/e/-/ɒ/ *pet-pot*	45
/d/ - /z/	7	100	/ʊ/-/ʌ/ *put-putt*	9
/θ/ - /ð/	1	6	/ʊ/-/uː/ *pull-pool*	7
/n/ - /ŋ/	Ø	18	/æ/-/ɑː/ *cam-calm*	4.5

(Catford 1987: 89-90)

Q6 What is the value of frequency counts and functional load for the teaching of sounds?

4. A hierarchy of difficulties based on contrastive analysis
Using a comparison of English and Spanish sounds, Stockwell and Bowen have established a hierarchy of difficulties on the basis of contrastive analysis. Their main assumption is that learners will have most difficulty with those items which do not exist in their native language (zero items) and which require them to learn two or more totally new allophones in the target language. English learners have to acquire [x], [x] and [ç] in German for example. Phonemes, which do not exist in the learners' native language, also prove to be difficult. Germans, for instance, have to learn /θ/ and /ð/ in English. Least difficult are intrinsic allophones, which are identical in the native tongue and the target language. Thus Germans will have no difficulty in learning aspirated [pʰ] in stressed initial position.

In the following table of Stockwell and Bowen's hierarchy of difficulties, the following abbreviations are used. 'R' stands for 'rule', 'G'
for 'grammar', 'G1' for 'native tongue' and 'G2' for 'target language',
'Op' for 'optional choice' for a possible selection among phonemes
to be learned, 'Ob' for 'obligatory choice' for a possible selection of
conditioned allophones to be learned and zero choice (Ø) for the existence of a certain sound in one language which has no counterpart in
the learners' mother tongue. Stockwell/Bowen's hierarchy of difficulties is as follows:

Degree of Difficulty		R (G1)	R (G2)
I	1	Ø	Ob
(maximal)	2	Ø	Op
	3	Op	Ob
II	4	Ob	Op
	5	Ob	Ø
	6	Op	Ø
III	7	Op	Op
(minimal)	8	Ob	Ob

Q7 Study the hierarchy in more detail and comment on its value.

5. Error Analysis

Error analysis examines actual mistakes made by students. The steps
in error analysis are as follows:

Step 1: **Identification of mistakes**
Step 2: **Description and classification of mistakes**
Step 3: **Evaluation of mistakes**
Step 4: **Elimination of mistakes**

5.1 Identification of mistakes
The identification of mistakes is one of the most difficult tasks faced
by foreign language teachers. As non-natives, teachers are usually not
fully competent in the target language and have difficulty in identifying lexical, grammatical and stylistic mistakes. Furthermore, those
changes in the language collectively described under the heading of

modern English usage complicate the correction of mistakes in the foreign language.

As far as pronunciation is concerned, students and teachers are confronted with two problems. First, they have to know how a word is pronounced in isolation and in context. Second, students and teachers must be able to perceive sounds correctly, ie to hear the sounds properly. Some students and teachers have a natural talent for making delicate discriminations of sound and are consequently in a position to pass sound judgments on mispronunciations. Students and teachers who are less talented are often not able to recognize differences in pronunciation and consequently misjudge mispronunciations and even correct pronunciations. It seems advisable that a course in phonetics should include several ear training sessions.

The difficulty in identifying mispronunciations is increased by the fact that sounds are not necessarily correct or incorrect, but can be graded on a scale. As far as English consonants and vowels in isolation and connected speech are concerned, they are not produced in one fixed place in the mouth, but within a certain variable area in the mouth. This can be seen in vowel diagrams, where circles are used to illustrate the areas of production. Sounds produced near or at the border of these areas can easily be misinterpreted and identified as incorrect.

5.2 Description and classification of mistakes

Mistakes in pronunciation can be described and classified in several ways. Broadly speaking, one can analyse mistakes from the point of view of the target language system and can distinguish between phonemic and phonetic mistakes as in */zen/ for *then* or */bRɪm/ for *brim*. One can also analyze mistakes from the point of view of the two languages involved and can distinguish between interlingual and intralingual mistakes as in */bɛk/ for *back* and */wæn/ for *van*. In a more specific analysis of mistakes, one can take the mother tongue and target language features as a basis and describe and classify mistakes in terms of incorrect features as in */ret/ for *red*, where the final consonant has the incorrect features 'fortis' and 'voiceless' instead of 'lenis' and 'devoiced'.

5.3 Evaluation of mistakes

The evaluation of mistakes in pronunciation is a linguistic as well as a pedagogical problem. The criteria for the evaluation often vary and are applied differently, so that different solutions are offered (cf. chapter 10).

5.4 Elimination of mistakes

The elimination of mistakes in pronunciation is a linguistic as well as a pedagogical problem. There are certain well-established and well-tried methods, which help students to overcome (some of) their problems (cf. chapter 10).

Q8 List your own psychomotoric phonetic problems in order of difficulty and analyze them.
- very difficult:
- difficult:
- quite difficult:
- neutral:
- quite easy:
- easy:
- very easy:

Q9 What is the contribution of error analysis to the teaching of sounds? Has error analysis contributed to a modification of hierarchies of difficulties? Should a student's perception of difficulty be taken into consideration when establishing a hierarchy of difficulties?

6. Typical mistakes in pronunciation

1. *[dʒestədeɪ]	14. *[bɛk] for *back*	27. *[plʌmbə] for *plumber*
2. *[bʌʃ]	15. *[sauθ θaɪd]	28. *[tʃəufə] for *chauffeur*
3. *[sɪn] for *thin*	16. *[rɪŋk] for *ring*	29. *[weri wel]
4. *[kləuðəz]	17. *[wuːl] for *wool*	30. *[hɒnə] for *honour*
5. *[fɪŋə]	18. *[ɒnjən]	31. *[mɪn] for *men*
6. *[smuːθ]	19. *[kraɪzɪz] for *crisis*	32. *[riːkəmend]
7. *[piːs] for *peas*	20. *[kwiːn ɒv ɪŋlənd]	33. *[kvɪə]
8. *[jʌŋə]	21. *[vɒt] for *what*	34. *[kɒnfɜːm]
9. *[daɪʔænə]	22. *[hændkətʃiːf]	35. *[ækʰtʃən]
10. *[æni] for *any*	23. *[laɪf] for *live* (adj.)	36. *[priːfeɪs]
11. *[tʃɜːni] for *journey*	24. *[pɒl] for *poll*	37. *[lʌndn]
12. *[letə frɒm dʒɒn]	25. *[mɔː ðæn ten]	38. *[æt həum]
13. *[weə] for *were*	26. *[aɪərən] for *iron*	39. *[wɒks] for *wax*

Q10 Explain the mispronunciations listed above.

Key to some questions

Q6 The relative frequency of sounds in a language determines the general setting of the articulatory organs. The general peculiarities of all the utterances in a language that characterize speech movements as a whole make up the **basis of articulation**. In some languages, the lips may remain largely passive, in others the whole level of the tongue may be quite high and yet in others it may be low. In French, the tongue is more tense and the movements are quicker than in English. Furthermore, the lips are quite active in French. One can conclude that French is usually spoken from a high and tense forward basis of articulation. English is spoken from a relatively low and relaxed basis of articulation, which can be explained, for example, by the relatively high frequency of /ə/ and /ɪ/, which make up 19% of the relative frequency of sounds, and by the existence of final lenis consonants. German tends to be between English and French as far as the basis of articulation is concerned.

From a language learning point of view, the relative frequency counts give the learners a clear indication of the general articulatory basis of the language to be learned and how to modify their own articulatory behaviour. The second point concerns the **relative functional load**, which refers to the quantification of the importance of linguistic contrasts in a language. The highest functional load is represented by 100 and the remainder are represented as percentages of this maximum. The relatively high functional load of the contrast between /p/ and /b/ means that a lot of English words are distinguished by this contrast and that consequently learners should be able to make this distinction. The contrast between /θ/ and /ð/ or /ʃ/ and /ʒ/ in initial position has a relatively low functional load and is thus less important than the contrast between /p/ and /b/. From a teaching point of view, the relative functional load should be taken into account because of its importance in communication. With the help of the quantification of contrasts, teachers can set clear priorities in their teaching of phonetics.

Suggested readings

Bialystok, E. (1990) *Communication Strategies*. Oxford: Basil Blackwell

Catford, J.C. (1987) "Phonetics and the teaching of pronunciation: a systematic description of English phonology", 87-100, in: Morley, J., ed. *Current Perspectives on Pronunciation: Practices Anchored Theory*. Washington, D.C.: TESOL

Corder, P. (1973/89) *Introducing Applied Linguistics*. Harmondsworth: Penguin

Delattre, P. (1965) *Comparing the Phonetic Features of English, German, Spanish and French*. Heidelberg: Julius Groos

Fisiak, J., ed. (1981/85) *Contrastive Linguistics and the Language Teacher*. Oxford: Pergamon

Heffner, R.-M. S. (1950/75) *General Phonetics*. Madison: The University of Wisconsin Press

James, C. (1980) *Contrastive Analysis*. London: Longman

Kasper, G./C. Færch (1983) *Strategies in Interlanguage Communication*. London: Longman

Kohler, K. (1977/97) *Einführung in die Phonetik des Deutschen*. Berlin: Erich Schmidt

Larsen-Freeman, D./M.H. Long (1991/92) *An Introduction to Second Language Acquisition Research*. London: Longman

Meinhold, G./E. Stock (1980/82) *Phonologie der deutschen Gegenwartssprache*. Leipzig: Bibliographisches Institut

Richards, J.C., ed. (1974) *Error Analysis*. London: Longman

Schumann, J.H./N. Stenson (1974/78) *New Frontiers in Second Language Learning*. Rowley, Mass.: Newbury House

Selinker, L. (1992) *Rediscovering Interlanguage*. London: Longman

Stockwell, R.P./J.D. Bowen (1965) *The Sounds of English and German*. Chicago: The University of Chicago Press

Note on pronunciation

apparatus /ˌæpəˈreɪtəs/, pedagogical /ˌpedəˈgɒdʒɪkəl/, version /ˈvɜːʃən/, angle /ˈæŋgəl/, transfer /trænsˈfɜː/, interference /ˌɪntəˈfɪərəns/, inappropriate /ˌɪnəˈprəʊpriət/, media /ˈmiːdiə/, eliminate /ɪˈlɪmɪneɪt/, to complement /ˈkɒmplɪment/, elimination /ˌɪlɪmɪˈneɪʃən/, confront /kənˈfrʌnt/, advisable /ədˈvaɪzəbəl/, criteria /kraɪˈtɪəriə/, priority /praɪˈɒrəti/.

10. LEARNING, TEACHING AND TESTING PRONUNCIATION

10.1 OBJECTIVES

1. General Objectives

The general aim in teaching pronunciation is the internalized, instantaneous and correct identification as well as the internalized, fluent and correct production of English sounds. Correct production of sounds means that advanced learners and future teachers of English will acquire a subphonemic or phonetic accuracy in the target language, which may be defined as near-nativeness. The model can be any standard national variety, where English is used as a mother tongue. It can be AmE, BrE, Australian English, New Zealand English, SAfrE, Irish English or Canadian English. It goes without saying that the type of pronunciation taught should be that with the highest social prestige in the country concerned, since an acrolect usually combines its prestige with a high degree of national and international intelligibility. As far as registers are concerned, a colloquial and possibly a formal style of pronunciation should be acquired. From a receptive point of view, advanced learners and future teachers of English should be able to understand all registers from very intimate to very formal style and the most important national and some (socio-)regional varieties of English.

Two basic sets of skills are involved in the process of learning a foreign pronunciation, **psychomotoric skills** and **cognitive skills**, which are organized in a hierarchical manner. Before one can attempt to pronounce an English word, one has to *know* how it is pronounced (**cognitive domain**: knowledge → understanding → application → analysis → synthesis → evaluation). Once one knows how to pronounce a word such as *indict, horizon* or *prosaic*, one has to try to *articulate* it properly (**psychomotoric domain**: perception → imitation or conscious production → internalized or automatic production → interpretation → creation. Interpretation and creation may be implemented by students who have achieved a native-like accent). Furthermore, the **affective**

domain (receiving → responding → valuing → organization of value system → characterization) also plays an important part in the acquisition of a foreign pronunciation. Whereas children and younger students usually enjoy imitating foreign sounds, one should not underestimate the **psychological** difficulty experienced by many adult speakers, who often have great problems imitating unfamiliar sounds. Adult learners' difficulties may be determined by biological factors, personality factors and sociocultural factors . The 'critical period hypothesis' holds that the vast majority of adult learners, in contrast to children, cannot achieve a native-like pronunciation in a foreign language. It might be more fitting to claim that, depending on their character, adults may actively enjoy or dislike imitating foreign sounds, or they may simply have a neutral attitude. Similarly, adults will enjoy playing a different role, be indifferent or feel uncomfortable adopting a different role. The more strongly they identify with members of a second language culture, the more successful they can be in mastering the foreign pronunciation. On the other hand, learners might prefer to preserve their own identity which would involve retaining their foreign pronunciation. As foreign learners normally do not achieve full competence in the target language, their whole personality is in any case reduced to a certain extent. Thus some foreign learners may be reluctant to relinquish their foreign accent, which to them is a sign of their identity.

In teaching a new sound system, various exercises combined with accurate phonetic and phonological descriptions and explanations, audio and audiovisual aids, and the insights gained from contrastive analysis, error analysis and interlanguage studies can all help to overcome some of the difficulties learners have with the production of foreign sounds. Obviously the teacher's skills and experience also play a decisive role.

2. Detailed taxonomy of pronunciation skills

A very detailed taxonomy of the skills to be learned in pronunciation is suggested by Munby (1978/81) and is reproduced here with slight alterations.
1. Discriminating sounds in isolate word forms
1.1 phonemes, especially phonemic contrasts
1.2 phoneme sequences
1.3 allophonic variants

1.4 assimilated and elided forms (esp. reduction of vowels and consonant clusters)

1.5 permissible phonemic variation

2. Articulating sounds in isolate word forms
2.1 phonemes, especially phonemic contrasts
2.2 phoneme sequences
2.3 allophonic variants
2.4 assimilated and elided forms (esp. reduction of vowels and consonant clusters)
2.5 permissible phonemic variation

3. Discriminating sounds in connected speech
3.1 strong and weak forms
3.2 neutralization of weak forms
3.3 reduction of unstressed vowels
3.4 modification of sounds, esp. at word boundaries, through
    - assimilation
    - elision
    - liaison
3.5 phonemic changes at word boundaries
3.6 allophonic variation at word boundaries

4. Articulating sounds in connected speech
4.1 strong and weak forms
4.2 neutralization of weak forms
4.3 reduction of unstressed vowels
4.4 modification of sounds, esp. at word boundaries, through
    - assimilation
    - elision
      liaison
4.5 phonemic changes at word boundaries
4.6 allophonic variation at word boundaries

5. Discriminating stress patterns within words
5.1 characteristic accentual patterns
5.2 meaningful accentual patterns
5.3 complex words

6. Articulating stress patterns within words
6.1 characteristic accentual patterns
6.2 meaningful accentual patterns
6.3 complex words

7. Recognizing the use of stress in connected speech
7.1 for indicating information units
   - content words and form words
   - rhythmic patterning
7.2 for emphasis, through location of nuclear accent
7.3 for contrast and comparison, through location of nuclear stress or nuclear shift
7.4 for feelings, through location of nuclear stress or shift

8. Manipulating the use of stress in connected speech
8.1 for indicating information units
   - content words and form words
   - rhythmic patterning
8.2 for emphasis, through location of nuclear accent
8.3 for contrast and comparison, through location of nuclear stress or nuclear shift
8.4 for feelings, through location of nuclear stress or shift

9. Recognizing variation in stress in connected speech
9.1 variation of word accentual patterns for rhythmic considerations
9.2 variation of word accentual patterns in stressed and unstressed words for meaningful prominence
9.3 variation of word accentual patterns distinguishing between the two types of complex words

10. Manipulating variation in stress in connected speech
10.1 variation of word accentual patterns for rhythmic considerations
10.2 variation of word accentual patterns in stressed and unstressed words for meaningful prominence
10.3 variation of word accentual patterns distinguishing between the two types of complex words

11. Recognizing and understanding intonation patterns: neutral position of nucleus and use of tone, in respect of
11.1 falling tone with declarative clauses
11.2 falling tone with interrogative clauses beginning with a question-word
11.3 falling tone with imperative clauses
11.4 rising tone with 'yes/no' interrogative clauses
11.5 rising tone with non-final clauses
11.6 fall-rise tone with any clause type
11.7 rise-fall with any clause type
11.8 level tone with any clause type

11.9 multi-nuclear patterns
11.10 tones with question tags

12.   Producing intonation patterns: neutral position of nucleus and use of tone, in respect of
12.1 falling tone with declarative clauses
12.2 falling tone with interrogative clauses beginning with a question-word
12.3 falling tone with imperative clauses
12.4 rising tone with 'yes/no' interrogative clauses
12.5 rising tone with non-final clauses
12.6 fall-rise tone with any clause type
12.7 rise-fall with any clause type
12.8 level tone with any clause type
12.9 multi-nuclear patterns
12.10 tones with question tags

13.   Recognizing and understanding intonation patterns: interpreting attitudinal meaning through variation of tone or nuclear shift, viz.
13.1 rising tone with declarative clauses
13.2 rising tone with interrogative clauses beginning with a question-word, having the nucleus in either end position or front position
13.3 falling tone with interrogative clauses beginning with a question-word, but with a shift to front position
13.4 rising tone with imperative clauses
13.5 falling tone with 'yes/no' interrogative clauses
13.6 rising tone with 'yes/no' interrogative, but nuclear shift to front position
13.7 level tone with declarative clauses, non-final clauses and enumerations

14.   Producing intonation patterns: expressing attitudinal meaning through variation of tone or nuclear shift, viz.
14.1 rising tone with declarative clauses
14.2 rising tone with interrogative clauses beginning with a question-word, having the nucleus in either end position or front position
14.3 falling tone with interrogative clauses beginning with a question-word, but with a shift to front position
14.4 rising tone with imperative clauses
14.5 falling tone with 'yes/no' interrogative clauses

10.2 METHODOLOGY

1. Introduction

As with any teaching, the teaching of foreign sounds is done in stages, which are as follows: a **presentation phase**, a **practice phase** and a **production phase**. A further teaching principle to be applied concerns the isolation of difficulties and their practice in steps of increasing complexity, which is known as the **bottom-up approach**. In phonetics, one should begin with the perception of sounds, then concentrate on the conscious imitation of sounds and finish with the automatic production of sounds. These stages should start with an isolated sound, then with the new sound in one word, in various words, in a phrase, in a sentence and finally in a text. Teachers can modify the tempo of their speech and even freeze individual sounds where necessary.

Teaching is obviously supported by **verbal explanations** and **audio materials** as well as **audiovisual materials**. The verbal explanations can include a detailed phonological and phonetic description with special emphasis on the relevant new feature(s) of sounds and practical hints on how to articulate the new sound. Audio materials are usually tapes and cassettes with recordings of native speakers. Visual aids can include pictures, charts, drawings, tables, phonetic and phonemic symbols, photos and specific diagrams of the speech organs. Audiovisual materials, which come closest to representing natural speech situations with their combination of sound and vision, can also be used. Sophisticated computer assisted language learning (CALL) programmes combine sound and vision and allow interactive learning to take place. In the case of phonetics, an automatic comparison of the native speakers' model pronunciation with the learners' pronunciation is now possible with the help of a specialized programme. In this respect, the new computer technology with its learning programmes is superior to the language laboratory. Two main things have been criticized as far as language laboratory work is concerned, ie the lack of a concomitant visual display and the fact that students very often reinforce their own mistakes, because in the practice and production stage, only one student's pronunciation can be checked by the teacher at any one time. An automatic, simultaneous assessment of the pronunciation of every student has not yet been possible in the language laboratory. Supervised exercises and drills with immediate or automatic corrections and certain well-tried, effective techniques can help students from the outset to learn the new sound system properly.

Any well-founded phonetic teaching programme starts with **ear training**, because in order to produce a new sound, one first has to hear the sound properly. To this purpose, minimal pairs or triplets can be used to improve students' discrimination of sounds, eg *thin-fin* or *thin-fin-thin* the sequence of which can be altered. Students have to identify the new sound or the known sound. One can also contrast native with non-native sounds like *back-back-Beck* or *when-wenn-when* for example. Regrettably, in many foreign language courses not enough time is devoted to ear training, although ear training is vital to the acquisition of foreign sounds. It is unfortunately the case that inadequate phonetic teaching very quickly leads to **fossilized mistakes**, ie incorrect linguistic features in the learners' speech which become permanent. Furthermore, it can be noted that fossilized mistakes in grammar and lexis can be corrected even in later stages of learning, whereas fossilized mistakes in pronunciation can only rarely be eradicated. While the individual teacher plays a decisive role in the initial stages of pronunciation, it is the individual student who has to minimize dependence and maximize self-reliance in later stages especially outside the formal teaching situation. In this respect, ear training is of paramount importance, since it helps learners in their development of self-correcting and self-monitoring abilities.

Whereas the bottom-up approach begins with the articulation of individual vowels and consonants and proceeds towards intonation, it is also feasible to have a **top-down approach**, where one begins with patterns of intonation and then looks at separate sounds. Although the top-down approach seems more attractive, because it emphasizes the communicative aspect in language learning and teaching, it has not proved very successful: too many problems arise at any one time. The number of bundled difficulties with which students are confronted makes the teaching and learning of a combination of segmentals and suprasegmentals nearly impossible. As far as suprasegmentals and especially intonation are concerned, the following sequence in teaching can be recommended:
- (segmentals: vowels and consonants)
- word stress
- weak forms
- sentence stress
- assimilation, elision and linking
- neutral intonation patterns
- attitudinal intonation patterns.

Detailed descriptions of and suggestions for teaching segmentals and suprasegmentals can be found in specialised books on teaching pronunciation (cf. suggested readings).

2. Phases

The following procedural method can serve as one example of how to teach a new sound like /θ/. It should be noted that any activities can be repeated in any phase if necessary and that a certain degree of overlap is normal and often useful.

Presentation phase
1. Introduction of a new sound. Production of a new sound by the teacher.

- teacher pronounces the new sound in isolation.
- teacher pronounces the new sound in a word which otherwise contains familiar sounds only.
- teacher pronounces the new sound in various words where the new sound occurs in different positions. Except for the new sound, all the words contain familiar sounds only.
- teacher repeats his/her presentation.
2. Teacher supports his/her presentation by verbal explanations and visual aids.
3. Teacher uses audio materials and audio-visual materials.
4. Teacher repeats the new sound in minimal pairs or triplets such as *thin-fin, thin-fin-thin.*
5. Students listen to the presentation and try to identify the new sound in isolation, in a word, in several words where the new sound occurs in different positions and in minimal pairs or triplets.
6. Teacher pronounces the new sound in a phrase, a short sentence and a long sentence.
7. Students listen to the presentation and try to identify the new sound in a phrase, a short sentence and a long sentence.

Practice phase
1. Students mimic the new sound in isolation.
2. Students mimic the new sound in a word.
3. Teacher supports the students' efforts by
- repeating the new sound in isolation and in a word.
- giving concrete advice to the students on how to modify incorrect or slightly incorrect articulation.
- by repeating students' incorrect articulation and contrasting an incorrect sound with the correct one using minimal pairs or triplets such as */sɪn/-/θɪn/ or /θɪn/-*/sɪn/- /θin/ and */sɪn/-/θin/-*/sɪn/.
4. Students contrast the new sound with a similar sound in the target language, ie *thin-sin-thin* or *fin-thin-thin.*
5. Teacher pronounces the new sound in a phrase and a short sentence.
6. Students mimic the new sound in a phrase and a short sentence.
7. Teacher pronounces the new sound in a long sentence and in a short text.
8. Students read the long sentence and short text with the new sound.
9. Students learn the long sentence and short text by heart and pronounce them.

Production phase
1. Students read a longer text with the new sound.
2. Students produce the new sound in a one-word-sentence in response to cues.
3. Students produce the new sound in a phrase in response to cues.
4. Students produce the new sound in a sentence, in several sentences and in texts in response to cues.
5. Students produce the new sound in a word, in a phrase, in a sentence, in several sentences and in texts automatically.

3. Increasing the articulatory difficulties in the production of a new sound

As far as the difficulty in the correct use of a newly learned sound is concerned, the length of an utterance and the different environments play an important role. The increase in difficulty of /θ/ in isolation, in a word, a phrase and in sentences with different sound environments, especially /s/ and /z/ and other /θ/ and /ð/ sounds, can be illustrated in the following exercise.

Elementary stage
- /θ/.
- *Thin.*
- *A thin book.*

Intermediate stage
- *I have bought a thin book.*
- *I have bought two thin books.*
- *Susan bought two thin books.*

Advanced stage
- *I bought three thin books.*
- *Susan has bought three thin books.*
- *Elizabeth has sold six thin sensational books and seven thick sensational books.*

Q1 Can the language laboratory help the learner to pronounce the foreign language more accurately?

Q2 How would one teach English /θ/, /ð/, /r/, /w/, /l/, /æ/, final lenis consonants, rhythm, and intonation?

10.3 TESTING AND EVALUATING PRONUNCIATION

1. Pronunciation tests

A student's pronunciation is obviously tested orally. Paper-and-pencil tests can be used for listening tasks and for cognitive difficulties in pronunciation, but the psychomotoric aspect of pronunciation can only be tested orally. Students can either read words, phrases, sentences or texts or use free speech. Free speech can consist of prepared or unprepared items such as a one-word-sentence, a phrase, a sentence, several sentences, a short text or a long text.

Since the spoken word is not permanent, students' pronunciations should always be taped to make the assessment more objective. The tests can be arranged in an interpersonal interview situation or in the language laboratory, where the tasks can be given in a written or an oral form. The advantage of a reading test lies in the fact that all students have the same task and are examined under the same conditions. Enabling students to hear the text spoken by a native speaker first means that they will all be at the same level with respect to the cognitive aspect of pronunciation, ie cognitive problems cannot interfere with their psychomotoric performance. Furthermore, in a reading task the student's performance cannot be affected by other linguistic difficulties such as grammar or lexis, or any other cognitive difficulties.

Q3 Can one test a student's pronunciation objectively? Which approach seems most reliable, valid, objective and practical?

2. Evaluation of mistakes in pronunciation

The question of the seriousness of mistakes obviously arises in the assessment of a student's pronunciation. In a first attempt by Dretzke/Martin (1975) to evaluate mistakes in pronunciation objectively, an evaluative chart was developed. A slightly modified version of the chart can be seen below. In the right hand column, typical mistakes in the pronunciation of (mainly northern) German students are listed in order of difficulty as observed over a certain period of time. The most difficult items are listed at the top and the least difficult items at the bottom. On the top horizontal line, a hierarchy of skills is suggested, where the stages of perception, imitation and production are ordered in a sequence of increasing difficulty. The individual mispronunciations are matched to a weighting factor, which is determined by the effect a mispronunciation has on communication as well as on native speakers and by the degree of difficulty of learning. The chart can be changed especially with regard to the weighting factor. Since different interpretations of the weighting factor can lead to subjective marking, an approach is now favoured whereby each individual mistake is weighted equally to avoid any problems of subjectivity. The order of difficulty can also be modified, because students may have different problems depending on variables such as age, gender, class and region for example.

3. Evaluative chart of phonology (model)

Evaluative Chart of Phonology

	1 aware	2 hears word	3 hears sentence	4 sa/s sound	5 says word	6 says phrase	7 says sentence	8 reads	9 conscious control	10 full use	weighting factor	points per item
rhythm											4	
sentence stress											2	
weak forms											4	
statement											1	
question											1	
wh-question											1	
series											1	
or-either											1	
or-one											1	
tag Q-info											1	
tag Q-conf.											1	
tag Q-name											4	
devoicing											2	
θ											2	
ð											2	
w+v											1.5	
æ											1	
r											1	
dark l											2	
word stress											1.5	
c											1.5	
dʒ											1.5	
tʃ											1.5	
s+z											1.5	
ʒ											2	
vowel length											2	
juncture											2	
closing diphth.											0.5	
centring diphth.											0.5	
ɑː											0.5	
ɔ											0.5	
ɒ											0.5	
ɪ											1.0	
ŋ												

total points
percentage

total points = percentage of system mastered
5

4. Native speakers' evaluation of mistakes in pronunciation

The criteria chosen for the evaluation of pronunciation in the above chart were not entirely satisfactory, since no empirical research was carried out to determine the effect of mispronunciations on communication with native speakers. Furthermore, a more thorough study of the criteria applied would be necessary. Basically, the above criteria were based on linguistic, pedagogical and psycholinguistic insights. In an alternative approach, functional-linguistic, sociolinguistic and pragmalinguistic criteria are applied. The traditional approach to the evaluation of mistakes in pronunciation has been dominated by the functional-linguistic approach: from the point of view of a phonological system, phonemes, which distinguish between meanings, are more important and decisive for communication than allophones. In practice, the replacement of /θ/ by /s/ is judged to be a more serious mistake than the replacement of [ɹ] by [r] or [ʁ]. From the sociolinguistic viewpoint, the evaluation is complicated by the fact that pronunciation plays a very important social role in England and that [ʁ] for instance, which occurs in the North East of England ('Northumbrian burr'), has very low social prestige. Consequently, an [ʁ]-pronunciation can be evaluated as a grave mistake. If one applies the pragmalinguistic criterion, which can be understood in terms of the success of one's communicative effort only, an [ʁ]-pronunciation can be seen as a slight mistake. As far as the success of the communicative message is concerned, matters are even further complicated if one takes into account the functional load, textual frequency of functional load, grammatical class of words and the redundancy involved in pronunciation, which some phoneticians estimate to be over fifty per cent. There is no doubt that psycholinguistic and pedagogical considerations are also relevant to the question of evaluation, but it is clear that the application of several criteria can lead to different and even contradictory results, so that ultimately no unambiguous and definitive answers can be given.

In real life situations, a non-native speaker's pronunciation will obviously be evaluated by native speakers. In some research carried out on this issue, native speakers' standards of linguistic acceptability were elicited. In a listening experiment, 225 Northern English students with an average age of 17 were asked to assess 24 texts, in each of which one of twenty-four typical German mispronunciations of English occurred between 12 to 14 times. The texts were read by a female native English speaker, who is bilingual in German and English. Two placebo texts served as control tasks. One of these texts was read in perfect English and another contained no mistakes but was filled with pauses at arbitrarily chosen points. The informants were asked to rate the pronunciation in each text on a seven-point scale under the headings of intelligibility, social prestige and pleasantness. The informants' judgements are summarized in the following table.

Assessment of mistakes in pronunciation	
degree of seriousness	**mistake**
serious mistake	1 [p] instead of [b̥]
	2 [k] instead of [g̥]
	3 [n] instead of [ŋg]
	4 [s] instead of [θ]
	5 (high) rising intonation instead of level or falling intonation
	6 syllable-timed rhythm instead of stress-timed rhythm
	7 [ʁ] instead of [ɹ]
	8 [ʋ] instead of [w]
medium mistake	9 [ŋk] instead of [ŋ]
	10 incorrect word stress instead of correct word stress
	11 [ʃ] instead of [ʒ]
	12 [ɛ] instead of [æ]
	13 [l] instead of [ɫ]
	14 [f] instead of [v̥]
	15 [t] instead of [d̥]
slight mistake	16 [z] instead of [ð]
	17 'saw blade-like intonation' instead of 'wave-like intonation'
	18 [tʃ] instead of [dʒ]
	19 strong forms instead of weak forms
	20 [oː] instead of [əʊ]
	21 [s] instead of [z̥]
	22 [ʔ] + stressed vowel instead of Ø + stressed vowel
	23 [ʋ] instead of [v]

(Dretzke 1985: 203)

Q4 Which of the following criteria are important for the evaluation of a student's pronunciation? Which other criteria could be taken into consideration?
- phonemic accuracy
- phonetic accuracy
- native speakers' impression
- pedagogical considerations
- students' learning difficulties
- effect on communication

5. Priorities in the teaching of English sounds

The assessment of typical mistakes in pronunciation by native speakers can also be used to establish a list of learning priorities. It should be clear that this list can only offer signposts and that other considerations in the teaching of sounds can overrule these recommendations.

Priorities in teaching sounds		
degree of priority		sounds to be learned
high	1	final voiced consonants
	2	medial [ŋg]
	3	[θ] and [ð]
	4	intonation, rhythm, weak forms
	5	[ɹ]
	6	[w]
	7	final [ŋ]
	8	word stress
	9	[ʒ]
	10	[æ]
	11	[ɫ]
	12	[dʒ]
	13	[əʊ]
	14	Ø + stressed vowel
low	15	[v]

(Dretzke 1985: 207)

6. Conclusion

Theoretical as well as applied linguistics, sociolinguistics, psycholinguistics, pragmalinguistics and methodology have all made a contribution to the theoretical and practical issues involved in phonetics and phonology and will continue to do so in the future. The learning and teaching of phonetics and phonology, which are sometimes neglected in schools and universities, deserve more attention, because of the effect a person's pronunciation has on listeners in terms of intelligibility, pleasantness and general ease of communication. Moreover, one's personality can be judged positively or negatively depending on the degree of one's phonetic competence. Although there is a certain degree of tolerance as far as one's pronunciation in a foreign language is concerned, certain stereotyped attitudes should not be underestimated. This is especially true for future foreign language teachers, whose goal should be a near-native pronunciation. It is to be hoped that the above contribution to the discussion of the various issues involved in phonetics and phonology will prove helpful to students and teachers alike.

Suggested readings

Avery, P./S. Ehrlich (1992) *Teaching American English Pronunciation.* Oxford: Oxford University Press

Bloom, B.S./J.Th. Hastings/G.F. Madaus (1971) *Handbook on Formative and Summative Evaluation of Student Learning.* New York: McGraw-Hill

Bowen, T./J. Marks (1996) *The Pronunciation Book.* London: Longman

Brown, G./G. Yule (1983) *Teaching the Spoken Language.* Cambridge: Cambridge University Press

Bygate, M. (1986) *Teaching Oral English.* Oxford: Oxford University Press

Byrne, D. (1986) *Teaching Oral English.* London: Longman

Dalton, C./B. Seidlhofer (1994) *Pronunciation.* Oxford: Oxford University Press

Dretzke, B. (1985) *Fehlerbewertung im Aussprachebereich.* Hamburg: Buske

Dretzke, B. (1987) "Beurteilung von Aussprachefehlern im Englischen", *Die Neueren Sprachen* 86, 507-517

Dretzke, B. (1998) "Zur Vermeidung von Sanktionen: Ausspracheschulung", 268-275, in: Jung, U.O.H., Hg. *Praktische Handreichung für Fremdsprachenlehrer.* Frankfurt/M.: Lang

Dretzke, B./J.N. Martin (1975) "Assessment of a Student's Phonological Command of English. An Evaluative Chart of Phonology", *Die Neueren Sprachen* 74, 326-333

Hancock, M. (1996) *Pronunciation Games*. Cambridge: Cambridge University Press

Haycraft, B. (1971/75) *The Teaching of Pronunciation*. London: Longman

Kenworthy, J. (1987) *Teaching English Pronunciation*. London: Longman

Laroy, C. (1995) *Pronunciation*. Oxford: Oxford University Press

Munby, J. (1978/81) *Communicative Syllabus Design*. Cambridge: Cambridge University Press

Underhill, N. (1987) *Testing Spoken Language*. Cambridge: Cambridge University Press

Note on pronunciation

instantaneous /ɪnstən'teɪniəs/, indict /ɪn'daɪt/, prosaic /prəʊ'zeɪɪk/, audio /'ɔːdiəʊ/, taxonomy /tæk'sɒnəmi/, liaison /li'eɪzən/, viz. /vɪz/ (= usually read out as *namely),* assessment /ə'sesmənt/, technique /tek'niːk/, triplet /'trɪplət/, alter /'ɔːltə/, inadequate /ɪn'ædɪkwət/, eradicate /ɪ'rædɪkeɪt/, paramount /'pærəmaʊnt/, monitoring /'mɒnɪtərɪŋ/, procedural /prəʊ'siːdʒərəl/, empirical /ɪm'pɪrɪkəl/, pragmalinguistic /prægməlɪŋ'gwɪstɪk/, burr /bɜː/, arbitrarily /'ɑːbɪtrərəli/.

Part II:

A COURSE IN TRANSCRIPTION AND PRONUNCIATION EXERCISES

1.0 BASIC STAGE: INDIVIDUAL WORDS

1. Basic words

plant, life, man, get, arm, house, sad, father, bed, lame, ago, bird, there, but, it, better, wish, son, care, bee, here, no, not, beat, law, belief, low, long, all, boy, look, do, oil, push, moon, poor, sure, player, fire, employer, slower, tower.

blind, head, this, friend, go, long, sing, beg, home, youth, Indian, keep, lamp, might, night, paper, red, yes, ship, church, catch, voice, love, rob, water, zeal, these, pleasure, leisure, jam, object, thank, thin, death, smooth.

2. Various words

separate, well, bad, does, car, make, arrange, bullet, age, chair, the, us, was, loose, that, big, Thames, sad, bus, bar, say, general, chalk, this, thick, thing, yes, promise, as, damage, tremble, go, noted, caravan, tar, play, butcher, change, chin, they, them, throw, kiss, easy, preface, says, marry, shut, master, strange, pudding, itch, their, these, through, author, hiss, music, minute, said, wax, hurry, rather, to eliminate, pull, showman, gentleman, postman, chairman, chairwoman, chairperson, just, catcher, then, thus, miss, senate, set, waggon, curry, commander, journal, colonel, graduate, to graduate, put, urgent, journey, method, month, bath, mouth, basis, fantasy, else, cease, his, is, case, decrease, decrees, to lose, oath, north, either, father, other, prophet, moderate, any, dozen, govern, many, path, youth, nothing, although, thousand, more than that, tune, duke, value, failure, issue, casual, huge, actual, human, curry, courage, harm, men, women, hum, cloth, cross, slower, player, Mrs, Ms, Messrs, put, putt, putty.

3. Words containing written <r>

tar, far, dark, verse, stir, corn, short, former, turn, born, care, to tear, beer, dear, near, tour, moor, pure, pear, mere, cure.

4. Words containing written <ng> or <nk> (<nc>, <ndk>, <nqu>, <nx>)

hang, king, sing, tongue, hanging, singing, singer, long, longish, slangy, strongly, longer, youngest, bungalow, language, lingo, singular, angle, Angles, England, English, single, angry, anger, finger, hunger, linger, anxious, drink, sink, think, among, evening, spring, wrong, young, younger, youngest, youngish, conclusion, unkind, handkerchief, inquire, ingredient, unknown, anchor, inquest, ungrateful.

5. Length or no length?

always, basket, chewing, record, coffee, fill, old, all, small, pot, speaker, speed, sport, borrow, spit, John, jaundice, good, blood, book, suit, soot, half, each, rather, mother, itch, magazine, cook, wool, want, look, last, card, car, gone, loop, loot, pool, new, avenue.

6. Words containing written <th>

Anthony, asthma, isthmus, Thomas, thing, thought, then, thin, author, breath, smooth, the, them, their, father, earth, earthen, thus, though, this, northern, southern, worthy, worth, those, there, bath, path, mouth, youth, baths, paths, mouths, youths, month, months, booth, breathe, Thames, thesis, thyme.

7. Words containing written <s> or <ss>

sell, satan, us, this, as, his, crisis, crises, oasis, oases, to use, the use, cease, basin, was, wisdom, house, houses, blossom, the desert, to desert, dessert, scissors, fasten, to dissolve, possess, newspaper, hypothesis, hypotheses.

8. Voiced or voiceless final consonants

tins, hands, tents, belongs, belonged, hymns, developed, drenched, dressed, doubled, dropped, comes, it's, notes, nods, possessed, asked,

I used to, let's, delayed, minutes, kills, clubs, seems, sings, longs, longings, backs, begs, legs, stabbed, heads, clothes, paths, arms, tops, hats, lives, smiths, Jacks, stops, bags, rides, buses, boxes, chooses, wishes, watches, suffixes, sins, since, hens, hence, fence, fens, tense, tens.

9. More difficult words containing written <r>

parents, hero, pirate, tyrant, rural, various, serious, furious, luxurious, severe, sincere, secure, career, aeroplane, liqueur, cashier, we're, they're, infuriating, curiosity, experience, persevere, persevering, invariably, prepare, preparation, reassure, bearable.

10. Various other words

any, Mary, marry, merry, where, really, children, careful, again, to wonder, correspondence, urgent, many, years, very, exhibition, to exhibit, too, two, examine, occasion, great, showman, radio, says, worried, during, extraordinary, at last, at once, at home, honour, hour, heir, to represent, representation, because, manifold, hotel, historical, herbs, suite.

2.0 INTERMEDIATE STAGE: TEXTS, PROPER NAMES AND GEOGRAPHICAL NAMES

2.1 Texts

The following texts can also be used for pronunciation practice. Each text contains one typical problem in pronunciation (cf. chapter 10).

2.1.1 A Lesson in Faith   **Ø +stressed vowel**
A foolish young man once astonished an old clergyman by boasting that he didn't believe in anything he could not see or understand. The clergyman was curious about the young man's attitude and proceeded to question him about it. „Do you believe that there's such a country as Austria?" asked the clergyman. The young man was prepared for such a question and answered calmly: "Yes I do, because though I have never seen it, my friend Diana and other people I know have been there." "Then you refuse to believe in anything that you or others haven't seen?" "Most certainly", said the youth. "Have you ever seen your own brains?" "Of course not." "Do you know anybody who has seen them?" "No." "Do you think you have got any?" The young man didn't reply thinking it was wiser to stop arguing with the clergyman.

2.1.2 One Dark Night   [əʊ]
A man was walking home from the railway station one dark night. As the road was quite lonely, he was hurrying along. Suddenly he noticed that someone was following him at a short distance. The faster he walked, the faster followed the stranger. At last, he came to the church-yard and wishing to know if the stranger was after his life or his purse, he entered. When the stranger followed him in, he had no more doubts about the stranger's intentions. He paused for a moment, took courage, picked up a big stone, and, turning round to the stranger, said: "What do you want? Why are you following me? Keep away from me." "Wait a minute, sir," said the stranger, "I'm going to Mr. Brown's with a parcel and the porter at the station said that if I followed you, I should find the place, as Mr. Brown lives next-door to you."

2.1.3 How Can you Teach a Dog Tricks [v]

One day, a Londoner was driving through the Surrey countryside. The sun was shining and the sky was a vivid blue. He stopped to admire the view and noticed a vast crowd outside some caravans parked near a village. He went closer and saw a man in a red vest entertaining the crowd with his dog's tricks. He went up to the man and asked. "Excuse me. How did you manage to train your dog like that. I would be grateful if you could advise me. I tried very hard with mine, but it was in vain. Your dog must be quite valuable by now." The man in the vest looked up at him and said calmly. "Well, you see, it's this way. You must know more than the dog. Otherwise you can't teach him anything."

2.1.4 The Strange Letters [d̥]

Two brothers convicted of stealing sheep were branded on the forehead with the letters ST for sheep thief.

One brother, unable to bear the shame, tried to bury himself in a foreign land. But people there asked him about the strange letters. He wandered restlessly, and at length, full of bitterness, died and was buried in a forgotten grave.

The other brother said: "I can't run away from the fact that I stole sheep. I will stay here and win back the respect of my neighbours and myself."

As the years passed he built up a reputation for integrity. One day, a stranger saw the old man with the letters on his forehead. He asked a native what they meant. "It happened a while ago." said the villager. "I've forgotten the particulars; but I think the letters are an abbreviation of *Saint*."

2.1.5 How to Choose Geese for a Special Occasion [ʒ]

The manager of a small hotel once had occasion to be very pleased with his staff, so he came to the decision to give them an extra treat. Instead of going on the usual pleasure outing, he arrived at the conclusion that a good meal would give them more pleasure. As they were all fond of poultry he decided on this occasion to choose geese. He went to the poulterer's shop and saw twenty geese exposed for sale. "I want you to pick up the ten toughest of these geese," he said. "That's an unusual request," said the shopkeeper. "That may be, but anything will do for bad workers," said the manager. So in some confusion, the shopkeeper set to work and selected the toughest of the geese. "Thank you," said the manager casually, "on this occasion I am providing for good workers, so I'll take the other ten, please."

2.1.6 Turning the Tables   **intonation**

A noted artist was recently visited by a reporter, who fired at him from a question sheet questions such as these: "Who were your parents? Which of your paintings do you consider your best work? When, where and why did you paint it? Who is your favourite dead master? Who is your favourite living master? What is your income from art? How old are you?"

But at this point the artist seized the interviewer by the arm and began in his turn: "Just a moment, please. What is your name, age, and salary? Is journalism with you a lifework or merely a means to a higher literary end? How do you like your editor? What was the best interview you ever wrote? Have you ever been fired? How does it feel? Where do you live? How much ..." But here the reporter, jerking his arm from the painter's grasp, fled from the studio, and the artist resumed his work.

2.1.7 A Vain Pursuit   **[w]**

In order to occupy his time when imprisoned in the Tower of London, Sir Walter Raleigh started to write a history of the world. Looking out of the window one day, he observed some sort of disturbance in the street. After a short time, a friend came in to see him. The friend had witnessed the event; Raleigh had seen him from the window, and now engaged him in conversation about the occurrence. It turned out that the visitor's impression of what had taken place was completely different from Raleigh's own.

Raleigh immediately proceeded to tear up the manuscript of his world history. "Why on earth are you doing that?" cried his friend. "If our views about this happening, which we've both experienced, are so at odds, how am I in any position to give an account of matters which took place decades and centuries ago?" answered Raleigh resolutely.

2.1.8 The Iron Duke's Bed   **[æ]**

"Last night, madam," said the tourist, "a man informed me that the Duke of Wellington once stayed in this hotel. Is it a fact?" "It is, sir," beamed the landlady "a solemn fact! He slept in the very room you had last night." The guest went away, but wasn't satisfied with her answer. He came back and kept on asking questions. "Was it just the same as it is now?" "Just the very same." "Same bed in it?" "The very identical bed and the story goes that he spent a comfortable night in it," answered the landlady smilingly. "Did the duke really sleep in the same bed?" asked the tourist again. The landlady had nothing more to add and nodded smilingly. "Good gracious!" exclaimed the tourist. "How did he manage that? No wonder they called him the Iron Duke."

2.1.9 The Don and his Letters   [z̦]
Dr. Bull was a professor living in Oxford. One day he said to his butler, "I have to go to London to see a friend of mine. I'll be there for about four weeks. Would you please send me my letters every day." The servant said he would and went off to pack Dr. Bull's bag. Dr. Bull went to London and the days passed but no letters arrived. Finally, after a fortnight, Dr. Bull received a letter from his servant and this is what it said: "Dear Sir, I'm sorry I cannot send all the letters which have arrived for you as you have locked up the letter-box and taken the key with you." So Dr. Bull wrote back: "Dear James, how silly of me. I'm sending you the key of the letter-box in this letter." Needless to say, he still received no letters.

2.1.10 English and American Gentry   [ŋg]
At a dinner party in New York, one of the guests, who was the younger brother of and English nobleman, began to speak rather freely about America and its people as seen from his angle. He said that he did not like America as much as England because they had no gentry. One of the company who had stronger feelings about this than the others and who could no longer stand such insults angrily asked him what he meant by gentry. The young Englishman replied: "Well, you know, gentry are those who never lift a finger themselves, and whose fathers before them never worked either." Then overcoming his anger, the American said: "Oh, we have plenty of those in America; there are plenty of idle fellows here who linger about all over the place, but we do not call them gentry; we just call them tramps."

2.1.11 The Doctor and the Chauffeur   **intonation**
One day a doctor was rung up by a lady who lived in a large villa just outside the town. "Doctor," she said, "I should be so glad if you would come and have a look at our chauffeur. He's ill, and it's most inconvenient, for my husband is going to London tomorrow and can't drive the car himself."
The doctor called at the house, and climbed the stairs to the chauffeur's room. To his surprise he found the patient sitting up in bed, smoking a pipe and looking as well as could be.
"Well," said the doctor, "what's the matter with you?" "Nothing", said the chauffeur, "but they're not paying me my wages, so I thought

I'd have a rest in bed till they do." "A good idea," said the doctor. "Move up and I'll lie down beside you. They don't pay me either."

2.1.12 Not Eligible   **intonation**

In Boston, there was a very exclusive church which was frequented by very rich, white people only. One day, a coloured gentleman cheerfully walked into the church and asked if he could become a member. The vicar, who was in charge of this exclusive church and who was proud of his achievement, answered rather hesitantly: "Well, you know ... we are all God's children, but I think my people don't like ... Why don't you go home and pray about it to the Almighty." Two days later, the coloured gentleman was back. "Well," said the man, "I have changed my mind, vicar. The Almighty said to me 'The people in this church have cherished their exclusiveness for so long that it is too difficult to change their ideas. You won't have a chance especially since I've been trying to get into it myself for the last fifteen years, and I haven't succeeded yet.'"

2.1.13 A Miser's Promise   [v̥]

A miser was rushed into hospital because he was seriously ill. A doctor examined him and said to him: "You must be very brave. You are a very sick man; you only have another month to live." The miser who was fond of his life replied: "Can't you save my life? Can't you give me the best treatment? If I live another year, I'll leave five thousand pounds to this hospital."

A year later, the doctor met his former patient in the street. "How are you?" he asked. "I'm feeling marvellous doctor," replied the man. "I've been meaning to speak to you," continued the doctor, "have you thought of your donation? You wanted to leave five thousand pounds to our hospital." "I said that? What are you talking about?" the former patient exclaimed. "Now you see how ill I was."

2.1.14 The Poisonous Snake   [g̊]

A gentleman lived on an island where poisonous snakes were a common plague. Because of this plague, he had dug a deep trench round his garden.

Late one evening, he was taking his dog for a walk. He had the vague feeling that there were snakes nearby. Suddenly his dog started to bark. He felt something against his leg and noticed what he thought was a big snake. So he hurried off for an axe and bravely cut the creature to pieces.

Next morning, his gardener came running to him in a troubled state: "It is all cut to pieces, sir. I've collected all the bits in this bag. Some rogue must have done it." "I beg your pardon. It was no rogue. I did it myself. I was brave enough to kill the big snake." "Big snake? But it wasn't a snake. It was the new garden hose."

2.1.15 A Very Long Root   [θ]

A boy had tooth ache. His cheek was swollen, and so his mother took him to the dentist's to have the tooth pulled out. But as soon as he was in the armchair, he thought the dentist was going to hurt him a lot and he refused to open his mouth. The dentist tried several things, but nothing worked. At last, the dentist thought of a good way to make him open his mouth. He took a pin and pricked the boy's thigh. While the boy opened his mouth to cry out, the dentist quickly pulled the tooth. "I didn't hurt you as much as you thought, did I?" asked the dentist. "No, you didn't," answered the boy, putting his hand on the spot where he had been pricked, "but I didn't think that the root of my tooth went down as far as that."

2.1.16 A Useful Mushroom   **intonation**

A French tourist happened to be in Switzerland at a roadside inn where German was the only language spoken; and as he could not speak German, he had some difficulty in making known his wants. Among other things he wanted mushrooms, but he couldn't make his landlord understand this. The Frenchman looked at him, he looked at the Frenchman, but neither could understand the other. The situation was not, both had to confess, easy to deal with. That the landlord regretted it, goes without saying. The tourist who had tried many ways to make himself understood had a good idea at last. He got out a pencil and drew a rough picture of a mushroom. At this the innkeeper was delighted and hurried off to fulfil his guest's wish. He returned in a few minutes, carrying - not the mushrooms, for that was not how he understood the picture - but an umbrella.

2.1.17 A Teacher in Court   [ð]

The other day a policeman stopped a woman driver, because she had been driving too fast. He gave her a ticket to appear in court the following Monday. The woman was a teacher and as she had arranged a school outing for Monday, she went at once to the judge. She told him about her traffic offence and about her arrangement for that day, and then asked if the judge could take her case immediately.

"So," said the judge sternly, after hearing her statement, "you're a school teacher. That's fine. For years, I have longed to have a school teacher in this court. For years I have longed to be in the same position as a teacher. And now," he shouted, "you sit down at that table over there and write 'I must not drive too fast' five hundred times."

2.1.18 The Telephone Call   **word stress**
A successful old lawyer, known to be a character, records the following story about the beginning of his career.
"I was still unknown and had just moved into my new office. I had put in a phone and prepared myself for the first client. I was beginning to feel melancholy when I suddenly noticed a shadow through the glass-door. I was uncertain at first what to do, but then I dropped the magazine I was reading and grabbed the telephone receiver and plunged into an imaginary dialogue.
"Yes, Mr. Jones," I said as the stranger came in. "I can confirm your doubts. Some of my clients did object to your programme, but I'll deal with it somehow. Yes, alright. Good-bye."
"Having thus impressed my prospective client, I hung up and turned to him." "Excuse me, sir," said the man, "I've come to connect your telephone."

2.1.19 The Big-Game Hunter   [dʒ]
One morning, Major James Morton was found dead on the pavement in his pyjamas. He had obviously fallen from a window on the second floor. When questioned by the police, his widow said: "My husband James, who was very courageous, had enjoyed a long life as a big-game hunter. Last night, he fell asleep just before midnight. Suddenly, I awoke and saw him getting out of bed. He was sleepwalking dreaming that he was on a big-game hunt. A jaguar rushed out of the jungle towards him. He must have imagined it was going to jump at him. He aimed at the jaguar but the rifle misfired and he had to flee. He ran to the open window. I screamed and he awoke immediately - but lost his balance and fell."
The police were genuinely sympathetic, but then they asked a simple question: "How do you know his dream?"

2.1.20 A Common Curiosity   [b̥]
A witty man had a job as editor of an American magazine. His friend was Bob Barnum, the noted showman. Nevertheless, the two liked to rib each other and to play tricks on one another.

One day, the editor jumped out of a cab and rushed into Barnum's exhibition: "Hello Bob," he said, "I'm writing an article about the Indian tribe that killed Captain Cook. Have you the club that killed him? I'm having a job finding it." Barnum said he would go and look for the club. Relating the story later, Barnum said: "I just had to grab the biggest club I could find. When I gave it to Bob, he said: 'I know you must have the club. Every other small museum in the country has it, so a large establishment like yours could not afford to be without it.' Then he left, delighted to have caught me out."

2.1.21 A Salesman's Job   [ɬ]

"Madam", said the book salesman, making certain that his foot was inside the door, "you can't remember me."

"Well, I remember your foot," said the woman, "and I'll thank you to remove it."

"That was twelve weeks ago," said the agent, who was used to speaking through cracks. "I was trying to sell towels then. You didn't want any."

"No, and I don't want anything now," said the woman, "good day, sir."

"Yes, it is a beautiful day," said the agent. "Anyway, I'm offering something else now, something quite different."

"Nothing is different from a door-to-door salesman," replied the woman. "It's always the same: vacuum cleaners, little handy whatnots. No thanks. Good afternoon."

"It is still morning," said the agent "and I represent the Bell Publishing Company."

"And I," said the woman in an angry voice "represent my husband. He'll be down in a minute I can tell you."

2.1.22 The Rat-Killer   [ɹ]

A tramp one day came to a farm which was full of rats. They were everywhere, behind the curtain, under the beds, on the kitchen tables and sometimes even in the children's boots. The barn and the cow-shed were full of them. As the tramp was hungry and thirsty, he thought of a way to get a good meal. He said to the farmer: "I will kill all the rats in your house if you will give me a good dinner." The farmer's wife was very pleased with this suggestion and said that he should have the best dinner they could get for him if he would do as he promised.

After he had his dinner, the tramp called for an axe, rolled his sleeves up, and said to the farmer: "I can start now. Bring in the rats, please."

2.1.23 Not a Customer   [ŋ]

Out on his daily rounds, a commercial traveller had entered a grocer's shop where he was waiting patiently to see the shopkeeper as he was busy serving. His assistant, a young, inexperienced girl, was standing on a ladder trying to reach a tin of peas. Unfortunately, the tin she chose was underneath many others. Before she knew what was happening dozens of tins came tumbling down from the shelf, one of them crashing down on the commercial traveller's head. Fortunately he was wearing a hard hat, otherwise he might have been knocked unconscious. However, he only got a shock. He was feeling bad enough having been thus humiliated, but his self-respect was lowered even more when the shopkeeper seeing what had happened, snapped at the girl: "Hey, watch what you're doing. That man might have been a customer."

2.1.24 A Practical Lesson   **weak forms**

Dr. John Brown, the famous biblical scholar, was well known for being short of money. On one occasion, he wanted to buy cheese from the local shopkeeper. He had hardly any money left, so he asked the shopkeeper for a pennyworth of cheese. The shopkeeper protested that nobody could possibly cut such a small quantity. "Then, what's the smallest quantity you can cut?" enquired the doctor. "Twopence worth," replied the grocer firmly. He at once took the cheese and cut a small piece off. After having weighed it, he placed it on the counter expecting the doctor to pay the twopence. "Now," said the doctor, taking up the knife, "I'll show you how to sell a pennyworth." So he cut the piece of cheese in two, gave the shopkeeper one half, picked up the other half and left the shop with a big smile.

Note: The texts, which are slightly modified in this book, are taken from Frerichs, W. (1971/74) *Texte für englische Nacherzählungen.* 5. Heft, Unter- und Mittelstufe. Frankfurt/Main: Hirschgraben, Hoffmann, H.G. (1964/71) *Neue englische Nacherzählungen.* I, Unterstufe bis Mittelstufe. München: Hueber and Jones, D. (1955/69) *Phonetic Readings in English.* Heidelberg: Carl Winter.

2.2 Proper names

Phyllis, Cedric, Kathy, Katie, Ian, Iain, Sean, Deirdre, Daryl, Abraham, Adam, Agatha, Albert, Alice, Andrew, Anthony, Archibald, Eve, Stephen, Stephanie, Geoffrey, Graham, Jean, Joan, Matthew, Michael, Philip, Maude, Eileen, Mervyn, Clare, Alison, Adrian, Marjorie,

Margaret, Susan, Christopher, Basil, Buchanan, Samuel, Arnold, Janine, Cherie, Sarah, Miriam.

Yeats, Keats, Augustine, Boleyn, Canute, Chaucer, Cleopatra, Crusoe, Douglas, Falstaff, Guinness, Gulliver, Guy Fawkes, Holmes, Lincoln, Maugham, Monroe, Raleigh, Ulysses, Xerxes, Wallace, St.John, Beauchamp, Prestige.

2.3 Geographical names

2.3.1 Great Britain and Northern Ireland

Hawick, Mousehole, Uttoxeter, Derby, Bournemouth, Carlisle, Plymouth, Portsmouth, Cambridge, Coventry, Durham, Edinburgh, Folkestone, Glasgow, Gloucester, Leicester, Worcester, Greenwich, Harwich, Lincoln, Southampton, Warwick, Windsor, London, Shrewsbury, Swansea, Salisbury, Reading, Oxford, Norwich, Llandudno, Gateshead, Penzance.

Berkshire, Cheshire, Shropshire, Merseyside, Hertfordshire, Suffolk, Gloucestershire, Leicestershire, Tyne and Wear, Cumbria, Warwickshire, Hereford, Worcester, Staffordshire.

Gwynedd, Clwyd, Dyfed, West Glamorgan, Gwent, Powys.

Fife, Strathclyde, Lothian, Hebrides.

Magherafelt, Limavady, Colraine, Ballymoney, Larne, Ballymena.

Thames, Tyne, Ouse, Severn, Cam, Clyde, Avon.

2.3.2 U.S.A., Canada, Australia, New Zealand

Arkansas, Connecticut, Illinois, Massachusetts, Michigan, Missouri, Tennessee, Louisiana, Utah, Idaho, Colorado, Delaware, Iowa, Minnesota, Nevada, Oregon, Vermont, Wisconsin, Wyoming, Chicago, Gettysburg, Harvard, Juneau, Phoenix, Tallahassee, Des Moines, Baton Rouge, Lincoln, Concord, Albany, Salem, Madison, Cheyenne, Niagara, Mississippi.

Yukon, Manitoba, Saskatchewan, Alberta, Newfoundland, Ottawa, Winnipeg,
Charlottetown.

Fremantle, Adelaide, Melbourne, Sydney, Brisbane, Canberra.

Auckland, Wellington.

2.3.3 Europe

Oslo, Gothenburg, Stockholm, Leningrad, Copenhagen, Moscow, Dublin, Hamburg, Munich, Hanover, Berlin, Aix-la-Chapelle, Cologne, Dresden, Leipzig, The Hague, Brussels, Paris, Bordeaux, Marseilles, Madrid, Lisbon, Strasbourg, Zurich, Geneva, Genoa, Barcelona, Milan, Venice, Rome, Naples, Warsaw, Prague, Vienna, Budapest, Belgrade, Bucharest, Istanbul, Ankara, Athens, Calais, Florence.

Belgium, (the) Netherlands, Liechtenstein, Malta, Cyprus, Luxembourg, Romania, Hungary,
Iceland, Gibraltar, Ireland (= Eire), Greece, Germany, Lithuania, Estonia, Latvia, Poland, Austria, Armenia, Portugal, Spain, France, United Kingdom, Switzerland, Italy, Bulgaria, Czech Republic, Slovakia, (Czechoslovakia), Albania, Turkey, Sweden, Norway, Finland, Denmark, Belarus, Russia, Moldova, Ukraine, (the Soviet Union), Andorra, Gibraltar, Yugoslavia, Slovenia, Croatia, Bosnia-Herzegovina, Macedonia (= Fyrom), Monaco, San Marino.

2.3.4 Rest of the World

Afghanistan, Algeria, Angola, Anguilla, Antigua, Argentina, the Argentine, Bahamas, Bahrein, Bangladesh, Barbados, Belize, Benine, Bermuda, Bhutan, Bolivia, Botswana, Brazil, Brunei, Burkina Faso, Burma, Burundi, Cambodia, Cameroon, (the) Caribbean, Central African Republic, Chad, Chile, China, Colombia, Congo, Costa Rica, Cuba, Djibouti, Dominica, Ecuador, Egypt, El Salvador, Equatorial Guinea, Ethiopia, Fiji, Gabon, Gambia, Ghana, Grenada, Guatemala, Guiana, Guinea, Guyana, Haiti, Honduras, Hong Kong, India, Indonesia, Iran, Iraq, Israel, Ivory Coast, Jamaica, Japan, Java, Jordan, Kampuchea, Kashmir, Kenya, Korea, Kuwait, Laos, Lebanon, Lesotho, Liberia, Libya, Madagascar, Malawi, Malaysia, Mali, Mauritania, Mauritius, Melanesia, Mexico, Micronesia, Mongolia, Morocco, Mozambique, Namibia, Nauru, Nepal, Nicaragua, Niger, Nigeria, Oman, Pakistan, Panama, Papua New Guinea, Paraguay, Peru, (the) Philippines, Polynesia, Puerto Rico, Qatar, Qatar, Rwanda, Samoa, Saudi Arabia, Senegal, (the) Seychelles, Sierra Leone, Singapore, Somalia, South Africa, Sri Lanka (Ceylon), Sudan, Sumatra, Surinam, Swaziland, Syria, Tahiti, Taiwan, Tanzania, Thailand, Tibet, Togo, Tonga, Trinidad, Tunisia, Uganda, Uruguay, Venezuela, Vietnam, Yemen, Zaire, Zambia, Zimbabwe.

3.0 ADVANCED STAGE: LIST OF DIFFICULT WORDS AND THE POEM THE CHAOS

3.1 List of difficult words

3.1.1 antiquary, category, laboratory, monastery, promontory, solitary, matrimony, testimony, parsimony, accuracy, intimacy, delicacy, democracy, diplomacy, admiralty, sovereignty, apoplexy, controversy, melancholy, parachutist, the accent, to accent, the conduct, to conduct, the import, to import, the permit, to permit, the conflict, to conflict, the digest, the export, to export, frequent, to frequent, the object, to object.

3.1.2 the produce, to produce, the project, to project, the rebel, to rebel, the present, to present, the protest, to protest, the record, to record, the subject, to subject, the transport, to transport, the cement, to cement, the comment, to comment, the contact, to contact, the dispute, to dispute, the interview, to interview, the misprint, to misprint, the process, to process, the report, to report, the purchase, competitive, modal, model, paralysis, register, heroic, hero, heroine, suicide.

3.1.3 anger, the wind, to wind, hind, to hinder, kind, kindred, wild, wilderness, bewilder, pneumonia, barbarian, atrocious, glazier, legion, trivial, optician, capricious, decision, vicious, discretion, onion, ingenious, experience, experiment, maniac, manual, lenient, transient, penal, demon, horizon, apparatus, hyena, trophy, tenant, liquor, liqueur, manor, valour, lemon, echo, atomic.

3.1.4 acid, strategic, exasperate, brass, giraffe, slander, avalanche, psychopath, morass, asset, sarcastic, ant, pant, askance, romance, cancel, aftermath, I ate, Pall Mall, squash, swallow, waffle, quack, pretty, petty, sacrilegious, fête, fiancé, suede, précis, fatigue, litre, litter, mosquito, prestige, regime.

3.1.5 accomplish, column, common, comrade, donkey, hover, affront, borough, combat, comely, compass, conduit, 'conjure, con'jure, constable, covet, dove, front, monkey, oven, shove, shovel, slovenly, smother, stomach, thorough, ton, tongue, worry, bosom, wolf, tomb, betroth, sloth, comb, frost, froth, bull, pull, dull, gull, hull, skull, bullet, pulley, pulpit, culprit, pulp.

3.1.6 bush, bushel, cushion, push, brush, crush, flush, put, hut, nut, butcher, butler, pudding, puddle, poodle, fuss, pussy (= cat), pussy (= adj. of pus), futile, pupil (= part of the eye), pupil (= student), tumult, tulip, ducat, duke, duchess, punish, bury, study, busy, persuade, suave, suite, juice, fruit, tune, chew, cellulose, dissoluble.

3.1.7 ceremony, obsolete, prejudice, chaotic, geography, diagonal, tuition, ambiguous, antenna, spontaneous, carcass, trespass, sepulchre, children, chicken, kitchen, linen, siren, women, specimen, spinach, lettuce, minute, goose, gooseberry, two, twopence, three, threepence, boatswain, forecastle, forehead, gunwale, halfpenny, housewife, housewife, income, saucepan, vineyard, waistcoat.

3.1.8 lead (= metal), to lead, dead, tread, bead, plead, pheasant, heathen, heather, jealous, zealous, feasible, yeast, wreath, clean, cleanly, cleanse, realm, treachery, sweat, steak, head, heat, great, idea, create, meander, area, era, Eire, guinea, reassure, beer, earn, heart, clear, bear, rehearse, beard, hearken, hearth, dreary, sheaf, sheer, shear, tear (= liquid from eye), tear (= rip), wear and tear, pear, swear, heir, weird, weir.

3.1.9 connoisseur, chauffeur, pier, peer, cashier, fiery, boor, Boer, boar, moor, devour, scour, adjourn, journal, courteous, courtesy, bourgeois, contour, ally, baptize, cadet, canal, kennel, campaign, catarrh, esquire, hotel, lapel, machine, police, perilous, liaison, lieutenant, utensil, advertise, advertisement, aggrandize, aggrandizement, demonstrate, demonstrative, contemplate, illustrate, illustrative.

3.1.10 abandon, already, amortize, canary, clandestine, committee, electrode, enamel, examine, rococo, subjunctive, to attribute, the attribute, contribute, develop, envelop, envelope, immobile, immodest, immoral, improper, impassive, inclement, impious, impotent, infinite, finite, infamous, philosophy, photographer, psychiatrist, speedometer, academy, academician, administer, administration, anticipate, anticipation, centralize, centralization, nationalize, nationalization, reconcile, reconciliation, superior, superiority, temperament.

3.1.11 ascertain, attain, disdain, retain, bargain, chaplain, captain, Britain, curtain, villain, addressee, refugee, auctioneer, career, profiteer, acquiesce, convalesce, grotesque, antique, oblique, physique, technique, balloon, cartoon, festoon, monsoon, economic, ecclesiastic, statistics, Arabic, arithmetic, catholic, choleric, lunatic, politics, rhetoric, insipid, valid, invalid, the invalid.

3.1.12 deposit, depot, explicit, deficit, personify, modify, specify, austerity, sincerity, validity, similitude, casual, habitual, perpetual, impetuous, particular, ceremonious, notorious, advantage, advantageous, miscellaneous, initiate, demonstrate, resuscitate, autumn, autumnal, decorum, decorous, desire, desirous, refer, reference, prefer, preference, ignore, ignorance, decay, decadent, oppose, opponent, comparable, reparable, disputable, applicable, admirable.

3.1.13 negative, relative, narrative, executive, interrogative, predicative, comparative, conservative, imaginative, explanatory, business, medicine, venison, nicety, blessed, cursed, learned, crooked, wretched, advisedly, designedly, plural, baron, barren, occurrence, adversary, comfort, effort, query, clerk, Derby, sergeant, worm, attorney, chalk, palm, qualm, the salve, to salve, salmon, alderman, almanac, appal, basalt, walnut, malt, squall, wallet, revolt, patrol, petrol, folk, Holborn, yolk, yoke, droll, poll, roll, toll.

3.1.14 dough, furlough, bough, drought, plough, slough (= swamp), slough (= cast-off skin), brougham, chough, clough, rough, slough, tough, cough, trough, draught, laughter, daughter, haughty, slaughter, fowl, growl, browse, bowels, bowl, bow (n.) (= act of bending, front of boat), bow (n.) (= knot), to bow, mow (= cut down), mow (= grimace), row (= quarrel), row (= line), to row, sow (n.), sow (v.), to sew.

3.1.15 plaid, plait, quay, Aegean, aesthetic, anaesthesia, diarrhoea, homeopathy, aerial, manoeuvre, gauze, laundry, vault, haunt, launch, sausage, gauge, beau, bureau, settee, breeches, freight, height, sleigh, cease, seize, cider, neither, leisure, deuce, Teutonic, dew, ewe, Sioux, Sue, to sue, pewter, to sew, to sow, niece, nice.

3.1.16 quiet, quite, diet, handkerchief, mischief, mischievous, sieve, medieval, roam, broad, foe, woe, canoe, shoe, poet, room, brook, rook, hood, soot, wool, blood, flood, brooch, soul, sole, blouse, couch, foul, acoustics, vouch, bouquet, camouflage, coupon, wound, argue, pursue, virtue, catalogue, plague, bruise, nuisance, suit, biscuit, guitar, annuity, continuity.

3.1.17 bilingual, bicycle, bigamy, menace, preface, terrace, diplomacy, obstinacy, supremacy, damage, garage, message, mirage, accurate, climate, candidate, delegate, legitimate, prelate, inmate, innate, separate, to separate, the advocate, to advocate, duplicate, courteous, hideous, bitterest, banquet, closet, planet, valet, ballet, cabaret, cadet, déjà vu.

3.1.18 device, suffice, caprice, malice, police, domicile, fertile, infantile, missile, profile, imbecile, famine, genuine, margarine, divine, porcupine, serpentine, benzine, magazine, routine, practise, practice, promise, treatise, franchise, merchandise, definite, favourite, hypocrite, plebiscite, finite, dynamite, satellite, Labourite.

3.1.19 sceptic, niche, sandwich, archaic, archangel, architect, archives, chameleon, choir, mechanism, chagrin, champagne, chaperon, chauffeur, moustache, parachute, angel, Angles, gypsy, exaggerate, longitude, gin, ginger, goal, gaol, ghastly, gherkin, ghetto, ghost, anguish, linguist, angle, finger, longer, kangaroo, longing, belonging, longish, youngish, hinge, lounge, sponge, edge, hue, huge, human, humane.

3.1.20 Stephen, nephew, queue, cosmetic, dismal, measles, husband, to husband, clumsy, observe, absolve, the use, to use, the excuse, to excuse, the house, to house, the louse, to louse, the mouse, to mouse, paradise, asylum, muscle, scheme, schooner, schedule, dessert, desert, to desert, dissolve, hussar, possess, scissors, panther, bequeath, booth, betroth, smooth, bath, baths, lath, laths, sheath, sheaths, wreaths, mouth, mouths, oath, oaths, truth, truths, youth, youths, bomb, bomber, climb, dumb, plumber, yacht, dignity, malignant, repugnant, signal, signature, blackguard, pseudonym, psychology, psyche, iron, muzzle, mussel, zeugma.

3.2 *The Chaos*

Dearest creature in Creation,
Studying English pronunciation,
I will teach you in my verse
Sounds like corpse, corps, horse and worse.

It will keep you, Susy, busy,
Make your head with heat grow dizzy;
Tear in eye your dress you'll tear.
So shall I! Oh, hear my prayer.

Pray, console your loving poet,
Make my coat look new, dear, sew it!
Just compare heart, beard and heard,
Dies and diet, lord and word,

Sword and sward, retain and Britain,
(Mind the latter, how it's written!)
Made has not the sound of bad,
Say-said, pay-paid, laid but plaid.

Now I surely will not plague you
With such words as vague and ague,
But be careful how you speak,
Say break, steak, but bleak and streak.

Previous, precious, fuchsia, via;
Pipe, snipe, recipe and choir,
Cloven, oven; how and low;
Script, receipt; shoe, poem, toe.

Hear me say, devoid of trickery:
Daughter, laughter and Terpsichore,
Typhoid, measles, topsails, aisles,
Exiles, similes, reviles;

Wholly, holly; signal, signing;
Thames; examining, combining;
Scholar, vicar and cigar,
Solar, mica, war and far.

From 'desire': desirable - admirable from 'admire';
Lumber, plumber, bier but brier;
Chatham, brougham; renown but known,
Knowledge, done, but gone and tone.

One, anemone, Balmoral;
Kitchen, lichen, laundry, laurel,
Gertrude, German; wind and mind,
Scene, Melpomene, mankind.

Tortoise, turquoise, chamois-leather,
Reading, reading, heathen, heather.

This phonetic labyrinth
Gives moss, gross, brook, brooch, ninth, plinth.

Billet does not end like ballet;
Bouquet, wallet, mallet, chalet.
Blood and flood are not like food,
Nor is mould like should and would.

Banquet is not nearly parquet,
Which is said to rhyme with khaki.
Viscous, viscount, load and broad;
Toward, to forward, to reward.

And your pronunciation is O.K.,
If you can say ricochet and croquet.
Rounded, wounded; grieve and sieve,
Friend and fiend; alive and live.
Liberty, library, heave and heaven;
Rachel, ache, moustache; eleven.
We say hallowed, but allowed
People, leopard, towed but vowed.

Mark the difference, moreover,
Between mover, plover, Dover,
Leeches, breeches; wise, precise,
Chalice, but police and lice.

Camel; constable, unstable,
Principle, disciple; label;
Petal, penal, and canal,
Wait, surmise, plait, promise; pal,

Suit, suite, ruin, circuit, conduit,
Rhyme with 'shirk it' and 'beyond it'.
But it is not hard to tell,
Why it's pall, mall, but Pall Mall.

Muscle, muscular; goal, iron;
Timber, climber, bullion, lion.
Worm and storm, chaise, chaos, chair,
Senator, spectator, mayor.

Ivy, privy, famous, clamour
And enamour rhyme with 'hammer'.
Pussy, hussy and possess,
Desert, but dessert, address.

Golf, wolf; countenance; lieutenants
Hoist, in lieu of flags, left pennants.
River, rival; tomb, bomb, comb,
Doll and roll and some and home.

Stranger does not rhyme with anger,
Neither does devour with clangour.
Soul, but foul and gaunt, but aunt;
Font, front, wont; want, grand and grant.

Shoes, goes, does. Now first say: finger,
And then singer, ginger, linger.
Real, zeal; mauve, gauze and gauge,
Marriage, foliage, mirage, age.

Query does not rhyme with very,
Nor does fury sound like bury.
Dost, lost, post and doth, cloth, loth,
Job, job, blossom, bosom, oath.

My oppugnant, keen oppugners,
Bowing, bowing, banjo-tuners,
In their yachts or their canoes;
Puisne, truism; use, to use.

Though the difference seems little,
We say actual, but victual.
Seat, sweat; chaste, caste; Leigh, eight, height;
Put, nut; granite, but unite.

Reefer does not rhyme with 'deafer',
Feoffer does and zephyr, heifer.
Dull, bull; Geoffrey, George; ate, late;
Hint, pint, Senate, but sedate.

Scenic, Arabic, pacific;
Science, conscience; scientific.
Tour, but our and succour, four;
Gas, alas and Arkansas!

Sea, idea, guinea, area;
Psalm, Maria, but malaria;
Youth, south, southern; cleanse and clean,
Doctrine, turpentine, marine.

Compare alien with Italian,
Dandelion with battalion,
Sally with ally; yea, ye
Eye, I, ay, aye, why, whey, key, quay!

Say aver, but ever, fever,
Neither, leisure, skein, receiver.
Never guess - it is not safe:
We say calves, valves, half, but Ralph!

Heron, granary, canary,
Crevice and device, and eyrie,
Face, but preface, but efface,
Phlegm, phlegmatic, ass, glass, bass.

Large, but target, gin, give, verging;
Ought, out, joust and scour, but scourging;
Ear, but earn; and wear and tear
Do not rhyme with 'here', but 'ere'.

Seven is right, but so is even;
Hyphen, roughen; nephew, Stephen;
Monkey, donkey; clerk and jerk;
Asp, grasp, wasp, and cork and work.

Pronunciation - think of psyche! -
Is a paling, stout and spiky.
Won't it make you lose your wits,
Saying fruit, suit, but conduits.

It's a dark abyss or tunnel,
Strewn with stones, like rowlock, gunwale,
Islington and Isle of Wight,
Housewife, verdict and indict!

Don't you think so, reader, rather,
Saying lather, bather, father?
Finally: which rhymes with 'enough',
Though, through, plough, cough, hough or tough?
Hiccough has the sound of 'cup'
My advice is -
Give it up!

(George N. Trenité)

4.0 DIAGNOSTIC PASSAGE

Let me tell you my friend that when students from other countries come to study in Britain, their lectures and tutorials are certainly not their only job, are they. For a little while, the problems of adjustment to the new environment may make it impossible to devote very much thought to university work. The recently arrived students must find out for themselves the answers to many questions. Should they change the customs they have always followed in eating their three full meals each day? What clothing should they choose? Ought they to wear those wretched blue jeans some students here have, or should they cling to the clothes they had usually preferred at home? They are inclined to feel admiration for the scale of living, the big university grounds, the well-kept houses, and the good educational equipment. But they don't understand how everyone can be in such a hurry, as if time were a god to be worshipped.

5.0 KEY TO SOME EXERCISES

1.0 BASIC STAGE: INDIVIDUAL WORDS

1. Basic words

plant /plɑːnt/, life /laɪf/, man /mæn/, get /get/, arm /ɑːm/, house /haʊs/, sad /sæd/, father /ˈfɑːðə/, bed /bed/, lame /leɪm/, ago /əˈgəʊ/, bird /bɜːd/, there /ðeə/, /ðə/, but /bʌt/, /bət/, it /ɪt/, better /ˈbetə/, wish /wɪʃ/, son /sʌn/, care /keə/, bee /biː/, here /hɪə/, no /nəʊ/, not /nɒt/, beat /biːt/, law /lɔː/, belief /bɪˈliːf/, low /ləʊ/, long /lɒŋ/, all /ɔːl/, boy /bɔɪ/, look /lʊk/, do /duː/, /du/, /dʊ/, /də/, /d/, oil /ɔɪl/, push /pʊʃ/, moon /muːn/, poor /pɔː/, /pʊə/, sure /ʃɔː/, /ʃʊə/, player /ˈpleɪə/, fire /ˈfaɪə/, employer /ɪmˈplɔɪə/, slower /ˈsləʊə/, tower /ˈtaʊə/.

blind /blaɪnd/, head /hed/, this /ðis/, friend /frend/, go /gəʊ/, long /lɒŋ/, sing /sɪŋ/, beg /beg/, home /həʊm/, youth /juːθ/, Indian /ˈɪndiən/, keep /kiːp/, lamp /læmp/, might /maɪt/, night /naɪt/, paper /ˈpeɪpə/, red /red/, yes /jes/, ship /ʃip/, church /tʃɜːtʃ/, catch /kætʃ/, voice /vɔɪs/, love /lʌv/, rob /rɒb/, water /ˈwɔːtə/, zeal /ziːl/, these /ðiːz/, pleasure /ˈpleʒə/, leisure /ˈleʒə/, jam /dʒæm/, object (n.) /ˈɒbdʒɪkt/, object (v.) /əbˈdʒekt/, thank /θæŋk/, thin /θɪn/, death /deθ/, smooth /smuːð/.

2. Various words

separate (adj., n.) /ˈsepərət/, separate (v.) /ˈsepəreɪt/, well /wel/, bad /bæd/, does /dʌz/, /dəz/, /dz/, /z/, /s/, car /kɑː/, make /meɪk/, arrange /əˈreɪndʒ/, bullet /ˈbʊlɪt/, age /eɪdʒ/, chair /tʃeə/, the /ðiː/, /ði/, /ðɪ/, /ðə/, us /ʌs/, /əs/, was /wɒz/, /wəz/, loose /luːs/, that /ðæt/, /ðət/, big /bɪg/, Thames /temz/, sad /sæd/, bus /bʌs/, bar /bɑː/, say /seɪ/, general /ˈdʒenərəl/, chalk /tʃɔːk/, this /ðɪs/, thick /θɪk/, thing /θɪŋ/, yes /jes/, promise /ˈprɒmɪs/, as /æz/, /əz/, damage /ˈdæmɪdʒ/, tremble /ˈtrembəl/, go /gəʊ/, noted /ˈnəʊtɪd/, caravan /ˈkærəvæn/, tar /tɑː/, play /pleɪ/, butcher /ˈbʊtʃə/, change /tʃeɪndʒ/, chin /tʃɪn/, they /ðeɪ/, them /ðem/, /ðəm/, throw /θrəʊ/, kiss /kɪs/, easy /ˈiːzi/, preface /ˈprefəs/, says /sez/, marry /ˈmæri/, shut /ʃʌt/, master /ˈmɑːstə/, strange /streɪndʒ/, pudding /ˈpʊdɪŋ/, itch /ɪtʃ/, their /ðeə/, these /ðiːz/, through /θruː/, author /'ɔːθə/, hiss /hɪs/, music /'mjuːzɪk/, minute (n.) /'mɪnɪt/, minute (adj.) /maɪ'njuːt/, said /sed/, wax /wæks/, hurry /'hʌri/, rather /'rɑːðə/, to eliminate /tʊ ɪ'lɪmɪneɪt/, pull /pʊl/, showman /'ʃəʊmən/, gentleman /'dʒentəlmən/, postman /'pəʊsmən/, chairman /'tʃeəmən/, chairwoman /'tʃeəwʊmən/, chairperson /'tʃeəpɜːsən/, just (adj.) /dʒʌst/, just (adv.) /dʒəst/, catcher /'kætʃə/, then /ðen/, thus /ðʌs/, miss /mɪs/, senate /'senət/, set /set/, waggon /'wægən/, curry /'kʌri/, commander /kə'mɑːndə/, journal /'dʒɜːnəl/, colonel /'kɜːnəl/, graduate /'grædʒuət/, to graduate /tə 'grædʒueɪt/, put /pʊt/, urgent /'ɜːdʒənt/, journey /'dʒɜːni/, method /'meθəd/, month /mʌnθ/, bath /bɑːθ/, mouth /maʊθ/, basis /'beɪsɪs/, fantasy /'fæntəsi/, else /els/, cease /siːs/, his /hɪz/, /ɪz/, is /ɪz/, /z/, /s/, case /keɪs/, decrease (n.) /'diːkriːs/, decrease (v.) /diː'kriːs/, decrees /dɪ'kriːz/, to lose /tə luːz/, oath /əʊθ/, north /nɔːθ/, either /'aɪðə/, father /'fɑːðə/, other /'ʌðə/, prophet /'prɒfɪt/, moderate /'mɒdərət/ (n., adj.), moderate (v.) /'mɒdəreɪt/, any /'eni/, dozen /'dʌzən/, govern /'gʌvən/, many /'meni/, path /pɑːθ/, youth /juːθ/, nothing /'nʌθɪŋ/, although /ɔːl'ðəʊ/, thousand /'θaʊzənd/, more than that /'mɔː ðən 'ðæt/, tune /tjuːn/, duke /djuːk/, value /'væljuː/, failure /'feɪljə/, issue /'ɪʃuː/, /'ɪsjuː/, casual /'kæʒuəl/, huge /hjuːdʒ/, actual /'æktʃuəl/, human /'hjuːmən/, curry /'kʌri/, courage /'kʌrɪdʒ/, harm /hɑːm/, men /men/, women /'wɪmən/, hum /hʌm/, cloth /klɒθ/, cross /krɒs/, slower /'sləʊə/, player /'pleɪə/, Mrs /'mɪsɪz/, Ms /mɪz/, Messrs /'mesəz/, put /pʊt/, putt /pʌt/, putty /'pʌti/.

3. Words containing written <r>

tar /tɑː/, far /fɑː/, dark /dɑːk/, verse /vɜːs/, stir /stɜː/, corn /kɔːn/, short /ʃɔːt/, former /'fɔːmə/, turn /tɜːn/, born /bɔːn/, care /keə/, to tear /tə teə/, beer /bɪə/, dear /dɪə/, near /nɪə/, tour /tʊə/, moor /mʊə/, pure /pjʊə/, pear /peə/, mere /mɪə/, cure /kjʊə/.

4. Words containing written <ng> or <nk> (<nc>, <ndk>, <nqu>, <nx>)

hang /hæŋ/, king /kɪŋ/, sing /sɪŋ/, tongue /tʌŋ/, hanging /'hæŋɪŋ/, singing /'sɪŋɪŋ/, singer /'sɪŋə/, long /lɒŋ/, longish /'lɒŋɪʃ/, /'lɒŋgɪʃ/, slangy /'slæŋi/, strongly /'strɒŋli/, longer (adj.) /'lɒŋgə/, longer (n.) /'lɒŋə/, youngest /'jʌŋgɪst/, bungalow /'bʌŋgələʊ/, language /'læŋgwɪdʒ/, lingo /'lɪŋgəʊ/, singular /'sɪŋgjʊlə/, angle /'æŋgəl/,

Angles /'æŋgəlz/, England /'ɪŋglənd/, English /'ɪŋglɪʃ/, single /'sɪŋgəl/, angry /'æŋgri/, anger /'æŋgə/, finger /'fɪŋgə/, hunger /'hʌŋgə/, linger /'lɪŋgə/, anxious /'æŋkʃəs/, drink /drɪŋk/, sink /sɪŋk/, think /θɪŋk/, among /ə'mʌŋ/, evening /'iːvnɪŋ/, spring /sprɪŋ/, wrong /rɒŋ/, young /jʌŋ/, younger /'jʌŋgə/, youngest /'jʌŋgɪst/, youngish /'jʌŋɪʃ/, /'jʌŋgɪʃ/, conclusion /kən'kluːʒən/, unkind /ʌn'kaɪnd/, handkerchief /'hæŋkətʃɪf/, inquire /ɪn'kwaɪə/, ingredient /ɪn'griːdiənt/, unknown /ʌn'nəʊn/, anchor /'æŋkə/, inquest /'ɪŋkwest/, ungrateful /ʌn'greɪtfəl/.

5. Length or no length?

always /'ɔːlweɪz/, /'ɔːlwɪz/, basket /'bɑːskɪt/, chewing /'tʃuːɪŋ/, record (v.) /rɪ'kɔːd/, record (n., adj.) /'rekɔːd/, coffee /'kɒfi/, fill /fɪl/, old /əʊld/, all /ɔːl/, small /smɔːl/, pot /pɒt/, speaker /'spiːkə/, speed /spiːd/, sport /spɔːt/, borrow /'bɒrəʊ/, spit /spɪt/, John /dʒɒn/, jaundice /'dʒɔːndɪs/, good /gʊd/, blood /blʌd/, book /bʊk/, suit /suːt/, /sjuːt/, soot /sʊt/, half /hɑːf/, each /iːtʃ/, rather /'rɑːðə/, mother /'mʌðə/, itch /ɪtʃ/, magazine /mægə'ziːn/, cook /kʊk/, wool /wʊl/, want /wɒnt/, look /lʊk/, last /lɑːst/, card /kɑːd/, car /kɑː/, gone /gɒn/, loop /luːp/, loot /luːt/, pool /puːl/, new /njuː/, avenue /'ævənjuː/.

6. Words containing written <th>

Anthony /'æntəni/, asthma /'æsmə/, /'æsθmə/, isthmus /'ɪsməs/, /'ɪsθməs/, Thomas /'tɒməs/, thing /θɪŋ/, thought /θɔːt/, then /ðen/, thin /θɪn/, author /'ɔːθə/, breath /breθ/, smooth /smuːð/, the /ðiː/, /ði/, /ðɪ/, /ðə/, them /ðem/, /ðəm/, their /ðeə/, father /'fɑːðə/, earth /ɜːθ/, earthen /'ɜːθən/, /'ɜːðən/, thus /ðʌs/, though /ðəʊ/, this /ðɪs/, northern /'nɔːðən/, southern /'sʌðən/, worthy /'wɜːði/, worth /wɜːθ/, those /ðəʊz/, there /ðeə/, /ðə/, bath /bɑːθ/, path /pɑːθ/, mouth /maʊθ/, youth /juːθ/, baths /bɑːðz/, /bɑːθs/, paths /pɑːðz/, mouths (n.) /maʊðz/, youths /juːðz/, /juːθs/, month /mʌnθ/, months /mʌnθs/, /mʌns/, booth /buːð/, /buːθ/, breathe /briːð/, Thames /temz/, thesis /'θiːsɪs/, thyme /taɪm/.

7. Words containing written <s> or <ss>

sell /sel/, satan /'seɪtən/, us /ʌs/, /əs/, /s/, as /æz/, /əz/, his /hɪz/, /ɪz/, crisis /'kraɪsɪs/, crises /'kraɪsiːz/, oasis /əʊ'eɪsɪs/, oases /əʊ'eɪsiːz/, to use /tə juːz/, the use /ðə juːs/, cease /siːs/, basin /'beɪsɪn/, was /wɒz/,

/wəz/, wisdom /'wɪzdəm/, house /haʊs/, houses /'haʊzɪz/, blossom /'blɒsəm/, the desert /ðə 'dezət/, to desert /tə dɪ'zɜːt/, dessert /dɪ'zɜːt/, scissors /'sɪzəz/, fasten /'fɑːsən/, to dissolve /tə dɪ'zɒlv/, possess /pə'zes/, newspaper /'njuːspeɪpə/, /'njuːzpeɪpə/, hypothesis /haɪ'pɒθəsɪs/, hypotheses /haɪ'pɒθəsiːz/.

8. Voiced or voiceless final consonants

tins /tɪnz/, hands /hændz/, tents /tents/, belongs /bɪ'lɒŋz/, belonged /bɪ'lɒŋd/, hymns /hɪmz/, developed /dɪ'veləpt/, drenched /drentʃt/, dressed /drest/, doubled /'dʌbəld/, dropped /drɒpt/, comes /kʌmz/, it's /ɪts/, notes /nəʊts/, nods /nɒdz/, possessed /pə'zest/, asked /ɑːskt/, I used to /aɪ juːst tə, tu/, let's /lets/, delayed /dɪ'leɪd/, minutes /'mɪnɪts/, kills /kɪlz/, clubs /klʌbz/, seems /siːmz/, sings /sɪŋz/, longs /lɒŋz/, longings /'lɒŋɪŋz/, backs /bæks/, begs /begz/, legs /legz/, stabbed /stæbd/, heads /hedz/, clothes /kləʊðz/, /kləʊz/, paths /pɑːðz/, arms /ɑːmz/, tops /tɒps/, hats /hæts/, lives (n.) /laɪvz/, lives (v.) /lɪvz/, smiths /smɪθs/, Jacks /dʒæks/, stops /stɒps/, bags /bægz/, rides /raɪdz/, buses /'bʌsɪz/, boxes /'bɒksɪz/, chooses /'tʃuːzɪz/, wishes /'wɪʃɪz/, watches /'wɒtʃɪz/, suffixes /'sʌfɪksɪz/, sins /sɪnz/, since /sɪns/, hens /henz/, hence /hens/, fence /fens/, fens /fenz/, tense /tens/, tens /tenz/.

9. More difficult words containing written <r>

parents /'peərənts/, hero /'hɪərəʊ/, pirate /'paɪərət/, tyrant /'taɪərənt/, rural /'rʊərəl/, various /'veəriəs/, serious /'sɪəriəs/, furious /'fjʊəriəs/, luxurious /lʌg'zjʊəriəs/, severe /sɪ'vɪə/, sincere /sɪn'sɪə/, secure /sɪ'kjʊə/, career /kə'rɪə/, aeroplane /'eərəpleɪn/, liqueur /lɪ'kjʊə/, cashier /kæ'ʃɪə/, we're /wɪə/, they're /ðeə/, infuriating /ɪn'fjʊərieɪtɪŋ/, curiosity /kjʊəri'ɒsəti/, experience /ɪk'spɪəriəns/, persevere /pɜːsɪ'vɪə/, persevering /pɜːsɪ'vɪərɪŋ/, invariably /ɪn'veəriəbli/, prepare /prɪ'peə/, preparation /prepə'reɪʃən/, reassure /riːə'ʃɔː/, /riːə'ʃʊə/, bearable /'beərəbəl/.

10. Various other words

any /'eni/, Mary /'meəri/, marry /'mæri/, merry /'meri/, where /weə/, really /'rɪəli/, children /'tʃɪldrən/, careful /'keəfəl/, /'keəfʊl/, again /ə'gen/, /ə'geɪn/, to wonder /tə 'wʌndə/, correspondence /kɒrəs'pɒndəns/, urgent /'ɜːdʒənt/, many /'meni/, years /jɪəz/, /jɜːz/, very /'veri/, exhibition /eksɪ'bɪʃən/, to exhibit /tʊ ɪg'zɪbɪt/, too /tuː/, two /tuː/, examine /ɪg'zæmɪn/, occasion /ə'keɪʒən/, great /greɪt/, showman /'ʃəʊmən/, radio /'reɪdiəʊ/, says /sez/, worried /'wʌrid/, during /'djʊərɪŋ/, extraordinary /ɪk'strɔːdənəri/, at last /ət 'lɑːst/, at once /ət 'wʌns/, at home /ət 'həʊm/, honour /'ɒnə/, hour /'aʊə/, heir /eə/, to represent /tə reprɪ'zent/, representation /reprɪzen'teɪʃən/, because /bɪ'kɒz/, /bɪ'kəz/, manifold /'mænɪfəʊld/, hotel /həʊ'tel/, /əʊ'tel/, historical /hɪs'tɒrɪkəl/, /ɪs'tɒrɪkəl/, herbs /hɜːbz/, suite /swiːt/.

2.0 INTERMEDIATE STAGE: TEXTS, PROPER NAMES AND GEOGRAPHICAL NAMES

2.2 Proper Names

Phyllis, Cedric, Kathy, Katie, Ian, Iain, Sean, Deirdre, Daryl, Abraham, Adam, Agatha, Albert, Alice, Andrew, Anthony, Archibald, Eve, Stephen, Stephanie, Geoffrey, Graham, Jean, Joan, Matthew, Michael, Philip, Maude, Eileen, Mervyn, Clare, Alison, Adrian, Marjorie, Margaret, Susan, Christopher, Basil, Buchanan, Samuel, Arnold, Janine, Cherie, Sarah, Miriam.

/'fɪlɪs/, /'sedrɪk/, /'kæθi/, /'keɪti/, /'iːən/, /'iːən/, /ʃɔːn/, /'dɪədri/, /'dærəl/, /'eɪbrəhæm/, /'ædəm/, /'ægəθə/, /'ælbət/, /'ælɪs/, /'ændruː/, /'æntəni/, /'ɑːtʃɪbɔːld/, /iːv/, /'stiːvən/, /'stefəni/, /'dʒefri/, /'greɪəm/, /dʒiːn/, /dʒəʊn/, /'mæθjuː/, /'maɪkəl/, /'fɪlɪp/, /mɔːd/, /'aɪliːn/, /'mɜːvɪn/, /kleə/, /'ælɪsən/, /'eɪdriən/, /'mɑːdʒəri/, /'mɑːgrət/, /'suːzən/, /'krɪstəfə/, /'bæzəl/, /bjuː'kænən/, /'sæmjuəl/, /'ɑːnəld/, /dʒə'niːn/, /ʃə'riː/ (/ʃe'riː/), /'seərə/, /'mɪriəm/.

2.3 Geographical names

2.3.1 Great Britain and Northern Ireland
Hawick, Mousehole, Uttoxeter, Derby, Bournemouth, Carlisle, Plymouth, Portsmouth, Cambridge, Coventry, Durham, Edinburgh,

Folkestone, Glasgow, Gloucester, Leicester, Worcester, Greenwich, Harwich, Lincoln, Southampton, Warwick, Windsor, London, Shrewsbury, Swansea, Salisbury, Reading, Oxford, Norwich, Llandudno, Gateshead, Penzance.

/hɔɪk/, /ˈmaʊzəl/, /juˈtɒksɪtə/, /ˈdɑːbi/, /ˈbɔːnməθ/, /kɑːˈlaɪl/, /ˈplɪməθ/, /ˈpɔːtsməθ/, /ˈkeɪmbrɪdʒ/, /ˈkɒvəntri/ (/ˈkʌvəntri/), /ˈdʌrəm/, /ˈedɪnbərə/, /ˈfəʊkstən/, /ˈglɑːzgəʊ/ (/ˈglɑːsgəʊ/, /ˈglæz-/, /ˈglæs-/), /ˈglɒstə/, /ˈlestə/, /ˈwʊstə/, /ˈgrenɪtʃ/ (/ˈgrɪn-/, /-ɪdʒ/), /ˈhærɪdʒ/ (/-ɪtʃ/), /ˈlɪŋkən/, /saʊθˈhæmptən/ (/saʊˈθæmptən/), /ˈwɒrɪk/, /ˈwɪnzə/ (/ˈwɪndzə/), /ˈlʌndən/, /ˈʃrəʊzbəri/, /ˈswɒnzi/, /ˈsɔːlzbəri/, /ˈredɪŋ/, /ˈɒksfəd/, /ˈnɒrɪdʒ/ (/-ɪtʃ/), /lænˈdɪdnəʊ/, /ˈgeɪtshed/, /penˈzæns/.

3.0 ADVANCED STAGE: LIST OF DIFFICULT WORDS AND THE POEM *THE CHAOS*

3.1.4 acid, strategic, exasperate, brass, giraffe, slander, avalanche, psychopath, morass, asset, sarcastic, ant, pant, askance, romance, cancel, aftermath, I ate, Pall Mall, squash, swallow, waffle, quack, pretty, petty, sacrilegious, fête, fiancé, suède, précis, fatigue, litre, litter, mosquito, prestige, regime.

/ˈæsɪd/, /strəˈtiːdʒɪk/, /ɪgˈzæspəreɪt/ (-ˈzɑːs-), /brɑːs/, /dʒəˈrɑːf/, /ˈslɑːndə/, /ˈævəlɑːntʃ/, /ˈsaɪkəʊpæθ/, /məˈræs/, /ˈæset/ (/ˈæsɪt/), /sɑːˈkæstɪk/, /ænt/, /pænt/, /əˈskæns/ (/əˈskɑːns/), /rəʊˈmæns/ (/ˈrəʊmæns/), /ˈkænsəl/, /ˈuːʃtəmæθ/ (/-mɑːθ/), /aɪ et/ (/aɪ eɪt/), /pæl ˈmæl/, /skwɒʃ/, /ˈswɒləʊ/, /ˈwɒfəl/, /kwæk/, /ˈprɪti/, /ˈpeti/, /sækrəˈlɪdʒəs/, /feɪt/, /fiˈɒnseɪ/ (/fiˈɑːnseɪ/), /sweɪd/, /ˈpreɪsiː/, /fəˈtiːg/, /ˈliːtə/, /ˈlɪtə/, /məsˈkiːtəʊ/ (mɒs-), /preˈstiːʒ/, /reɪˈʒiːm/.

3.1.8 lead (= metal), to lead, dead, tread, bead, plead, pheasant, heathen, heather, jealous, zealous, feasible, yeast, wreath, clean, cleanly, cleanse, realm, treachery, sweat, steak, head, heat, great, idea, create, meander, area, era, Eire, guinea, reassure, beer, earn, heart, clear, bear, rehearse, beard, hearken, hearth, dreary, sheaf, sheer, shear, tear (= liquid from eye), tear (= rip), wear and tear, pear, swear, heir, weird, weir.

/led/, /tə liːd/, /ded/, /tred/, /biːd/, /pliːd/, /ˈfezənt/, /ˈhiːðən/, /ˈheðə/, /ˈdʒeləs/, /ˈzeləs/, /ˈfiːzəbəl/, /jiːst/, /riːθ/, /kliːn/, /klenli/ (adj.), /kliːnli/ (adv.), /klenz/, /relm/, /ˈtretʃəri/, /swet/, /steɪk/, /hed/, /hiːt/, /greɪt/, /aɪˈdɪə/, /kriˈeɪt/, /miˈændə/, /ˈeəriə/, /ˈɪərə/, /ˈeərə/, /ˈgɪni/, /riːəˈʃɔː/ (/riːəˈʃʊə/), /bɪə/, /ɜːn/, /hɑːt/, /klɪə/, /beə/, /rɪˈhɜːsəl/, /bɪəd/, /ˈhɑːkən/, /hɑːθ/, /ˈdrɪəri/, /ʃiːf/, /ʃɪə/, /ʃɪə/, /tɪə/, /teə/, /weər ən teə/, /peə/, /sweə/, /eə/, /wɪəd/, /wɪə/.

3.1.19 sceptic, niche, sandwich, archaic, archangel, architect, archives, chameleon, choir, mechanism, chagrin, champagne, chaperon, chauffeur, moustache, parachute, angel, Angles, gypsy, exaggerate, longitude, gin, ginger, goal, gaol, ghastly, gherkin, ghetto, ghost, anguish, linguist, angle, finger, longer, kangaroo, longing, belonging, longish, youngish, hinge, lounge, sponge, edge, hue, huge, human, humane.

/ˈskeptɪk/, /niːʃ/ (/nɪtʃ/, /nɪʃ/), /ˈsænwɪdʒ/ (/ˈsænwɪtʃ/), /ɑːˈkeɪɪk/, /ˈɑːkeɪndʒəl/ (/ɑːkˈeɪndʒəl/), /ˈɑːkɪtekt/, /ˈɑːkaɪvz/, /kəˈmiːliən/, /ˈkwaɪə/, /ˈmekənɪzm/, /ˈʃægrɪn/, /ʃæmˈpeɪn/, /ˈʃæpərəʊn/, /ˈʃəʊfə/, /məˈstɑːʃ/ (/mə-/, /-ˈstæʃ/), /ˈpærəʃuːt/, /eɪndʒəl/, /ˈæŋgəlz/, /ˈdʒɪpsi/, /ɪgˈzædʒəreɪt/, /ˈlɒndʒɪtjuːd/ (/ˈlɒŋgɪtjuːd/), /dʒɪn/, /ˈdʒɪndʒə/, /gəʊl/, /ˈdʒeɪl/, /ˈgɑːstli/, /ˈgɜːkɪn/, /ˈgetəʊ/, /gəʊst/, /ˈæŋgwɪʃ/, /ˈlɪŋgwɪst/, /ˈæŋgəl/, /ˈfɪŋgə/, /ˈlɒŋgə/ (adj.), /ˈlɒŋə/ (n.), /kæŋgəˈruː/, /ˈlɒŋɪŋ/, /bɪˈlɒŋɪŋ/, /ˈlɒŋɪʃ/ (/ˈlɒŋgɪʃ/), /ˈjʌŋɪʃ/ (/ˈjʌŋgɪʃ/), /hɪndʒ/, /laʊndʒ/, /spʌndʒ/, /edʒ/, /hjuː/, /hjuːdʒ/, /ˈhjuːmən/, /hjuˈmeɪn/.

INDEX